REPRESENTATIONS IN MIND AND WORLD

Essays Inspired by Barbara Tversky

"This remarkable volume celebrates and documents the accomplishments of a remarkable cognitive scientist, Barbara Tversky. In their investigations of psychological representation Barbara and her students elegantly bridge at least three formidable gulches: between mental and physical representation, between lab and field, and between disciplines that not only include philosophy and psychology but also the visual arts, design, and computer science.

This work not only honors George Miller's exhortation to give psychology away, but closes the circle by using an analysis of physical representation in the field to shape and inform psychological theory. Each chapter shows the benefits and wisdom of establishing a permanent dialogue between academic theory and phenomena and challenges in the real world, creating not 'applied' science but science that is richer and more complete by virtue of worrying about its applicability."

—**Elke U. Weber**, Princeton University

"Barbara Tversky is our premier cognitive ethologist. She observes cognition at work in the wild, then brings it into the lab. This illuminating Festschrift shows the range and power of the work now being done by her numerous students and collaborators. I recommend it strongly."

—**C. R. Gallistel**, Rutgers University—New Brunswick

This volume pulls together interdisciplinary research on cognitive representations in the mind and in the world. The chapters—from cutting-edge researchers in psychology, philosophy, computer science, and the arts—explore how structured representations determine cognition in memory, spatial cognition information visualization, event comprehension, and gesture. It will appeal to graduate-level cognitive scientists, technologists, philosophers, linguists, and educators.

Jeffrey M. Zacks is Professor and Associate Chair of Psychological & Brain Sciences, and Professor of Radiology, at Washington University in St. Louis.

Holly A. Taylor is Professor of Psychology and Co-Director of the Center for Applied Brain & Cognitive Sciences at Tufts University.

REPRESENTATIONS IN MIND AND WORLD

Essays Inspired by Barbara Tversky

Edited by Jeffrey M. Zacks and Holly A. Taylor

NEW YORK AND LONDON

First published 2018
by Routledge
711 Third Avenue, New York, NY 10017

and by Routledge
2 Park Square, Milton Park, Abingdon, Oxon, OX14 4RN

Routledge is an imprint of the Taylor & Francis Group, an informa business

Library of Congress Cataloging-in-Publication Data
A catalog record for this book has been requested

ISBN: 978-1-138-82969-5 (hbk)
ISBN: 978-1-138-82970-1 (pbk)
ISBN: 978-1-315-16978-1 (ebk)

Typeset in Bembo
by Keystroke, Neville Lodge, Tettenhall, Wolverhampton

Paperback cover image courtesy Andrea Kantrowitz

Printed in Canada

CONTENTS

LIST OF CONTRIBUTORS

Kathleen M. Arnold, Department of Psychology & Neuroscience, Duke University, United States.

Thomas Barkowsky, Bremen Spatial Cognition Center, University of Bremen, Germany.

Mireille Bétrancourt, School of Education & Technology, University of Geneva, Switzerland.

Tad T. Brunyé, Center for Applied Brain & Cognitive Sciences at Tufts University; Department of Psychology, Tufts University; and Cognitive Science Team, U.S. Army Natick Soldier Research, Development, and Engineering Center, United States.

Roberto Casati, Institut Jean Nicod CNRS ENS EHESS, France.

Michel Denis, LIMSI-CNRS, Université Paris Sud, France.

Frank Dylla, Bremen Spatial Cognition Center, University of Bremen, Germany.

Zoe Falomir, Bremen Spatial Cognition Center, University of Bremen, Germany.

Nancy Franklin, Department of Psychology, Stony Brook University, United States.

Christian Freksa, Bremen Spatial Cognition Center, University of Bremen, Germany.

Michael Greenstein, Department of Psychology & Philosophy, Framingham State University, United States.

Zach D. Haga, Center for Applied Brain & Cognitive Sciences at Tufts University, United States.

Lindsay A. Houck, Center for Applied Brain & Cognitive Sciences at Tufts University and Cognitive Science Team, U.S. Army Natick Soldier Research, Development, and Engineering Center, United States.

Andrea Kantrowitz, Department of Art, State University of New York at New Paltz, United States.

Elizabeth J. Marsh, Department of Psychology & Neuroscience, Duke University, United States.

Chiara Meneghetti, Department of General Psychology, University of Padua, Italy.

Jeffrey V. Nickerson, School of Business, Stevens Institute of Technology, United States.

Jane Nisselson, Virtual Beauty, United States.

Ana-Maria Olteţeanu, Bremen Spatial Cognition Center, University of Bremen, Germany.

Francesca Pazzaglia, Department of General Psychology, University of Padua, Italy.

Holly A. Taylor, Center for Applied Brain & Cognitive Sciences at Tufts University and Department of Psychology, Tufts University, United States.

Jasper van de Ven, Bremen Spatial Cognition Center, University of Bremen, Germany.

Jeffrey M. Zacks, Department of Psychological & Brain Sciences and Department of Radiology, Washington University, United States.

1

INSIGHT IN MIND

Holly A. Taylor and Jeffrey M. Zacks

Representations of Barbara Tversky

How do representations in our heads and representations out in the world interact to produce human behavior? This is one of the great questions of contemporary cognitive science and the theme of this book. These questions also reflect the career of Barbara Tversky. The chapters presented here all take aim at cognitive representations in complex cognition. They emerged from a symposium held in Chicago in November, 2015, to honor Barbara Tversky's career. They extend beyond traditional definitions of cognitive science by representing a convergence of psychologists, artists, computer scientists, philosophers, and designers.

This volume is broad in scope, befitting the panoramic range of Barbara Tversky's scientific career. In a recent conversation with one of us, Tversky referred to Yuval Noah Harari's contrast between hunter-gatherers and farmers (Harari, 2014) and characterized herself as an intellectual hunter-gatherer. Indeed, her restless scientific mind has ranged over verbal memory, scenes, events, diagrams, and mental imagery. She has studied college students and children, architects and artists. With her collaborators, she has invented tasks, wrestled behaviors such as wayfinding, drawing, and graphing into the laboratory, and conjured methods to render the dynamic processes of free-range cognition accessible to quantitative analysis. At the same time, within this vast range of topics, she masterfully connects ideas both within and across topics, thus creating order and theory relevant for understanding and predicting complex cognition more generally.

This volume aims to reflect not only Barbara's research but also her theoretical approach, which is unique in its ability to provoke insight and connection. Across the wide range of her work stretches a common focus on the format of representations. Representations can be in one's mind or made explicit on a piece of paper or computer screen in the world. Barbara clearly also recognized that even considering both internal and external representations would be insufficient to understand complex cognition. The mind interacts with the world and it is important to understand fundamentals of how internal and external representations interact.

Another equally important factor to understanding complex cognition emerges in Barbara's research strategy. Just as she examines internal and external representations and their interaction, she takes the real world into the lab and the lab into the real world. In this way, she has been able to explore how cognition actually functions in important real-world situations. In her work and the work she has inspired, people have navigated environments without ever leaving the lab room, creating mental representations from spatial language, maps, and virtual reality. People have also navigated cities of the world and many a college campus. People have been asked to understand or explain diagrams created as experimental stimuli, and Barbara has set out to understand and find commonalities amongst diagrams others have published to explain a concept. She has explored how artists create, how designers design, and how scientists explain.

This wide-ranging curiosity is evident in her collaborators and students—and in the chapters assembled here. We have arranged the book in three sections, moving from representations in the mind to representations in the world to the interaction of mind and world. The chapters themselves reflect research emanating from the lab, "in the wild" of the real world, and conceptualized in the mind of her students, post-docs, and collaborators based on their inspiring interactions with her.

Representations in Mind

Roberto Casati opens with a philosophical grounding of mental representations. Building on the popular distinction between fast/automatic and slow/effortful modes of processing (e.g., Kahneman, 2011), Casati proposes a new mode that offloads some of the slow and effortful components of reasoning onto the environment. The view that human cognition can only be understood in terms of how it is embedded in the environment of things is called "situated cognition," and it is a view with which Tversky has long been engaged. One way to describe Casati's project is to say that he "situates situated cognition." Nancy Franklin and Michael Greenstein take ideas of mental representation to a highly constrained—and high-stakes—setting: legal testimony. Their chapter reviews how memory and storytelling interact during legal testimony. We anticipate that this chapter will be extremely valuable not just to cognitive scientists but also to legal practitioners. In the final chapter of this section, Tad Brunyé, Zach Haga, Lindsay Houck, and Holly Taylor take on another real-world application of memory: finding one's way around. This work, inspired by Taylor's early work with Barbara (Taylor & Tversky, 1992a, 1992b), explores how spatial mental representations impact knowledge of, and interactions with, the environment. All three of these chapters demonstrate the Tverskyan strategy of uncovering fundamental attributes of memory representations by looking at how they engage with complex, naturalistic tasks.

Representations in World

The second section focuses on the representational artifacts that humans create. It opens with a visual essay by Jane Nisselson, abstracting her short film based on Tversky's paper Visualizing Thought (Tversky, 2011). The essay and the film vividly illustrate how the elements of diagrams function. Michel Denis' chapter zooms in on one diagrammatic element, the arrow, wonderfully taking a common artifact that appears simple enough to take for granted and showing the actual cognitive complexity that underlies its functioning. Increasing the complexity of the representational artifacts, Mireille Bétrancourt takes on a particularly contemporary cognitive artifact: animation. It turns out to be surprisingly difficult to design effective animations; Bétrancourt's chapter investigates why this is so and suggests what can be done. Representational artifacts exist for people to use, even if only for the artifact's creator. Jeffrey Nickerson moves from the artifacts themselves to how practitioners really use them, showing how designers use artifacts to reason, to discover, to provoke themselves to new insights. Finally, Francesca Pazzaglia and Chiara Meneghetti show that there are dramatic differences in how people use cognitive artifacts to learn about spatial environments, and that these differences are systematic.

Interaction of Mind and World

We close, of course, with how representations in the mind and in the world interact. Elizabeth Marsh and Kathleen Arnold open this section by considering how using memory cycles back to influence memory representations. Much of Tversky's early research investigated the operations used by children and adults when encoding and remembering verbal materials (e.g., Tversky, 1973; Tversky & Teiffer, 1976). When Marsh and Tversky began collaborating, they focused on how these mechanisms function in the sorts of things that people actually do with verbal memories (Tversky & Marsh, 2000). When people use verbal memories, they interact in interesting ways with the world and come back to influence the mental representation. One important thing people do is tell others about what happened—and as Marsh and Arnold demonstrate, this affects not only the listener but also the memory of the teller. Christian Freksa et al's chapter applies this mind-world interaction analysis to spatial problem solving. Notably, the arrangement of objects in space, whether they be buildings in a city, rooms in a building, or matchsticks on a table, affects spatial problem solving related to those objects. Jeffrey Zacks's chapter applies a similar analysis to event representations, showing how our mental and neural representations of events determine our media—and vice versa. Finally, Andrea Kantrowitz illustrates (literally!) a fine-grained description of how artists go back and forth with their marks, shaping their creative cognition in real time.

The Complete Picture

Many of the authors represented have been committed to the field of cognitive science for long years. Others are recent converts or fellow travelers. We hope that this book will be useful to both old hands and new recruits. For ourselves, we think that the work collected here renders vivid the power, breadth, and creativity of what contemporary cognitive science can be. This only makes sense, given that it was inspired by Barbara Tversky.

Authors' Note

Preparation of this volume and the introductory chapter was a joint and equal effort. Order of authorship was determined by a coin flip.

References

Harari, Y. N. (2014). *Sapiens: A brief history of humankind*. Random House.

Kahneman, D. (2011). *Thinking, fast and slow*. Macmillan.

Taylor, H. A., & Tversky, B. (1992a). Descriptions and depictions of environments. *Memory and Cognition*, 20, 483–496.

Taylor, H. A., & Tversky, B. (1992b). Spatial mental models derived from survey and route descriptions. *Journal of Memory and Language*, 31, 261–282.

Tversky, B. (1973). Encoding processes in recognition and recall. *Cognitive Psychology*, 5, 275–287.

Tversky, B. (2011). Visualizing thought. *Topics in Cognitive Science*, 3(3), 499–535.

Tversky, B., & Marsh, E. (2000). Biased retellings of events yield biased memories. *Cognitive Psychology*, 40, 1–38.

Tversky, B., & Teiffer, E. (1976). Development of strategies for recall and recognition. *Developmental Psychology*, 12, 406–410.

Representations in Mind

2

TWO, THEN FOUR MODES OF FUNCTIONING OF THE MIND

Towards a Unification of "Dual" Theories of Reasoning and Theories of Cognitive Artifacts

Roberto Casati

The main aim of this contribution is to stabilize and generalize the use of the conceptual labels originating from "dual" theories of reasoning, so as to provide a theoretical unification with theories of cognitive artifacts, and to describe in an abstract way the mechanics of cognitive artifacts. Psychological literature has by and large accepted the distinction between two "systems", or – as I shall say – two *modes* of operation of the brain in certain tasks, mainly reasoning and decision-making tasks (Evans 2003, 2012, 2015 for reviews; Evans and Frankish 2009; Kahneman 2011). Mode 1 (M1, for brevity) is an automatic, autonomous, stimulus-driven, fast operating mode that delivers rough but locally acceptable results; M2 is modulated by will and attention, operates slowly and stepwise, intensely uses working memory, and is in general more accurate. I shall take the distinction for granted (with some caveats, in particular I shall argue that we do not need to endorse a substantive view of cognitive *systems*, as opposed to a more neutral talk of *modes*) and argue for an extension of the conceptualization to cover cases discussed in the literature of cognitive artifacts, with the goal of unifying the two fields. I'll first introduce M4, an operating mode that completely outsources the computations typically run by M1 and/or M2 to external artifacts. The M4 mode fully delegates the relevant mental activity – what I shall dub "core" computational tasks – and only makes its user care about the input and output of the computation. Then I'll vindicate the existence of a Mode 3, best understood as occupying an intermediate position between M2 and M4. In the third mode we interact with cognitive artifacts (such as maps, measuring instruments, written text) and this interaction is both essential to performing a certain task (as opposed to what happens in M1 and M2) and is not an instance of wholesale offload (as opposed to M4). Interactions with cognitive artifacts actually display proprietary computations, which give some hints about the architecture of cognition, and about its flexibility. Flexibility in turn creates room for the activity of designers of cognitive artifacts.

In this chapter I investigate the relationships between the M3, M1 and M2, and discuss some demarcation issues: whether M3 activities are a subclass of M2 activities, and whether we should postulate continuity between the four modes. More specifically, I look into some of the proprietary computations of M3 (such as shunting information, bridging cognitive modules, displacing search processes, or restructuring memory search). Other targets are popular metaphors such as the "extended mind" and "the world as external memory" that, by making the M3 look too much like M4, risk missing out on the specific properties of brain-artifact interaction.

M1 vs M2: An Example from Navigation

I grew up in a right-driving country. My parents taught me how to cross the street when I was very young. Over time I refined this practice. I moved from having no idea about crossing streets to being moderately skilled, to being an expert. When you acquire such a skill, the imperatives are to train and to aim at being error free. Over such a long, endless process of learning and perfecting, your responses inevitably become automatic: they involve a sense of your body, a sense of your target, time planning, quick decision making, and gut feelings. For instance, when you cross the street, you automatically expect and almost feel danger first on your left-hand side, then on your right-hand side. Navigation is computation (Hutchins 1995).[1] You assess time in relation to the space of travel, the contingencies of the street scene, your assessment of safe zones, the presence of other actors. You even break the law from time to time. You face, and make, quick decisions if an unexpected car shows up. Crossing the street has become second nature to you; you are *fluent* in crossing the street.

On my first visit to England, a left-driving country, I was back at square one. No more quick assessments, no more quick decisions, no more confidence: I was a child once more. I was warned over and over again about looking "in the other direction" or, if in doubt, "look in all directions". I paid attention to each step I took – an attitude that may even be dangerous in some circumstances, as I would often freeze in the middle of the street. I really planned each crossing in advance, aiming to figure out how to complete it and trying to avoid the prospect of needing a contingency plan (too difficult to figure out, almost impossible to implement). I could almost feel my thinking slowing down. I engaged in hypothetical reasoning, without relying on any past experience of crossing in a similar situation (Evans 2003.) People who have spent enough time in both driving cultures report that they adapt, becoming as skilled as the natives, or at least as fluent as proficient second-language speakers. I clearly did not spend enough time there. Statistics on road accidents in the UK confirm difficulties for right-hand-driving truck drivers (Danton, Kirk, Hill 2009).

There are many entry points to the two-mode metaphor and the reason I choose this one is mainly because it makes the important aspect vivid (if you ever had the experience of the other-driving habit): both a clear phenomenology and obvious behavioral differences are associated with the deployment of each mode in the two different cases respectively. Mode 1 is the way my brain operates when I cross the street in France, and Mode 2 when I do so in Great Britain. In the first case I think fast, in the second I think slow (Kahneman 2011). But what do "fast" and "slow" mean? It is partly a matter of decisions/calculations unfolding in time, but the time differences reflect architectural differences in the organization of thought.

What the Distinction Is and What It Is Not

The psychological literature has accepted a distinction between two "systems", or two modes of operation of the brain in certain tasks, mainly reasoning and decision-making tasks. Mode 1 is described as an automatic, fast and fluent operating mode that delivers rough but locally acceptable results; Mode 2 is described as modulated by will and attention, as operating slowly and stepwise, as taxing memory working, and as delivering comparatively more accurate results in many cases. There are now a number of ways to present the distinction and to relate it to other older distinctions (intuition vs. reason, heuristics and biases vs. logic, encapsulated "Fodorian" modules vs. central processing; see Evans 2003), but let me just say what I take the distinction *not* to be. First and most importantly, it is not a distinction between two *systems, strictly considered*, if by "system" we mean something like the visual system or the auditory system, although it may be so interpreted.[2] Kahneman himself insists on the fact that "System one" and "two" are akin to fictional characters. Second, it is not a distinction between two modules (like the vision module for face recognition and the vision module for line orientation). Both M1 and M2 rely on the operation of modules – although in addressing a particular task, they may tap into different modular resources, and deploy them in different ways. Third, and by (almost) the same token, it is not a distinction between having intuitions and not having intuitions. You have and use plenty of intuitions when you operate in M2. Finally, the distinction is not that of innate vs. acquired. Learning does make a difference in operating M2, but on the one hand a lot of learning is present in the myriad systems that operate in M1, and on the other hand – to mention but an example – reading is the result of learning, but competent reading clearly displays M1 automaticity and fluency.

On a positive characterization, M1 and M2 are best construed as *modes of operation* of the brain. This is to say that although based on a host of different competencies, they are better seen at the level of *performance* rather than at the level of *competence*. This is suggested by the literal adverbial reading of Kahneman's distinction between thinking "fast" and "slow". One may thus characterize the approach defended here as an "adverbial" construal of the relevant phenomena, as opposed to a "substantival" construal, typified by talk of "systems".

Generalizing the Distinction

Talk of modes is crucial to a first generalization. There are a large variety of mental engagements over and above verbal problem solving and decision making. As we have seen, navigation is hospitable to the two-modes distinction. Visual analysis is another example: you can just let vision process information automatically, or you may want to intervene on it by directing your overt attention to details (Cavanagh 2004).

Second, in the tasks standardly discussed in the literature on reasoning, the overarching "control concept" of M2 is *enhanced epistemic or pragmatic quality*.[3] This too can be generalized. You want to end up in a zone in which the quality of your representation or of your action is better than the one you would obtain in using the first thing that comes to mind, i.e. in using M1, relative to a certain task such as navigating or finding the solution to a logic problem.

For the present purposes, the main aspect of M2 is that it is a mode of operation in which various M1-like activities are modulated and regimented for performing a certain task such as navigation. When you address a certain problem in M2 mode, you do not trust, or you do not care about, the first thing that comes to mind; and you try to make sure that other, more trustworthy things come to mind. As an illustration, consider the difference between walking down to the cafeteria (something you did so many times that not only does it feel automatic, it is automatic to the point of making you forget that you wanted to go to the news-stand), on the one hand, and on the other hand going from to Place de la Concorde to the Eiffel Tower, unassisted by maps (something that requires you to plan, visualize, double check, and put together bits and pieces of spatial knowledge).

How does M2 work? After a long period of attention to how M1 can interfere with normative reasoning, the literature has produced a number of insights into the functioning of M2 activities. The mechanics of M2 is assumed to be a mix of inhibition and selective attention (Stanovich 2009), but it also includes designing strategies or learning tricks to generate good solutions. For instance, while M1 comes up with biased, perception-generated answers to logic problems such as that presented in the Wason selection task (Wason & Evans 1975), training in logic, or the use of local metacognitive strategies (Houdé et al. 2000) may inhibit the responses that actually come to everyone's minds (including to the logician's mind) and buy time and attention for solving the task, based on principles. Overriding M1 is an interesting design problem for cognition. Probably metacognitive feelings are involved in getting M2 started. For instance, we may detect a conflict and become suspicious; a certain outcome may feel "fishy"; expertise plays a role here.

Once the revision process has started, checking each step of your solution-generating process is a standardly applied strategy. This can only work, of course, if you are able to access the various steps of the computation. Some other strategies are generally available:

- Actually thinking twice, i.e. going over the process one more time: maybe the generated solution differs, or corrects the first one.
- Being systematically suspicious about the result, so that you may want to think twice.
- Learning by heart some partial solutions you are bound to use (for instance, the results of the multiplication table).
- Running the process in reverse, conditionally: if this is what I obtained, then . . .

But, as I said, the actual mechanics of M2 operation are as yet not fully understood (Stanovich 2009). For the present purposes, we can accept that as M2 operation is algorithmic in nature, action can take place at the input, at the computation, or at the output levels. Whether and how this is possible will depend on the type of process you plan to act upon.

Introducing M4

My proposal is to extend the M1/M2 metaphor to include another mode, M3. Actually, I propose to introduce *two* other operation modes, M3 and M4, and in order to exactly understand the import of the introduction of M3 I find it convenient to start from M4. M4 occupies an extreme of the spectrum of ways of operating under examination here. Working in M4 mode means *delegating* the *relevant* mental process to some external *device*, and only caring about the *solution* of the delegated process. M4 really is a proxy mode. For instance, you launch a navigation query ("Destination: Eiffel Tower"), and take directions from a GPS-based navigation device, by listening to the instructions dictated to you over a speaker. "Proceed to the intersection. At the intersection, make a left turn." You do not even look at the map on the display. This is a paradigmatic case of M4 in operation.

Let us spend some time on this particular example of the "talking navigator". First of all, this extreme type of human-machine interaction is only possible in heavily constrained environments, such as the road system, where decisions tend to be discrete, as the options are simplified: you rely on an ontology of networked one-dimensional objects (routes), left turns, right turns, and little else, where the only legal moves are going ahead or turning back – not, say, head for a 37° bearing.

Second, in most cases – and in this one in particular – you do not give up all of your mental life. You are still making decisions, you launch a navigation query, you listen to the verbal instructions and interpret them, you check them against your perception of the environment – conflicts may arise ("was it the first or the second exit at the intersection?") – and you should still be able to solve them. Yet, you are giving up most of the *relevant* mental life, if compared to a more engaged relationship with, say, a paper map. In particular, you are giving up *navigational* computations, that you outsource completely, in the same sense in which you outsource them to a taxi driver in an unknown city (Marconi 2005). In M4 mode you only access/perform at the input and/or the output of the computation, and you do not run any of the relevant computations in your brain.

Let me introduce a distinction between *core* computational tasks and *auxiliary* computational tasks. A core computational task, relative to a given performance, is a task that is essential to obtain the desired result. In navigation, core computational tasks are dead reckoning and determining a direction, for instance. You must be able to compute your local position and you must be able to compute your direction to target, either by finding a heading directly to target, or by laying down a sequence of waypoints and then finding a heading to each of them in sequence. In M4 mode the core computational task of navigation is clearly offloaded. You do not need to know where you are and you do not need to calculate any of the next steps. Still, you must compute something, i.e. how to launch a query (how to interact with the device) and how to interpret the result. Relative to navigation, these are auxiliary computational tasks, as they are not navigational computations. Besides, they are not specific to navigation and are actually shared by many other tasks (e.g. looking up an encyclopedia entry on your PC).

A signature feature of M4 is then that you do not need to access any steps of the core computational task that characterizes the performance. The nature of the performance changes: it is no longer "navigation", but "use of an instrument that finds the route for you."

Introducing M3

I sought to characterize M4 in order to gain a better understanding of M3. M3 is distinct from M2 in that it essentially uses external artifacts, and is however distinct from M4 insofar as, relative to a particular task, delegating to external artifacts is not wholesale – and definitely does not outsource some *core* computational task. As an instance, consider navigating an unknown environment by using a paper map. First, this is clearly different from navigating (M1-like) in a known environment for which your brain has constructed – you can't help it – an effective mental map. The notion of a mental map may itself be controversial (see Madl et al. 2015 for a review), but I assume that information is stored in the brain in map-like, i.e. spatially organized, format. The M1-like features of mental map representation and use, on the other hand, are not controversial. You do not need to consult an external map to find your way back to the elevators in this building: fluency and automaticity are granted here. Second, navigating with a paper map in an unknown environment is clearly different from taking directions from a GPS, or setting an autopilot, which are prime examples of M4 mode of operation. In an unknown environment, assisted by a map, you try in a careful, stepwise fashion to identify landmarks, to interpret and assess affordances, and to keep an explicit mental record of visited places; you are also inhibiting some of your powerful M1 routines (Stanovich 2009). (For instance, your perception-based intuitions suggest proceeding in a straight line, but the map signals an obstacle that is invisible from your current location, and so you take a detour; to take another example, your mental mapping system hooks on to whatever visual features are available in the landscape, including clouds and waves, which make for very ephemeral landmarks, and you have to inhibit or discard this hooking.) You interpret the map propositionally, not just as a depiction of the terrain, but as a set of instructions, of inferential cues, that are subject to distortions of various type (Tversky 1981; Tversky and Lee 1998, 1999; Denis 1997.) All this puts you in an M2-like mode of operation. But the map is essential here; interaction with the map modulates all the other activities you engage in. Map-assisted navigation at its core consists of deliberately thinking of and making a connection between you and your environment, which requires interpreting both the map (to make quick inferences about what to expect around you) and the environment (to assess the presence of landmarks), before trying to connect the one to the other.

A map stores information about a place in a specific, spatially structured way (Casati and Varzi 1999; Rescorla 2009; Kulvicki 2015.) For our present purposes, the important point is that it records information about places that you may or may not have visited, and in particular about places that you may not be able to perceptually access in the present moment. A map used for navigation should be capable of supporting certain specific queries. By asking the appropriate questions of the map, you can for instance determine that you are in a certain location, and that you should move in a certain direction if you want to reach your final destination. In order to perform these functions in navigation, a map needs *orienting.* Orienting can be explicit (as when you are able to have a meridian's representation on the map coincide with the represented meridian), or implicit (you master a set of rules for transforming each direction you establish on the map on a direction in the represented region; no matter the actual position of the map relative to you and your environment). In both cases you are establishing *physical relationships* between the map and the environment in which the map is situated, and this requires a certain set of skills on your part, which you must learn. Navigation is computation: you should be able to compute, on an oriented map, your current location, by finding the appropriate correspondences between represented landmarks and their representations (for instance, the bearings of two landmarks intersect on the map in a point that approximates your current location).

Are you "delegating" to a map, in the sense in which you were delegating to the talking navigator? Certainly not. When you interact with a map you engage in a specific mode of operation. To recap, you have to be able to ask questions that the map can provide answers to, and be able to find the answers on the map, in order to make decisions; you actively engage with the map, and this engagement lets you generate the mental representations that you need to make your decisions and start your motor routines. You are core-computing, on the map and with the map, position and route yourself. This way of interacting I take as definitional of M3.

The Mechanics of M3

M3 involves external cognitive, epistemic artifacts essentially, and we have to consider now the features of these artifacts. The first key distinction I have in mind here is that between representational vs. non-representational cognitive artifacts.[4]

Some artifacts are not cognitive: hammers, nails and scissors belong in this family. Although you have to cognitively engage with them in order to use them, and although they may have a cognitive effect on you, their function is not to impinge on your cognitive states; whatever they may do to cognition, they don't do it by design. On the other hand, epistemic artifacts, by design, are meant to have an effect on your cognitive states. For instance, they may have been designed to improve the quality of your cognitive states. How do they do this? The main sub-distinction here is between representational and non-representational artifacts. A pair of glasses with suitable lens correction will make you see better. If you have to read a road sign, you end up in a better cognitive situation relative to not wearing them. Glasses intervene on the incoming information by structuring it. However, glasses do not represent anything; they are not about anything. Wearing glasses does modify your mental representation – your visual image of the scene in front of you – but glasses (and their cognates mirrors, microscopes, telescopes, periscopes) are not like written words, maps or painted images, which are items that have representational content (over and above structuring the information that gets to your senses).

In the case of cognitive artifacts, the pragmatics condition the recruitment of cognitive functions and strategies and constrain the design of the artifact. Given the variety of uses, we observe some quite specific and at times interconnected ways cognitive artifacts interact with the brain, i.e. types of cognitive mechanics:

> freeing up working memory, storing information, making inferences visually available and available for inspection, priming action, bridging different modules, shunting information, providing hyper-stimuli to a module, making orienting and navigation possible, indexing, displacing complex searches to automatic brain routines.

This is, of course, an open-ended list. Here is where a key theoretical tool of the account I would like to propose finds its place. In all those cases we can point to some specific *cognitive advantage* linked to the adoption of a given artifact. One of the main tasks for psychology is then to find operationalizations of the advantages (e.g. in what is it easier to use a route display rather than a map display on an embarked navigation system? What makes certain types of diagrams better suited than others in order to extract inferences? (Tversky et al. 2000, Heiser & Tversky 2006 on arrows; Tversky 1995); Why are certain items in the multiplication table easier to remember than others?) And the main task for designers is to assess and exploit the trade-offs between cognitive advantages.

Let me give a few examples of quite specific interactions between cognitive artifacts and the brain along the lines I just drew.

Displacement. Suppose you are looking for the trains leaving between 9 and 11. You are presented with four timetables, each presenting the same facts, but in a different graphic style: Mixed Bag, Order, Highlight, Chunk. You shall notice a difference in retrieving the desired set of times.

(Mixed Bag): 10:20, 8:30, 11:40, 13:30, 9:25, 10:35, 16:40, 8:15
(Order): 8:15, 8:30, 9:25, 10:20, 10:35, 11:40, 13:30, 16:40
(Highlight): **10:20**, 8:30, 11:40, 13:30, **9:25**, **10:35**, 16:40, 8:15
(Chunk): 8:15 8:30, 9:25, 10:20,10:35, 11:40, 13:30, 16:40

Larkin and Simon (1987) would claim that the four timetables are informationally equivalent but computationally different. Tversky et al. (2007) distinguish here between the Principle of Congruence ("the structure and content of a visualization should correspond to the structure and content of the desired mental representation") and the Principle of Apprehension ("the structure and content of a visualization should be readily and accurately perceived and comprehended", p. 56). But these overarching distinctions do not tell us about the mechanics yet. What are the computational differences that matter for Apprehension? Why does it take longer to search in (Mixed Bag) than in any other style? If you think about your behavior in front of (Mixed Bag), unassisted by paper and pencil, you'll notice that you have to pay attention sequentially to each item in the series, you have to explicitly mentally label it as a positive or a negative, you have to store positives in memory, and possibly revisit the series for double checking. That means that both targets and distractors are processed and re-processed. You must remember what the target's content is, or where an encountered target was, in case you forgot the content. Both spatial and short-term memory are actively engaged and put under pressure, and paying attention to each item clearly locates your activity in an M2-like area. In the other three formats, powerful and fast computational routines of the visual system take up part of this chore, kicking it to M1 modes of operation. The visual system loves ordered series, color differences and chunks, and can instantly zero in on the positives as they have been singled out in a visual-system-friendly format (Healey and Enns 2012). Displacement of cognitive tasks is one of the key mechanisms of cognitive artifacts. The design implicit in (Order), (Highlight), and (Chunk) is an orchestration of M1-operating routines, that are more effective than the M2 work done when searching in (Mixed Bag).

Displacement is interesting in two other respects. First, it does not require learning, and thus is extremely effective, giving designers of cognitive artifacts great leverage. Second, moving computations to one part of the brain to another keeps the computations within the boundaries of the brain. The non-necessity of learning distinguishes Displacement from other shifts of cognitive load within the brain. For instance, in gaining expertise about paintings, art dealers train their brain so that certain complex step-by-step (M2) judgements about the quality of a painting are automatized and get compressed into intuitive, perception-like assessments (M1). Different parts of the brain are involved (Kirk et al. 2009; Houdé et al. 2000 talk of "shifting" for this latter mechanism), but automatization requires a fair deal of learning.

Shunting. When looking at a line drawing representing a chair, early phases of information processing are *shunted*: line extraction is directly interfaced with the recognition of a chair. An enormous cognitive advantage (quick recognition) is provided by the very parsimonious use of simple and uniform lines. The strong explanatory hypothesis here (Cavanagh 1999) is that at some level of visual architecture information is stored in a format that only specifies occlusion boundaries – precisely as line drawings do. This format is the mental target of line drawings. Thus, given the hypothesized architecture, drawings work efficiently because they allow shunting of information. This fact teams up with the simplicity of the production of drawings, as opposed to other representational styles (photorealistic images, silhouettes – Willats 1997): drawings are both representationally effective and easy to produce.

Bridging. External representations can act as *bridges* between representational systems that have no biological/evolutionary reason to team up. Bridging is the key to understanding reading and writing, for instance. Letters written on an external support are the external bridges between the visual recognition module and the phonological module. These two modules had no evolutionary ground for working together (Dehaene 2009). They team up in those who read because years of tireless and often painful education and operant conditioning have established the relevant neural connections between them. And they do team up very effectively, as you are not able to just look at the patterns on this page and see mere scribbles or decorations: you cannot help but read what is written here, thus moving from an M2 slow deciphering to an M1-type fluency. But they cannot team up without the written letters, without the relevant external bridges.

To take another example, numerals have been described (Spelke and Tsivkin 2001) as a linguistic and cognitive bridge between two modules incorporating "core" knowledge, that is, between precise subitization of small quantities and approximate representation of large quantities. By using numerals and counting, we can "see" small differences in large quantities that are not accessible to perceptual intuition (for instance, the difference between 58 and 59 apples).

The Mechanics Impose Design Constraints on Cognitive Artifacts

A generalization from the case of numerals is at hand: the cognitive mechanics imposes constraints on the design of cognitive artifacts. "Displacing" or redistributing cognitive load is but one of the characteristics of M3. In general, M3 intervenes in an M2-like way by orchestrating different M1-like activities and in an M1-like way in some nuts and bolts of the fine-grained interaction with artifacts.

Think again of the way you interact with a map. You M2-like engage in a complex back-and-forth between map and terrain; once a relevant bit of information has been gathered, you make progress, update your position, and you do not go to look for that piece of information a second time. Moving your head back-and-forth from map to terrain, in order to gather information by your internal spatial mapping system, on the other hand, is performed in an M1-like way. A contrast with photographs is useful here. *Portability* is the cognitive advantage and signature of maps over other environment representations such as photographs. Photographs are, by etiology and design, *viewpoint bound*. One may use a photograph as a guide to explore a certain environment, but the limits of this use are all too soon evident precisely because of the viewpoint-boundedness of photographs; if you move around, after a while some important landmarks the photograph represents will be out of view, and other landmarks, which the photograph does not represent, will become salient; parallax, hence perspective, changes dramatically as people move in the environment. This means that when using a photograph as an aid to navigation, the inferential load grows exponentially as one moves away from the photograph's viewpoint, and becomes more and more framed in hypothetical format. On the other hand, the inferential load required for using a map is constant over the whole territory mapped. The M2 engagement with maps fades into a number of automatic M1 routines as you start navigating, whereas the M1 immediacy of recognition of a landscape in a photograph turns quickly into M2 inferential reconstructions of the ground as you move away from the photograph's viewpoint.

Objections to the Present Proposal

Terminology: Mode vs. Substance

At the end of the day, M1 is an automatic, artifact-unassisted mode, M2 is a reflexive, controlled and possibly algorithmic mode of operation, M4 is an assisted, proxy mode, and M3 is an assisted, non-delegating mode of functioning of the brain. One may quarrel over the terminology, propose similar labels for carving out the field at different joints, or propose different labels. Stanovich (2009) suggested renaming M1, understood substantivally as a full-blown system, as TASS (The Autonomous Set of Systems). The renaming would have the advantage of not considering M1 as a single entity, but as a bunch of modules or non-modular systems, autonomy being the signature feature of each of them. Insofar as I restrict the label "M1" to a mode of operation, giving an adverbial reading of the label, I have no particular stance on this.

As can be seen from the previous discussion, some potential problems came precisely from a substantivized view of the "system" terminology. My suggestion is that we reserve the "system" labels derived from the now established "dual processes" tradition for modes of operation, not for modules or groups of modules (i.e. "systems" in the old sense in which we talk of the visual system).

There have been calls for systems (or modes of operation, or styles of processing) over and above M1 and M2. The main proposal is in Stanovich (2009) suggesting that within M2 one distinguishes between an algorithmic system and a reflective system. The reflective system is what allows overriding M1 operating activities, installing an algorithmic mechanism in their place (consider again thinking twice before crossing the street in London: you first stop and ponder – reflective activity; then decide to pay attention to each step – implementing the explicit crossing algorithm). Once more, I am happy with this as it is basically a differentiation within M2 in the sense described here. (Stanovich himself proposes new labels, talking of the "autonomous mind", "algorithmic mind", and "reflective mind": "The proposal is thus that just as mode 1 has been pluralized into TASS, we might now need to recognize two aspects of mode 2, the reflective and algorithmic" (p. 59). This proposal is echoed in Houdé and Borst (2014).)

Another potential criticism concerns the risk of overgeneralization (for instance, to the vision/observation distinction). However, I see a wide generalization as an advantage as opposed to former, more restrictive framing of the problem (e.g. talk of reason vs. intuition).

Classification Issues

A further criticism concerns the range of the concepts used here. It may be objected that M3 is actually an instance of M2; in M3 we would just be in M2 mode, only we would use cognitive artifacts, not only intracranial routines. Paper-and-pencil reasoning or computing is after all one of the prototypical examples of M2. But I would like to resist the subsumption move on the following grounds. First, subsumption would prevent us from seeing an aspect of M2, which is its being composed of a number of activities that are performed in M1 mode – here the paper-and-pencil example prevents us from providing a sufficiently articulate description of the phenomena. Second, M3 itself involves orchestrating not only slow and reflective activities, but also M1-like activities, as we have seen in the timetable example.

The Continuity Issue

A third potential criticism is that there is more continuity between the systems than the adopted, discrete labels may suggest. This is somewhat evident at the M4 end of the spectrum, where the amount of core computation that is outsourced appears to be a matter of degree, creating a soft gradient with M3. However, the distinction between the two "paradigm" cases of the talking GPS navigator and of the engaged use of a map should be sufficiently telling for the broad classification we are after. A more delicate issue may present itself at the M2-M3 interface, an issue different from that of subsumption discussed above. The problem is created in particular by the theoretical status of *spoken language*, which, being articulated in public, physical utterances, may be considered as a kind of external cognitive artifact. Most certainly, spoken language is involved in most of the tasks that are defining of the M1-M2 divide, if only because these tasks require interpreting instructions imparted in natural language. Furthermore, spoken language is certainly used in orchestrating various mental activities. On top of that, some elements of language look like more standard artifacts (numerals (Casati 2011) resemble maps; Tversky (2015) lists some spatial aspects of spoken language). Another delicate issue is the use of the body, in particular in gesturing interpreted as a kind of scaffolding, as a communication instrument or as a way of articulating thought (Goldin-Meadow 2003, Hostetter and Alibali 2008, Beilock and Goldin-Meadow 2010, Goldin-Meadow and Beilock 2010, Jamalian, Giardino and Tversky 2013, Giardino 2014). All these examples could invite skepticism about the M2-M3 demarcation proposed here. One line of defense of the proposed demarcation is that spoken language is the only clear singularity here, and that besides that it would be the only module-based cognitive artifact. Pursuing this line would lead to the suggestion that cognitive artifacts were (and still are) modeled on the relevant features of spoken language, which would constitute a sort of Ur-cognitive artifact. Bodily gestures may be less problematic, insofar as their public, "frozen" aspect is more in line with the paradigmatic examples of cognitive artifacts. But surely the continuity issue needs further exploring.

Open Questions

The demarcation issues lead us to some other open questions. One is the relation of the M3-M4 classification with existing philosophical theories of the extended or of the augmented mind (Clark 1999, Clark and Chalmers 1998). A demarcation issue lurks in the proposal of considering the use of cognitive artifacts as determining a form of "extension" of the mind. Without entering into the intricacies of the debate about the merit of redefining the mind's boundaries (Marconi 2005), the present proposal, by shifting the focus to distinctions within performance, may contribute to defusing a substantivalist reading of the opposition between assisted and unassisted cognizing. One may resist the inference from the fact that the mind interacts with artifacts, to the claim that these become actual parts of the mind. We may consider but one specific case discussed by Clark and Chalmers (1998), in which mental what-memories (remembering that one has to go to a certain event) are replaced by mental where-memories (remembering to look at the calendar to see what event one should go to). The strong reading of the extended mind thesis, according to which we have the right to consider as a part of our mind any element that functionally replicates mental functions, is the only one available here, in that it is not supplemented by a computational equivalence. Where-memory searches are computationally different from what-searches. Memory-deprived but notepad-assisted Otto and memory-efficient Inga may be functionally equivalent (Clark and Chalmers 1998), but they are computationally nonequivalent. For the present purposes, thus, we can be neutral as to the engaging claims of the metaphysical thesis.[5]

Why Use Those Metaphors?

Finally, a very general question. Why do we need these semi-metaphorical concepts in general? Why should we endorse them?

Although I defended only an adverbial reading of the labels, it may be argued that in the case of the M1/M2 distinction there may be more substance to it; it would be more than just a metaphorical re-description. M1 and M2 modes would then correspond to natural psychological kinds, tokened in different brain circuitries. The same can very well be the case for M3, and (relatively trivially) for M4. Some of the literature on the two *systems* clearly goes that way.

Be it as it may, the use of metaphors is important for mainly two reasons. The first is that we need to keep track of history and make room for interdisciplinarity in scientific development, so that we can link current research to research in different epochs and domains. Umbrella labels allow for a certain tolerance that future research may find too generous; but at the same time future research may just depend upon the present tolerance. The second is that we want research to reach out to life, sooner or later. This means that we need to employ easy-to-grasp, handy concepts. The proposal to introduce M3 and M4 builds on the relatively widespread acceptance of dual system language in some communities (e.g. behavioral economics, from where it is put to use in policy making and marketing; Samson and Voyer 2012, 2014). It purports to enrich our common-sense representation of psychological processes, so as to assist planning and decision making, in particular in areas such as education. This, I dare say, is all the more important today, as we are swamped by a flow of technological innovations that interact in complex, somewhat surprising, and mostly non-trivial ways with our brains.

Author Note

I first met Barbara Tversky many years back in the south of France, at a workshop on space representation. We have since been conference friends, mostly meeting at workshops that are at the borders of our respective disciplinary and competence areas. This may bear witness to our shared dissatisfaction with too-rigid disciplinary demarcations, and possibly with the desire to classify too much. And yet with this contribution I hoped to create a stable demarcation, for a reason. If you agree with me on the existence of a specific mode of operation of the mind that coincides with what I called here M3, there is no question that Barbara is the person who, more than anyone else, contributed to the understanding of how the mind works in M3 mode.

Thanks to Pierre Bonnier, Marco Fasoli, Valeria Giardino, Vittorio Girotto, Nicole Hall, John Kulvicki, Diego Marconi, Elena Pasquinelli, and Goffredo Puccetti, and to the participants to the 2015 Chicago meeting, and to students at the course on cognitive artifacts at the University of Turin, for insightful comments.

Notes

1 Computations are intended here in the sense of Marr (1982), who distinguished a computational level – as opposed to an algorithmic level and an implementational level – in his characterization of the workings of a cognitive system.
2 See Casati, Dokic, Le Corre (2014), for a discussion of the criteria used in demarcating sensory modalities.
3 The enhancement is not always available, though. Face recognition is a paradigm case of an M1 activity of the brain that is hard to improve by M2-like observation processes. But the point is that in some circumstances M1 may not be available, and we need to use M2-like processes (e.g. in creating and then using facial composites such as Identi-Kit). People with prosopagnosia (face blindness) learn some strategies that mitigate the socially indesirable consequences of their condition, e.g. they explicitly create memory association of identities with some distinctive features, such as gait or hair color. Their relatives and friends can help by stabilizing some of those features.
4 Some other ways of classifying cognitive artifacts are available in the literature. See Hutchins 1999; Kirsh 1995, Heersmink 2013; Bloom 1998. I stand by this minimal classification without making any claim as to its completeness or adequacy. As a matter of fact, classifications of artifacts tend to be theory laden, and little attention is in general paid to the underlying mechanics.
5 Other metaphors, such as "the world as external memory", can be resisted on similar grounds. For instance, if we set in sunlight an oriented model of a city to determine the impact of shadows from a building, we are reducing our computational load, but we are not offloading computations to the model, which is not computing anything.

References

Beilock, S. L. & Goldin-Meadow, S. (2010). Gesture changes thought by grounding it in action. *Psychological Science*, 21, 1605–1610.

Bloom, P. (1998). Theories of artifact categorization. *Cognition*, 66, 87–93.

Casati, R. & Varzi, A. C. (1999). *Parts and places*. Cambridge, MA: MIT Press.

Casati, R. (2011). Numerals and word sequences. In Reboul, A. (Ed.), *Mind, values, and metaphysics, philosophical essays in honor of Kevin Mulligan* (pp. 327–338). Springer International.

Casati, R., Dokic, J., & Le Corre, F. (2014). Distinguishing the commonsense senses. In Matthen, M., Stokes, D., Biggs, S. (Ed.), *Perception and its modalities* (pp. 462–480). Oxford University Press.

Cavanagh, P. (1999). Pictorial art and vision. In Robert A. Wilson & Frank C. Keil (Eds.), *The MIT encyclopedia of the cognitive sciences* (pp. 648–651). Cambridge, MA: MIT Press.

Cavanagh, P. (2004). Attention routines and the architecture of selection. In Michael Posner (Ed.), *Cognitive neuroscience of attention* (pp. 13–28). New York: Guilford Press.

Clark, A. (1999). *Being there*. Cambridge, MA: MIT Press.

Clark, A. & Chalmers, D. (1998). The extended mind. *Analysis* 58 (1), 7–19.

Danton, R., Kirk, A., & Hill, J. (2009). Mainland European Truck Accidents in the UK – Key Issues for Drivers. Vehicle Safety Research Centre, Paper Number 09–0238. Technical report presented at Enhance Safety Vehicles (ESV) conference. www-nrd.nhtsa.dot.gov/pdf/esv/esv21/09-0238.pdf, last accessed October 2015.

Dehaene, S. (2009). *Reading in the brain*. Penguin Viking.

Denis, M. (1997). The description of routes: A cognitive approach to the production of spatial discourse. *Cahiers de Psychologie Cognitive*, 16, 409–458.

Evans, J. S. B. (2003). In two minds: dual-process accounts of reasoning. *Trends in Cognitive Sciences*, 7(10), 454–459.

Evans, J. S. B. (2012). Dual process theories of deductive reasoning: facts and fallacies. *The Oxford Handbook of Thinking and Reasoning*, 115–133.

Evans, J. S. B. (2015). Thinking twice: Two minds in one brain. *Gogoa*, 1213. Retrieved from www.ehu.eus/ojs/index.php/Gogoa/article/viewFile/14071/12491

Evans, J. S. B. & Frankish, K. E. (Eds.) (2009). *In two minds: Dual processes and beyond*. Oxford University Press.

Evans, J. & Frankish, K. (2009). The duality of mind: An historical perspective. In Evans, J. S. B. & Frankish, K. E. (Eds.), *In two minds: Dual processes and beyond*. Oxford University Press.

Giardino, V. (2014). Diagramming: connecting cognitive systems to improve reasoning. In Benedek, A. & Nyíri, K. (Eds.), *Visual learning, Vol. 4: Emotion, expression, explanation* (pp. 23 – 34). Peter Lang Verlag, Frankfurt/M.

Goldin-Meadow, S. (2003). *Hearing gesture: how our hands help us think*. Cambridge, MA: Harvard University Press.

Goldin-Meadow, S. & Beilock, S. L. (2010). Action's influence on thought: the case of gesture. *Psychological Science*, 5(6), 664–674.

Healey, C. G. & Enns, J. T. (2012). Attention and visual memory in visualization and computer graphics. *IEEE Transactions on Visualization and Computer Graphics*, 18, 7, 1170–1188.

Heersmink, R. (2013). A taxonomy of cognitive artifacts: function, information, and categories. *Review of Philosophy and Psychology*, 4, 465–481.

Heiser, J. & Tversky, B. (2006). Arrows in comprehending and producing mechanical diagrams. *Cognitive Science*, 30, 581–592.

Hostetter, A. B. & Alibali, M. W. (2008). Visible embodiment: gestures as simulated action, *Psychonomic Bulletin and Review*, 15(3), 495–514.

Houdé, O., Zago, L., Mellet, E., Moutier, S., Pineau, A., Mazoyer, B., & Tzourio-Mazoyer, N. (2000). Shifting from the perceptual brain to the logical brain: The neural impact of cognitive inhibition training. *Journal of Cognitive Neuroscience*, 12(5), 721–728.

Houdé, O. & Borst, G. (2014). Measuring inhibitory control in children and adults: brain imaging and mental chronometry. *Frontiers in Psychology*, 5(June), 1–7. doi: 10.3389/fpsyg.2014.00616

Hutchins, E. (1995). *Cognition in the wild*. Cambridge, MA: MIT Press.

Hutchins, E. (1999). Cognitive artifacts. In Wilson, R. A., Keil, F. C. (Eds.), *The MIT encyclopedia of the cognitive sciences* (pp. 126–128). Cambridge, MA: MIT Press.

Jamalian, A., Giardino, V., & Tversky, B. (2013). Gestures for thinking. In M. Knauff, M. Pauen, N. Sabaenz, and I. Wachsmuth (Eds.) *Proceedings of the 35th Annual Conference of the Cognitive Science Society*. Austin, TX: Cognitive Science Society.

Kahneman, D. (2011). *Thinking, Fast and Slow*. New York: Farrar, Straus and Giroud.

Kirk, U., Skova, M., Christensen, M. S., & Nygaard, N. (2009). Brain correlates of aesthetic expertise: A parametric fMRI study, *Brain and cognition*, 69, 2, 306–315.

Kirsh, D. (1995). The intelligent use of space. *Artificial Intelligence*, 73, 31–68.

Kulvicki, J. (2015). Maps, pictures, and predication. *Ergo* 2(7), 149–174.

Larkin, J. & Simon, H. (1987). Why a diagram is (sometimes) worth 10,000 words. *Cognitive Science*, 11, 65–99.

Madl, T., Chen, K., Montaldi, D., & Trappl, R. (2015). Computational cognitive models of spatial memory in navigation space: A review. *Neural Networks*, 65, 18–43.

Marconi, D. (2005). Contro la mente estesa, *Sistemi intelligenti*, XVII, 3, 389–98.

Marr, D. (1982). *Vision*. New York: Freeman.

Rescorla, M. (2009). Predication and cartographic representation, *Synthese,* 169, 175–200.

Samson, A. & Voyer, B. (2012). Two minds, three ways: Dual system and process models in consumer psychology. *Academy of Marketing Science Review*, 2, 48–71.

Samson, A. & Voyer, B. (2014). Emergency purchasing situations: Implications for consumer decision-making. *Journal of Economic Psychology*, 44, 21–33.

Spelke, E. S. & Tsivkin, S. (2001). Initial knowledge and conceptual change: Space and number. In M. Bowerman & S. Levinson, (Eds.), *Language acquisition and conceptual development* (pp. 70–97). Cambridge, UK: Cambridge University Press.

Stanovich, K. E. (2009). Distinguishing the reflective, algorithmic, and autonomous minds: Is it time for a tri-process theory? In J. Evans & K. Frankish (Eds.), *In two minds: Dual processes and beyond* (pp. 55–88). Oxford University Press.

Stanovich, K. E., West, R. F., & Toplak, M. E. (2011). The complexity of developmental predictions from dual process models. *Developmental Review*, 31(2–3), 103–118.

Tversky, B. (1981). Distortions in memory for maps. *Cognitive Psychology*, 13, 407–433.

Tversky, B. (1995). Cognitive origins of graphic conventions. In F. T. Marchese (Ed.), *Understanding images* (pp. 29–53). New York: Springer-Verlag.

Tversky, B. (2015). The cognitive design of tools of thought. *Review of Philosophy and Psychology*, 6, 99–116.

Tversky, B. & Lee, P. U. (1998). How space structures language. In C. Freksa, C. Habel, & K. F. Wender (Eds.), *Spatial cognition: An interdisciplinary approach to representation and processing of spatial knowledge* (pp. 157–175). Berlin: Springer-Verlag.

Tversky, B. & Lee, P. U. (1999). Pictorial and verbal tools for conveying routes. In Freksa, C., & Mark, D. M. (Eds.), *Spatial information theory: cognitive and computational foundations of geographic information science* (pp. 51–64). Berlin: Springer.

Tversky, B., Zacks, J., Lee, P. U., & Heiser, J. (2000). Lines, blobs, crosses, and arrows: Diagrammatic communication with schematic figures. In M. Anderson, P. Cheng, and V. Haarslev (Eds.), *Theory and application of diagrams* (pp. 221–230). Berlin: Springer.

Tversky, B., Agrawala, M., Heiser, J., Lee, P. U., Hanrahan, P., Phan, D., et al. (2007). Cognitive design principles for generating visualizations. In G. Allen (Ed.), *Applied spatial cognition: From research to cognitive technology* (pp. 53–73). Mahwah, NJ: Lawrence Erlbaum Associates.

Wason, P. & Evans, J. S. B. (1975). Dual processes in reasoning? *Cognition*, 3(2), 141–154.

Willats, J. (1997). *Art and representations: New principles in the analysis of pictures*. Princeton: Princeton University Press.

Zacks, J. & Tversky, B. (1999). Bars and lines: A study of graphic communication. *Memory and Cognition*, 27, 1073–1079.

3

NOTHING BUT THE TRUTH?

An Assessment of Narrative Goals in the Criminal Justice System

Nancy Franklin and Michael Greenstein

Next to direct observation, people constitute the most universal category of information source we have. Humans are often goal-driven, for example, with an intention to inform, persuade, or entertain. This is a choice of framing, which more than once Tversky has demonstrated can profoundly affect a range of higher cognitive processes (Marsh, Tversky, & Hutson, 2005; Tversky & Kahneman, 1981; Tversky & Marsh, 2000). Specifically for memory, recounting an event with dramatic or persuasive goals can lead to predictable and lasting distortions of memory for the event through (at the very least) selective rehearsal, selective emphasis, and reorganization (e.g., Soleti, Curci, Bianco, & Lanciano, 2012). Dramatic or persuasive retellings prompt emotional rehearsal, which can reduce access to perceptual and contextual detail (Dudukovic, Marsh, & Tversky, 2004; Suengas & Johnson, 1988), but that can simultaneously increase framing-consistent elaborations and inferences at recall (Hashtroudi, Johnson, Vnek, & Ferguson, 1994). In shaping a story, a speaker reshapes his or her own memory. The listener whose only experience of the event is through that speaker's goal-directed retelling has no escape from distortions arising from this process, and they can be considerable.

In many domains, retelling with a goal-directed framing presents no particular harm to anyone. Sometimes the best retelling is a goal-directed one, as when both speaker and listener simply seek amusement from a colorful recap of a funny event. For other domains, goal-directed retellings, and their cognitive consequences, may pose tremendous risk. One such domain is criminal justice, where the perspectives and goals associated with all of those involved can have unexpected and unintended consequences. Some of the policies, conventions, and formal restrictions regarding retellings are uniquely characteristic of this system. In the current chapter, we consider how the many layers of people and procedures within it can systematically amplify risks to memory and judgment.

At the heart of many cases is a witness[1] report of the crime. As the case moves forward, the witness often retells details of the event many times to multiple audiences. Different retellings may have different goals (such as, for example, emphasizing emotional responses when speaking with friends but emphasizing event details when speaking with investigators). Some of these are given in rapid succession, often to the same person, immediately after the event. The arguably most impactful retelling (at trial) may not happen for years.

The Crime and Its Immediate Aftermath

For purposes of discussion, consider a rather typical crime. A man is approached on the street by a stranger and is robbed. His challenge is to remember the perpetrator well enough to describe and later identify him. Witness error in situations such as these is well established (see Castelli, Goodman, Edelstein, Mitchell, Paz-Alonso, Lyons, & Newton, 2006, for a review). The fundamental principle underlying this phenomenon is that human memory relies largely on reconstruction and is thus fallible. Not only does the stressful nature of incidents like this undermine the encoding of detail in the first place (Deffenbacher, Bornstein, Penrod, & McGorty, 2004), but much of the detail that is encoded is forgotten within minutes (Deffenbacher, Bornstein, McGorty, & Penrod, 2008).

The witness may be able to describe some physical characteristics of the perpetrator, but language is a frustratingly poor device for individuating a single human face. Worse, descriptions arising from stranger-perpetrator crimes typically include only around five descriptors (Flowe & Humphries, 2011), with no guarantee of their accuracy (e.g., Yuille & Cutshall, 1986). Stress during exposure, characteristic of many crimes, produces errors for most of the standard descriptive categories, including race, even when witnesses are provided with multiple options (Morgan, Southwick, Steffian, Hazlett, & Loftus, 2013), so there is ample reason for concern. Inaccurate descriptions may send the investigation off on the wrong track from the get-go, and both the act of providing a description (Schooler & Engstler-Schooler, 1990) and exposure to a police composite generated from the witness's description (Wells, Charman, & Olson, 2005) may further distort memory for the perpetrator before an identification can be made.

One might take some comfort in the witnesses' opportunity to make a factual report, in the form of the 911 call, right after the robbery. While the immediacy of this retelling might provide some protection against forgetting, even 911 reports are subject to rehearsal processes that can distort subsequent memory; for example, if the 911 operator asks selective or suggestive questions. Assuming that the 911 call is the witness's first communication about the crime and that the operator does nothing to direct his retelling, the witness's memory is still not entirely safe. First, distortion may occur based on self-suggestion, both during initial exposure (e.g., Kerstholt, Raaijmakers, & Valeton, 1992) and during a recall attempt (Hastie, Landsman, & Loftus, 1978). Suggestibility can actually be higher when free or cued recall precedes exposure to misinformation than when it does not (e.g., Chan, Thomas, & Bulevich, 2009; Wilford, Chan, & Tuhn, 2014). So, a witness whose 911 operator has not influenced his description is still at risk for subsequent memory contamination as the investigation moves forward. Second, if one or more co-witnesses are present, they are likely to discuss the crime with each other (Skagerberg & Wright, 2008) even before anyone calls 911, and co-witnesses can contaminate each other's memory (Gabbert, Memon, & Allan, 2003; Roediger, Meade, & Bergman, 2001), a phenomenon known as *social contagion*. To the extent that this is accompanied by contagion of co-witness emotion as well (Hatfield, Cacioppo, & Rapson, 1993), the emotional framing found by Barbara Tversky and her colleagues suggest further threats to the accuracy of witness retellings.

Decades of findings have demonstrated how easily incidental suggestion can produce false memories (Tversky & Tuchin, 1989), even shortly after the witnessed event (Loftus & Palmer, 1974) and even for salient moments in one's own life (Hyman, Husband, & Billings, 1995). Missing details and repeated retellings in the context of a criminal investigation provide a rich set of opportunities for incorporating imagined, inferred, or suggested details of all kinds into memory (e.g., Busey, Tunnicliff, Loftus, & Loftus, 2000). This could involve something as consequential as the presence of a gun during an incident (Morgan et al., 2013), a detail that might otherwise be unfalsifiable through other evidence and that might increase the severity of both the criminal charge and the sentence. Any "assistance" the officer gives by asking about or suggesting specific details (Wells, Memon, & Penrod, 2006) may prompt the witness to incorporate them into memory—one of many forms of post-event suggestion. Exposure to police suspects (Deffenbacher, Bornstein, & Penrod, 2006) and feedback in an ID procedure that is not double-blind (e.g., Wells & Bradfield, 1998) constitute other common and well-documented sources of memory distortion that can stem from this stage of the case.

Meanwhile, the investigator may press a witness by, for example, encouraging him to try again after the witness has expressed no or little memory for some specific detail (Tollestrup, Turtle, & Yuille, 1994). Such a practice is known for introducing error (Susa & Meissner, 2011). The more a witness is asked to repeat details, the more we must be concerned about this risk of memory intrusions (Bergman & Roediger, 1999; Chan & LaPaglia, 2011; Hanba & Zaragoza, 2007; Lane, Mather, Villa, & Morita, 2001).

During the investigation, the officer can choose to take measures that might help to preserve a witness's narrative over time and to minimize her own influence on this narrative. Among these are to use double-blind interview and identification procedures and to separate witnesses, ask open-ended questions, and use non-suggestive instructions. Witness interviews have historically involved a series of open-ended and closed questions, each aimed at a specific element of the crime. As we have seen, such questions can introduce distortions through suggestibility (e.g., Loftus & Palmer, 1974). The danger is particularly high in the context of witness interviews because the investigator typically has incomplete access to ground truth and is thus at risk of asking questions that are inappropriate or that include incorrect assumptions. So there is much opportunity for the investigator to ask misleading questions that lead to false memories.

By relying on open-ended questions, the Cognitive Interview technique, introduced by R. Edward Geiselman, Ronald Fisher, and colleagues, reduces these risks and provides many advantages for witness accuracy (Fisher & Geiselman, 1992; Geiselman, Fisher, Firstenberg, Hutton, Sullivan, Avetissian, & Prosk, 1984). But the findings we have discussed regarding retelling goals suggest the potential for trade-offs associated with even these best practices as a function of the witness's framing. The Cognitive Interview's broad, open-ended style of asking questions certainly appears to support idiosyncratic retrieval strategies and avoid suggestibility effects. On the other hand, distortions based on retelling goals are worst precisely in recall situations such as these, and particularly following an emotional retelling (Tversky & Marsh, 2000). A cue-driven interview method, consisting of a series of specific questions, may reduce the impact of retelling style through more effective memory prompts (Marsh et al., 2005), but then we once again face issues of suggestibility.

As the investigation moves forward, police and later attorneys ask questions in order to develop a theory of the case. Initially remembered details that don't fit the theory may remain selectively unrehearsed throughout these interactions, resulting in retellings (and memory) at risk for pointing coherently and singularly toward the police theory. This can result in a narrative that is reduced through the omission of details that could later prove relevant.

Another way that narratives can be reduced is through increased communicative efficiency between the questioner and the witness, which develops normally as two people converse. Speakers and listeners generally develop common ground over the course of their interactions, identifying mutually held knowledge, beliefs, and referents (Clark & Wilkes-Gibbs, 1986). This leads to increasingly efficient communication by eliminating the need to repeat elements that have become part of common ground (Clark & Haviland, 1977). A witness's task of continuing to give redundant and detailed descriptions, without making accommodations that are expected in almost every other setting, produces unnatural communication that likely impacts working memory and memory search processes.

Other, more indirect risks may be revealed as researchers consider emotional retelling effects specifically within the context of the criminal justice system. For example, emotionally-oriented speakers tend to intrude more personal commentary in their retellings (Marsh et al., 2005). An impatient police officer who finds the witness to be heading off on an irrelevant tangent may interrupt him, disrupting memory search processes as well as preempting the inclusion of potentially important crime details.

That is not to say the officer cannot protect against the introduction of further risk. During this interview process, her most important resource is the witness's memory, such as it is. Best practices require the officer to preserve witness evidence and to minimize contagion (National Research Council, 2014), much as they would for other forms of evidence. Early witness statements are not guaranteed to be accurate, but with time come multiple opportunities for contamination. Thus it is always important to obtain as immediate and complete an accounting as possible of both memory and confidence. While sealing a fingerprint in plastic is straightforward, we have no technique to prevent human memory from alteration through inference-making, forgetting, and incorporated post-event information. Humans are intelligent and social beings, and there is no sealing them in baggies.

Investigators' Reports

The police officer interacts with witnesses to develop a sufficiently detailed narrative of her own, both for purposes of future investigation and for purposes of filing one of the first formal reports in the case. She is one of many individuals who will ultimately provide detailed descriptions of the incident (Douglass, Brewer, Semmler, Bustamante, & Hiley, 2013). It is interesting to note that the officer also often generates the written statement to be signed by the witness. That is, the most factually-oriented report attributed to the witness during the early stages of investigation may actually be authored by someone else. Both types of report are written by someone who was not an eyewitness to the robbery and whose own representation of it is subject to a range of potentially problematic influences.

Given the investigator's prior experience with similar crimes, or with any suspect whose modus operandi fits this crime, or with specific details she may have about this case from a different source, the officer's own memory may be subject to distortions, omissions, intrusions, and binding errors even by the time she first meets the witness. These risks can be exacerbated by common police practices of delayed and incomplete notetaking (Cauchi & Powell, 2009), as well as the potential for confirmation bias (preferential seeking, processing or acceptance of evidence supporting her current view) to influence the broader investigation (Kassin, Dror, & Kukucka, 2013; O'Brien, 2009). The framing of officers' narratives to themselves and each other can influence bias toward a suspect, the scope of both witness and suspect interviews, and the officers' own subsequent courtroom testimony.

Interrogation of A Suspect

Whereas witnesses typically come forward to volunteer their retellings in the criminal justice process, suspect statements generally come about only after an officer brings them into the process. In part because of this, the nature of the suspect interview and the means by which the suspect's statements are obtained diverge in many ways from what we see with witnesses. Research regarding suspect statements has focused largely on social psychological influences during and after interrogation.

Any suspect, guilty or innocent, would have reason to deny involvement in the crime. Officers who interrogate suspects are trained in methods that are designed to extract useful details and inculpatory statements that presumably only a guilty suspect would supply. One major problem is that the coercive nature of some of these methods puts them at high risk for producing false inculpatory statements from innocent suspects. These statements are a form of retelling, and they enter into the criminal justice process, producing a myriad of downstream effects. We will next examine the generation of these statements.

The Reid technique (Inbau, Reid, & Buckley, 2013), which has been a standard tool for interrogating suspects for several decades, provides officers with methods to successfully challenge the (presumably guilty) suspect's resistance. It encourages officers to interrupt the suspect, refuse to allow or accept protestations of innocence, and bluff if necessary with claims of evidence against him. Interrogations may go for hours, during which the suspect may develop a fluently told narrative of the incident, coherent in structure and rich with details, many of which had been known only to the actual perpetrator and police but which the officer had referred to during the interrogation.

The suspect may be asked to repeat the full description of the event multiple times. A videotaped confession may come only after this is worked out and repeatedly rehearsed to the interrogator's satisfaction. The confession's apparent absence of emotion, which may actually arise from the suspect's exhaustion and potentially also from a lack of personal involvement in the crime, can be chilling for a juror to watch at trial. Only the suspect is shown in the video, with no sign of external influences on what appears to be a free recall of the incident. Jurors are not the only ones influenced by a confession; alibi witnesses who had previously reported a memory of the suspect being elsewhere at the time of the crime are also influenced when made aware of self-incriminating statements (Kassin et al., 2013).

More recent developments in interviewing suspects, such as the Scharff Method (Granhag, Oleszkiewicz, Strömwall, & Kleinman, 2015), make great headway toward distinguishing between innocent and guilty suspects by having interrogators strategically capitalize on their current knowledge of crime details. For example, interrogators can extract additional information by implying that they know more crime details than they actually do. Guilty suspects who are duped by this method may then freely volunteer information about the crime, believing they are referring to knowledge they and the interviewer have in common. The details the suspect provides may then be investigated further and assessed for their accuracy, improving the investigative process and reducing manipulation of the contents of the suspect's narrative.

The stakes are high, because prosecution of the wrong person or an incorrect verdict means not only that the actual perpetrator got away, but perhaps also that an innocent person has been wrongfully convicted. Examining only the sorts of phenomena we have discussed thus far, we get a glimpse of the problem's scope. In about three-quarters of cases where defendants were convicted and later exonerated, one or more eyewitness accounts had contributed to the conviction (Wells, Memon, & Penrod, 2006). In about one-quarter of exoneration cases, the innocent suspect had provided an untrue self-incriminating statement. That is, one or another form of retelling-gone-wrong at the outset of the case is responsible for two of the primary contributing factors toward wrongful conviction. Eyewitnesses are generally sincere, a stark reminder that adopting a factual style of retelling in no way guarantees accuracy. False confessors generally do not believe what they are compliantly reporting, but they do have an incentive to convince their interviewer of the veracity of their telling, with the expectation that they will be released when the interviewer is satisfied with their statement.

Deception Detection

Clearly, many suspects, as well as some witnesses, may be motivated to obfuscate or lie. Effective use of the evidence in the criminal justice system involves judging its veracity. Which details provided in which accounts of the event are to be incorporated into the "actual" narrative by which a defendant will be judged? Investigators and interrogators engage heavily in these questions, and so will attorneys, judges, and jurors when the case moves to trial.

Most of us are much worse at detecting liars than we think we are. In fact, average performance by adults is consistently found to be barely above chance (Bond & DePaulo, 2006). Fail at deception detection as an investigator or juror, and you may be woefully inadequate in your ability to evaluate witnesses' and suspects'/defendants' statements, with serious consequences. Unfortunately, police are no better than laypeople at this task, and in fact, they show a bias toward perceiving deception, with confidence increasing as a function of both seniority on the force (e.g., Meissner & Kassin, 2002; Vrij, 2008) and training in detection techniques (Masip, Alonso, Garrido, & Herrero, 2008). Interestingly, there do appear to be some promising techniques for improving detection, most of which rely on characteristics of narrative style (e.g., Vrij, Granhag, Mann, Leal, 2011). Unfortunately, however, the stylistic constraints imposed on witnesses at trial effectively thwart the emergence of these cues.

The Trial

As the case moves toward adjudication, the narrative enters the hands of two opposing attorneys. Their role is to construct arguments that are framed not to inform, but to convince. In most day-to-day experiences, in contrast to this environment, two disagreeing parties would engage in some sort of exchange with the goal of convincing each other. But here, the two attorneys will become locked in a storytelling contest, told largely by proxy through their witnesses.

The attorneys' audience will be those who wield the greatest power over verdicts, freedom, and sentencing—the judge and jurors. The jurors are essentially a captive audience of eavesdroppers, and their experience deviates substantially from typical language contexts from the beginning. Where else are people asked to invest enormous amounts of time listening to the deeply personal stories of strangers? In some ways, this is vaguely like watching a (days-long) movie, but in many ways, it is not. Involvement as a juror is required rather than freely chosen. Trial narratives, unlike educational or entertainment media, are told through stylized and refereed discourse, as we have discussed. These are far from ideal circumstances for providing decision-makers with a faithful, complete, and relevant set of facts or with the usual social cues they would normally use to evaluate them. The narratives they will consider come at the end of a long chain of cognitive and social influences on many different participants. They will have to sort out statements, presented in a unique and stylized form and provided by a wide range of sources who hold conflicting narrative goals.

Consider some of the unusual components of this process. The attorneys' narratives of the crime are first vetted over a long and formal process. In pre-trial motions to the judge, claims about the event are presented and the relevance and strength of these claims are bolstered by reference to authoritative strangers' previous decisions regarding other people's long-ago narratives told in other courtrooms. A set of decisions made in private between the judge and attorneys during these preliminary hearings shapes narrative design and often leads to suppression of elements that witnesses would have wanted to tell and jurors would have found important.

In this context, a good story is a simple and memorable one, creating order out of what may be chaotic, complex, incomplete, and potentially inconclusive or self-undermining evidence. The attorney narratives convey certainty, with the aim of satisfying the judge's and jurors' perceived desire for a sensible story (Pennington & Hastie, 1992). This perceived desire is one reason why defense attorneys often feel the need to generate an alternative narrative rather than simply argue that their client didn't do it.

For reasons that are legally quite sensible, trials start with the prosecution's case. The order of witnesses is determined not directly by the witnesses but by the attorney's practical and strategic considerations. In court, balance is purportedly achieved by allowing equal access to prosecution and defense perspectives. But we also know that timing of presentation of contradictory evidence can impact which of the contradictory views is believed (Dahl, Brimacombe, Lindsay, 2008; Ehrlich & Johnson-Laird, 1982; Gabbert, Memon, & Wright, 2006). Perhaps in everyday life, statements about a given topic that are presented earlier tend to be associated with greater authority or with higher confidence than those expressed later, but this cue normally available in spontaneous discourse is lost in the justice system. Compounding the problem, jurors may distort their understanding and memory for later statements to be consistent with those they had heard earlier.

A host of additional issues arise from the highly constrained speaking styles of the courtroom, even for a highly motivated and sincere witness with a factually-directed retelling goal. The form and content of statements are not under his control. Direct questioning and cross-examination constitute a tightly bound series of cued recall tasks, one detail at a time—a far cry from the witness's initially more free-form retelling. Instead, even on direct examination, answers must typically be brief and directly responsive. Witnesses are generally even more tightly constrained under cross-examination, often with answers limited to "yes" and "no." The order in which the event elements are addressed may not reflect chronological or causal relationships (Pennington & Hastie, 1992), further taxing working memory for both the witness and the jurors. These constraints give the attorneys, rather than the witness, control over how the courtroom narrative unfolds, and they almost certainly undermine the witness's use of idiosyncratic memory search strategies, which could reduce the informativeness of his testimony.

Testimony known to be inference or hearsay is formally disallowed in court. For example, the witness cannot testify that the robber had planned to harm him if he had resisted, simply because the witness had perceived the robber to be potentially violent. Such prohibitions are meant to provide important protections against unreliable factual evidence. In reality, however, trials take place long after the original incident. With time comes an ever-increasing likelihood that elements of prohibited categories will become incorporated into the witness's memory for the original event (Paterson, Kemp, & McIntyre, 2012). Because individual details aren't generally tagged in memory with their actual source, neither the witness nor a memory expert would be in a good position to identify the actual source of each individual reported detail (Johnson, Hashtroudi, & Lindsay, 1993).

Given the findings on witness memory discussed earlier in the chapter, the risk is, in fact, quite high that distortions from all manner of sources have been incorporated and rehearsed repeatedly by the time of trial. These errors are often consistent and enduring. We often speak of the unreliability of witness memory, but using standard terms from research methodology, what we actually mean by this is that eyewitness memory has low validity. Its reliability, in the form of errors intruding into memory and then staying there, can unfortunately be quite high for at least some parts of the witness account.

Thus far, we have discussed factually-oriented retelling goals at trial, but it would be naive to expect that witnesses are not also influenced at trial by emotionally-oriented goals. Despite explicit instructions they may receive to the contrary, there is no preventing emotionally-oriented retelling motivations from creeping into witness testimony. Indeed, one might expect that witnesses with a significant stake in the case (for example, the victim) would be especially prone to emotional retelling. The work by Tversky and colleagues on retellings showed clear impact on memories of the witnesses themselves. How might such communicative goals impact testimony, even under the strict rules of the courtroom, and influence jury decision making? One possibility is that the characteristics of emotionally-oriented retelling imply that the witness is particularly trustworthy. For example, emotionally-oriented speakers are less accurate at quoting dialogue (Wade & Clark,

1993). But this style of testimony, purportedly presenting remembered utterances from the incident word-for-word, may increase the jurors' trust in the witness.

Credibility may also be artificially inflated through common perceptual biases. Brief exposure to the perpetrator (Memon, Hope, & Bull, 2003) and substantial physical distance (Lampinen, Erickson, Moore, & Hittson, 2014) both make for poor witnessing conditions. But people reliably overestimate the duration of brief events that are unpredicted, stressful, and out of their control (Cutler, Penrod, & Martens, 1987; Loftus, Schooler, Boone, & Kline, 1987), and they reliably underestimate distance from themselves (e.g., Wiest & Bell, 1985). Both of these forms of systematic distortion can serve to strengthen the perceived reliability of their testimony by implying that they got a better view than they actually had. Both phenomena may also distort their beliefs about how much danger they themselves were in, which can in turn increase the witness's own vulnerability to further distortion by heightening the emotional qualities of the event (Drivdahl, Zaragoza, & Learned, 2009).

Even for a witness who takes a strictly factual approach to testimony at trial, there may be extensive and irrevocable damage done through prior emotionally-oriented retellings. The risk of this may be even higher for certain populations known to be particularly vulnerable to suggestion. These include elderly adults (Barber & Mather, 2014), who are less able to inhibit information irrelevant to the current goals (Hasher, Lustig, & Zacks, 2007; Hasher & Zacks, 1988).

Furthermore, specific questions and answers have often been rehearsed behind the scenes between the witness and attorney in preparation for testimony. With repeated retellings, selectively rehearsed details (accurate or not) become more accessible, more fluent, more organized, and more vivid (Hastie et al., 1978). Unsurprisingly, then, repeated retelling also increases confidence (Kelley & Lindsay, 1993). More than half of witnesses in the exoneration cases examined by Garrett (2011) expressed low confidence initially but expressed high confidence at trial.

With regard to jury decision making, in turn, the results are clear: Witness confidence that may have been largely manufactured over time and that is expressed at trial turns out to influence jurors' assessment of eyewitness evidence more than any other factor (Cutler, Penrod, & Dexter, 1990). Laypeople hold flawed beliefs about eyewitness accuracy, trusting identifications at trial that are made with high confidence (Schmechel, O'Toole, Easterly, & Loftus, 2006) and holding flashbulb memories to be highly accurate (Talarico & Rubin, 2003). Exacerbating this is the reduction in behavioral cues of uncertainty (such as hesitations and hedges) that jurors would have otherwise been able to use to assess the witness's credibility (Voss & Van Dyke, 2001).

As the trial is in full swing, claims are frequently and overtly challenged, more than just about anywhere else. These challenges do not just take the form of arguing that the witness is lying or mistaken, but also typically take the form of objections to the questions themselves. (Person A asks Person B a question, and Person C tries to convince Person D to make Person A withdraw the question. Person A, knowing that D will sustain C's objection, may nevertheless ask the question, simply to generate an implicature in the minds of Persons E through P).

What impact does all of this have on the jurors' own developing narrative? According to research on the continued influence effect (Johnson & Seifert, 1994; Lewandowsky, Ecker, Seifert, Schwarz, & Cook, 2012; see also Steblay, Hosch, Culhane, & McWethy, 2006), statements that are contradicted, retracted, or stricken will still persist in memory and impact judgment. This is understood in the legal community and expressed with the popular phrase, "You can't unring a bell."

Never do jurors observe direct interaction between witnesses, who may actually be in the best position to challenge and correct each other's memories. And never can they interrupt the proceedings to ask for clarifications. They do nevertheless form a memory for what they have encountered throughout the trial. And being imperfect, these memories will be partial and influenced by several somewhat arbitrary factors. Among them are the relative priorities that jurors have assigned to different narrative perspectives. Also among them is the relative fluency and imageability of details, with exaggerated statements often higher on both (Lawson & Strange, 2015). At the end of the trial process, jurors enter deliberation, essentially serving as co-witnesses who perform a collaborative memory task as they rehash the details of the case (Basden, Basden, Bryner, & Thomas, 1997; Barber & Rajaram, 2011). This, of course, creates new opportunities for selective rehearsal and forgetting.

Other Contributions to the Narrative

Other players sometimes impact the story of a criminal case. For example, given the more than 40 million foreign-born immigrants living in the U.S. as of 2017, it is common for witnesses and suspects who are not fluent in English to rely on an interpreter both during interviews and court proceedings. Since small linguistic and cultural nuances can impact comprehension and decision making, this poses its own set of complications.

A witness may seek help from a therapist after surviving a traumatic crime, which is an understandable and often advisable decision. The body of work by Tversky and colleagues concerning retellings, however, should caution us about how such interactions may impact memory for the crime. Once again, we see that many systemic and personal decisions within the criminal justice universe can create trade-offs between mutually competing goals.

Some particularly impactful cases may be covered by the media. The press has its own storytelling pressures that emphasize both informing the audience and maintaining its interest. When news stories, tabloids, and blogs amplify or mischaracterize events or goals, or when they suggest as-yet unsubstantiated details, they can sway people's representations of the case (Loftus & Banaji, 1989), even for those who rate the stories as not particularly credible (Lawson & Strange, 2015). And those bells cannot be unrung. Poor source monitoring (Lawson & Strange, 2015) can even lead jurors to remember inaccurate or sensationalized claims as having come directly from trial witnesses. Juror exposure to publicity may be reduced by moving trials to other jurisdictions or by imposing media blackouts, but such a system is not foolproof, with verdicts remaining vulnerable to influence (Ruva & McEvoy, 2008). The challenges of preventing witness exposure to media accounts are even greater, since they often live in the area where media are most concentrated, they possess a particular interest in the case, and they may themselves have participated as sources for the media.

Personal Interactions Along the Way

Crimes indeed have good odds of being retold to someone in an emotional style—if not to a 911 operator, co-witnesses, or police, then to friends. The more serious the crime, the more we might be concerned, both about the frequency of retellings in this style and about the damage that this manner of retelling can do. An emotionally-oriented retelling produces about twice as many major errors as does a factually-oriented one (Marsh et al., 2005). In fact, elaborating on emotional consequences of an event is one of the most effective ways of inducing false memory (Drivdahl, Zaragoza, & Learned, 2009). We should be concerned that memory for the original incident may suffer serious and permanent harm when witnesses retell the story of the crime in this way to friends and family (Marsh & Tversky, 2004). Their subjective experience concerning their memory will likely be quite different; with each retelling, their memory will seem to them to become stronger and more full of detail. But this is precisely what we would expect of memories that pick up additional detail, inferences, and fluency after the fact. The concern remains that the retellings may produce systematic losses and distortions to the *original* memory of the event itself—the only one that should be of interest during any part of the criminal justice process.

There is simply no avoiding risk. Factually-oriented and emotionally-oriented retelling contexts pose various risks, and avoiding any act of retelling or rehearsing also creates a risk of forgetting. Such is the nature of memory, which is why it can be such an unreliable form of evidence regardless of the witness's retelling goals. This is one major challenge for exoneration cases. It is not just the passage of time, but ironically also the prior acts of remembering, that may undermine faithful recovery from memory of what was originally experienced.

Conclusions

The justice system treats itself as a network of interacting but independent sources of information, sheathed in unbiased fact-finding and operating to impose checks and balances on any biases that do exist in order to effectively neutralize them. As psychologists, we know better. People start with expectations and biases, and they distort their own and each other's memory, judgment, and perception. Before any of that happens, they had encoded information far from perfectly in the first place. These various pieces amplify each other toward predictable, systematic error. Both laypeople and the guardians of the justice system, not fully understanding these risks, have been unable to protect against them.

The justice system serves many highly valued purposes, and it was developed thoughtfully with the intention of ensuring fair opportunities for all parties. But with regard to human factors, it leaves much to be desired. The phenomena we raise here are not problems specifically of the prosecution or defense, and they are not limited to criminal law. They arise in the interaction between human cognition and a formalized system that was not developed in ways that best support human memory, communication, or judgment.

Every single player in the judicial process—witness, investigator, attorney, judge, and juror—holds an important role with regard to memory and narrative construction. Communication is limited by what is remembered. And as Barbara Tversky and her colleagues have demonstrated, memory is shaped by what has been communicated (Marsh & Tversky, 2004; Marsh et al., 2005; Tversky & Marsh, 2000). Added to that, laypeople who are removed both in time and space from the crime itself have an enormously difficult task: to come to a simple guilty/not guilty decision after being exposed to complex and contradictory retellings, presented under conditions that are cognitively taxing, unfamiliar, and stripped of many of the common linguistic and social cues that might benefit them. They are not permitted to ask questions during testimony or even to back-channel cues regarding their comprehension (or lack thereof), further adding to the artificiality of the context for both the jurors and witnesses. Balances built into the system are meant to ensure fairness, but they cannot protect against these snowballing risks to memory and judgment. Worse, many of the very practices associated with criminal law exacerbate the risks.

Psychologists have sought to educate the public on some of these matters for decades. In the end, the goal is not to make jurors globally skeptical, but to equip them to better assess the actual probative value of witness evidence. The criminal justice system is becoming more receptive to techniques that might help to preserve and convey witnesses' memory, and research psychologists and the press continue to educate the public on its fallibility. There is much work ahead for the partnership between psychological scientists and the criminal justice community as we develop better ways of protecting evidence as it passes from witness to investigator to attorney to juror.

Note

1 We will use "witness" throughout the chapter as an inclusive term to refer to both victims and bystanders. Similarly, we will refer to the term "officer" to refer to members of the police response and investigative team. For simplicity of discussion, we will refer to witnesses as "he" and officers as "she."

References

Barber, S. J. & Mather, M. (2014). How retellings shape younger and older adults' memories. *Journal of Cognitive Psychology*, *26*(3), 263–279. doi: 10.1080/20445911.2014.892494

Barber, S. J. & Rajaram, S. (2011). Exploring the relationship between retrieval disruption from collaboration and recall. *Memory*, *19*, 462–469. doi.org/10.1080/09658211.2011.584389

Basden, B. H., Basden, D. R., Bryner, S., & Thomas III, R. L. (1997). A comparison of group and individual remembering: Does collaboration disrupt retrieval strategies? *Journal of Experimental Psychology: Learning, Memory, and Cognition*, *23*(5), 1176–1189. doi.org/10.1037/0278-7393.23.5.1176

Bergman, E. T. & Roediger, H. L. (1999). Can Bartlett's repeated reproduction experiments be replicated? *Memory & Cognition*, *27*(6), 937–947. doi:10.3758/BF03201224

Bond, C. F. & DePaulo, B. M. (2006). Accuracy of deception judgments. *Personality and Social Psychology Review*, *10*(3), 214–234. doi: 10.1207/s15327957pspr1003_

Busey, T. A., Tunnicliff, J., Loftus, G. R., & Loftus, E. F. (2000). Accounts of the confidence accuracy relation in recognition memory. *Psychonomic Bulletin & Review*, 7, 26–48.

Castelli, P., Goodman, G. S., Edelstein, R. S., Mitchell, E. B., Paz-Alonso, P. M. P., Lyons, K. E., & Newton, J. W. (2006). Evaluating eyewitness testimony in adults and children. In I. Weiner & A. K. Hess (Eds.), *The Handbook of Forensic Psychology* (pp. 243–304). Hoboken, NJ: Wiley.

Cauchi, R. & Powell, M. B. (2009). An examination of police officers' notes of interviews with alleged child abuse victims. *International Journal of Police Science & Management*, *11*(4), 505–515.

Chan, J. C. & LaPaglia, J. A. (2011). The dark side of testing memory: Repeated retrieval can enhance eyewitness suggestibility. *Journal of Experimental Psychology: Applied*, *17*(4), 418. doi: 10.1037/a0025147

Chan, J. C., Thomas, A. K., & Bulevich, J. B. (2009). Recalling a witnessed event increases eyewitness suggestibility: the reversed testing effect. *Psychological Science*, *20*(1), 66–73. doi:10.1111/j.1467-9280.2008.02245.x

Clark, H.H. & Haviland, S. E. (1977). Comprehension and the given-new contract. In R. O. Freedle (Ed.), *Discourse production and comprehension. Discourse Processes: Advances in Research and Theory*, Vol. 1 (1977) (pp. 1–40). Norwood, NJ: Ablex Publishing Corporation.

Clark, H. H. & Wilkes-Gibbs, D. (1986). Referring as a collaborative process. *Cognition*, *22*(1), 1–39. doi: 10.1016/0010-0277(86)90010-7

Cutler, B. L., Penrod, S. D., & Dexter, H. R. (1990). Juror sensitivity to eyewitness identification evidence. *Law and Human Behavior*, *14*, 185–191. doi: 10.1007/BF01062972

Cutler, B. L., Penrod, S. D., & Martens, T. K. (1987). The reliability of eyewitness identification: The role of system and estimator variables. *Law and Human Behavior*, *11*, 233–258. doi: 10.1007/BF01044644

Dahl, L. C., Brimacombe, C. E., & Lindsay, D. S. (2008). Investigating investigators: How presentation order influences participant–investigators' interpretations of eyewitness identification and alibi evidence. *Law and Human Behavior*, *33*(5), 368–380. doi:10.1007/s10979-008-9151-y

Deffenbacher, K. A., Bornstein, B. H., McGorty, E. K., & Penrod, S. D. (2008). Forgetting the once-seen face: estimating the strength of an eyewitness's memory representation. *Journal of Experimental Psychology: Applied*, *14*(2), 139–150. doi: 10.1037/1076-898X.14.2.139

Deffenbacher, K. A., Bornstein, B. H., & Penrod, S. D. (2006). Mugshot exposure effects:

Retroactive interference, mugshot commitment, source confusion, and unconscious transference. *Law and Human Behavior, 30*(3), 287–307.

Deffenbacher, K. A., Bornstein, B. H., Penrod, S. D., & McGorty, E. K. (2004). A meta-analytic review of the effects of high stress on eyewitness memory. *Law and Human Behavior, 28*(6), 687. doi: 10.1007/s10979-004-0565-x

Douglass, A. B., Brewer, N., Semmler, C., Bustamante, L., & Hiley, A. (2013). The dynamic interaction between eyewitnesses and interviewers: The impact of differences in perspective on memory reports and interviewer behavior. *Law and Human Behavior, 37*(4), 290–301. doi: 10.1037/lhb0000034

Drivdahl, S. B., Zaragoza, M. S., & Learned, D. M. (2009). The role of emotional elaboration in the creation of false memories. *Applied Cognitive Psychology, 23*(1), 13–35. doi:10.1002/acp.1446

Dudukovic, N. M., Marsh, E. J., & Tversky, B. (2004). Telling a story or telling it straight: The effects of entertaining versus accurate retellings on memory. *Applied Cognitive Psychology, 18*, 125–143. doi:10.1002/acp.953

Ehrlich, K. & Johnson-Laird, P. N. (1982). Spatial descriptions and referential continuity. *Journal of Verbal Learning and Verbal Behavior, 21*(3), 296–306. doi:10.1016/S0022-5371(82)90626-0

Fisher, R. P. & Geiselman, R. E. (1992). *Memory enhancing techniques for investigative interviewing: The cognitive interview*. Springfield, IL: Thomas.

Flowe, H. D. & Humphries, J. E. (2011). An examination of criminal face bias in a random sample of police lineups. *Applied Cognitive Psychology, 25*, 265–273. doi:10.1002/acp.1673

Gabbert, F., Memon, A., & Allan, K. (2003). Memory conformity: Can eyewitnesses influence each other's memories for an event? *Applied Cognitive Psychology, 17*(5), 533–543. doi:10.1002/acp.885

Gabbert, F., Memon, A., & Wright, D. B. (2006). Memory conformity: Disentangling the steps toward influence during a discussion. *Psychonomic Bulletin & Review, 13*(3), 480–485. doi:10.3758/BF03193873

Garrett, B. (2011). *Convicting the innocent: Where criminal prosecutions go wrong*. Cambridge: Harvard.

Geiselman, R. E., Fisher, R. P., Firstenberg, I., Hutton, L. A., Sullivan, S. J., Avetissian, I.V., & Prosk, A. L. (1984). Enhancement of eyewitness memory: An empirical evaluation of the Cognitive Interview. *Journal of Police Science and Administration, 12*, 130–138. www.worldcat.org/title/journal-of-police-science-and-administration/oclc/615557750

Granhag, P. A., Oleszkiewicz, S., Strömwall, L. A., & Kleinman, S. M. (2015). Eliciting intelligence with the Scharff technique: Interviewing more and less cooperative and capable sources. *Psychology, Public Policy, and Law, 21*(1), 100. doi: 10.1037/law0000030

Hanba, J. M. & Zaragoza, M. S. (2007). Interviewer feedback in repeated interviews involving forced confabulation. *Applied Cognitive Psychology, 21*(4), 433–455. doi:10.1002/acp.1286

Hasher, L. & Zacks, R. T. (1988). Working memory, comprehension, and aging: A review and a new view. *Psychology of Learning and Motivation, 22*, 193–225. doi: 10.1016/S0079-7421(08)60041-9

Hasher, L., Lustig, C., & Zacks, R. T. (2007). Inhibitory mechanisms and the control of attention. In A.B. Conway, C. Jarrold, M. J. Kane, A. Miyake, & J. N. Towse (Eds.), *Variation in working memory* (pp. 227–249). Cambridge: Oxford University Press.

Hashtroudi, S., Johnson, M. K., Vnek, N., & Ferguson, S. A. (1994). Aging and the effects of affective and factual focus on source monitoring and recall. *Psychology and Aging*, 9(1), 160–170. doi: 10.1037/0882-7974.9.1.160

Hastie, R., Landsman, R., & Loftus, E. F. (1978). Eyewitness testimony: The dangers of guessing. *Jurimetrics, 19*(1), 1–8. www.jstor.org/stable/29761641

Hatfield, E., Cacioppo, J. T., & Rapson, R. L. (1993). Emotional contagion. *Current Directions in Psychological Science. 2*(3), 96–99. www.jstor.org/stable/20182211

Haviland, S. E. & Clark, H. H. (1974). What's new? Acquiring new information as a process in comprehension. *Journal of Verbal Learning and Verbal Behavior, 13*(5), 512–521. www.sciencedirect.com/science/journal/00225371

Hyman, I. E., Husband, T. H., & Billings, F. J. (1995). False memories of childhood experiences. *Applied Cognitive Psychology, 9*, 181–197. doi:10.1002/acp.2350090302

Inbau, F. E., Reid, J. E., & Buckley, J. P. (2013). *Essentials of the Reid technique.* (2nd Edition). Burlington, MA: Jones & Bartlett Publishers.

Johnson, M. K., Hashtroudi, H., & Lindsay, D. S. (1993). Source monitoring. *Psychological Bulletin, 114*(1), 3–28. http://psycnet.apa.org/doi/10.1037/0033-2909.114.1.3

Johnson, H. M. & Seifert, C. M. (1994). Sources of the continued influence effect: When misinformation in memory affects later inferences. *Journal of Experimental Psychology: Learning, Memory, and Cognition, 20*(6), 1420–1436. doi: 10.1037/0278-7393.20.6.1420

Kassin, S. M., Dror, I. E., & Kukucka, J. (2013). The forensic confirmation bias: Problems, perspectives, and proposed solutions. *Journal of Applied Research in Memory and Cognition, 2*(1), 42–52. doi: 10.1016/j.jarmac.2013.01.001

Kelley, C. M. & Lindsay, D. S. (1993). Remembering mistaken for knowing: Ease of retrieval as a basis for confidence in answers to general knowledge questions. *Journal of Memory and Language, 32*(1), 1–24. www.journals.elsevier.com/journal-of-memory-and-language

Kerstholt, J. H., Raaijmakers, J. G. W., & Valeton, J. M. (1992). The effect of expectation on the identification of known and unknown persons. *Applied Cognitive Psychology, 6*, 173–180.

Lampinen, J. M., Erickson, W. B., Moore, K. N., & Hittson, A. (2014). Effects of distance on face recognition: Implications for eyewitness identification. *Psychonomic Bulletin & Review, 21*, 1489–1494. doi:10.3758/s13423-014-0641-2

Landry, K. L. & Brigham, J. C. (1992). The effect of training in criteria-based content analysis on the ability to detect deception in adults. *Law and Human Behavior, 16*(6), 663–676. doi: 10.1007/BF01884022

Lane, S. M., Mather, M., Villa, D., & Morita, S. K. (2001). How events are reviewed matters: Effects of varied focus on eyewitness suggestibility. *Memory & Cognition, 29*(7), 940–947. doi:10.3758/BF03195756

Lawson, V. Z. & Strange, D. (2015). News as (hazardous) entertainment: Exaggerated reporting leads to more memory distortion for news stories. *Psychology of Popular Media Culture, 4*(2), 188–198. doi: 10.1037/ppm0000015

Lewandowsky, S., Ecker, U. K., Seifert, C. M., Schwarz, N., & Cook, J. (2012). Misinformation and its correction: Continued influence and successful debiasing. *Psychological Science in the Public Interest, 13*(3), 106–131. doi: 10.1177/1529100612451018

Loftus, E. F. & Banaji, M. R. (1989). Memory modification and the role of the media. In V. A. Gheorghiu, P. Netter, H. J. Eysenck, & R. Rosenthal (Eds.), *Suggestion and suggestibility* (pp. 279–293). Berlin: Springer.

Loftus, E. F. & Palmer, J. C. (1974). Reconstruction of automobile destruction: An example of the interaction between language and memory. *Journal of Verbal Learning and Verbal Behavior, 13*, 585–589. doi: 10.1016/S0022-5371(74)80011-3

Loftus, E. F., Schooler, J. W., Boone, S. M., & Kline, D. (1987). Time went by so slowly: Overestimation of event duration by males and females. *Applied Cognitive Psychology, 1*, 3–13. doi:10.1002/acp.2350010103

Marsh, E. J. & Tversky, B. (2004). Spinning the stories of our lives. *Applied Cognitive Psychology, 18*, 491–503. doi:10.1002/acp.1001

Marsh, E. J., Tversky, B., & Hutson, M. (2005). How eyewitnesses talk about events: Implications for memory. *Applied Cognitive Psychology, 19*, 531–544. doi:10.1002/acp.1095

Masip, J., Alonso, H., Garrido, E., & Herrero, C. (2008). Training to detect what? The biasing effects of training on veracity judgments. *Applied Cognitive Psychology, 23*(9), 1282–1296. doi:10.1002/acp.1535

Meissner, C. A. & Kassin, S. M. (2002). "He's guilty!": Investigator bias in judgments of truth and deception. *Law and Human Behavior, 26*(5), 469–480. doi: 10.1023/A:1020278620751

Memon, A., Hope, L., & Bull, R. (2003). Exposure duration: Effects on eyewitness accuracy and confidence. *British Journal of Psychology, 94*(3), 339–354. doi:10.1348/000712603767876262

Morgan, C. A., III, Southwick, S., Steffian, G., Hazlett, G. A., & Loftus, E. F. (2013). Misinformation can influence memory for recently experienced, highly stressful events. *International Journal of Law and Psychiatry, 36*, 11–17. doi: 10.1016/j.ijlp.2012.11.002

National Research Council of the National Academies (2014). *Identifying the culprit: Assessing eyewitness identification*. Washington, D.C.: National Academies Press.

O'Brien, B. (2009). Prime suspect: An examination of factors that aggravate and counteract confirmation bias in criminal investigations. *Psychology, Public Policy, and Law, 15*(4), 315. doi: 10.1037/a0017881

Paterson, H. M., Kemp, R., & McIntyre, S. (2012). Can a witness report hearsay evidence unintentionally? The effects of discussion on eyewitness memory. *Psychology, Crime & Law, 18*(6), 505–527. doi: 10.1080/1068316X.2010.510117

Pennington, N. & Hastie, R. (1992). Explaining the evidence: Tests of the story model for juror decision making. *Journal of Personality and Social Psychology, 62*(2), 189–206. http://psycnet.apa.org/doi/10.1037/0022-3514.62.2.189

Roediger, H. L., Meade, M. L., & Bergman, E. T. (2001). Social contagion of memory. *Psychonomic Bulletin & Review, 8*(2), 365–371. doi:10.3758/BF03196174

Ruva, C. L. & McEvoy, C. (2008). Negative and positive pretrial publicity affect juror memory and decision making. *Journal of Experimental Psychology: Applied, 14*(3), 226–235. doi: 10.1037/1076-898X.14.3.226

Schmechel, R. S., O'Toole, T. P., Easterly, C., & Loftus, E. F. (2006). Beyond the ken? Testing jurors' understanding of eyewitness reliability evidence. *Jurimetrics, 46*, 177–214. www.jstor.org/stable/29762929

Schooler, J. W. & Engstler-Schooler, T. Y. (1990). Verbal overshadowing of visual memories: Some things are better left unsaid. *Cognitive Psychology, 22*(1), 36–71. www.sciencedirect.com/science/article/pii/001002859090003M

Skagerberg, E. M. & Wright, D. B. (2008). The prevalence of co-witnesses and co-witness discussions in real eyewitnesses. *Psychology, Crime & Law, 14*(6), 513–521.

Skagerberg, E. M. & Wright, D. B. (2009). Susceptibility to postidentification feedback is affected by source credibility. *Applied Cognitive Psychology, 23*, 506–523. doi:10.1002/acp.1470

Soleti, E., Curci, A., Bianco, A., & Lanciano, T. (2012). Does talking about emotions influence eyewitness memory? The role of emotional vs. factual retelling on memory accuracy. *Europe's Journal of Psychology, 8*(4), 632–640. doi: 10.5964/ejop.v8i4.526

Steblay, N., Hosch, H. M., Culhane, S. E., & McWethy, A. (2006). The impact on juror verdicts of judicial instruction to disregard inadmissible evidence: A meta-analysis. *Law and Human Behavior, 30*(4), 469–492. doi:10.1007/s10979-006-9039-7

Suengas, A. G. & Johnson, M. K. (1988). Qualitative effects of rehearsal on memories for perceived and imagined complex events. *Journal of Experimental Psychology: General, 117*(4), 377–389. doi: 10.1037/0096-3445.117.4.377

Susa, K. & Meissner, C. A. (2011). Cognitive processes governing the verbal description identification paradox. Paper presented at the Annual Meeting of the American Psychology-Law Society, Miami, FL.

Talarico, J. M. & Rubin, D. C. (2003). Confidence, not consistency, characterizes flashbulb memories. *Psychological Science, 14*(5), 455–461. doi:10.1111/1467-9280.02453

Tollestrup, P. A., Turtle, J. W., & Yuille, J. C. (1994). Actual victims and witnesses to robbery and fraud: An archival analysis. In D. F. Ross, J. D. Read., & M. P. Toglia (Eds.), *Adult eyewitness testimony: Current trends and developments*, pp. 144–159. Cambridge: Cambridge University Press.

Tversky, A. & Kahneman, D. (1981). The framing of decisions and the psychology of choice. *Science, 211*(4481), 453–458. www.jstor.org/stable/1685855

Tversky, B. & Marsh, E. J. (2000). Biased retellings of events yield biased memories. *Cognitive Psychology, 40*(1), 1–38. doi: 10.1006/cogp.1999.0720

Tversky, B. & Tuchin, M. (1989). A reconciliation of the evidence on eyewitness testimony: Comments on McCloskey and Zaragoza. *Journal of Experimental Psychology: General, 118*(1), 86–91. http://psycnet.apa.org/doi/10.1037/0096-3445.118.1.86

Voss, J. F. & Van Dyke, J. A. (2001). Narrative structure, information certainty, emotional content, and gender as factors in a pseudo jury decision-making task. *Discourse Processes, 32*(2&3), 215–243. doi: 10.1080/0163853X.2001.9651599

Vrij, A. (2008). Nonverbal dominance versus verbal accuracy in lie detection: A plea to change police practice. *Criminal Justice and Behavior, 35*(10), 1323–1336. doi:10.1177/0093854808321530

Vrij, A., Granhag, P. A., Mann, S., & Leal, S. (2011). Outsmarting the liars: Toward a cognitive lie detection approach. *Current Directions in Psychological Science, 20*(1), 28–32. doi:10.1177/0963721410391245

Wade, E. & Clark, H. H. (1993). Reproduction and demonstration in quotations. *Journal of Memory and Language, 32*(6), 805–819. www.journals.elsevier.com/journal-of-memory-and-language

Wells, G. L. & Bradfield, A. L. (1998). "Good, you identified the suspect": Feedback to eyewitnesses distorts their reports of the witnessing experience. *Journal of Applied Psychology, 83*, 360–376.

Wells, G. L., Charman, S. D., & Olson, E. A. (2005). Building face composites can harm lineup identification performance. *Journal of Experimental Psychology: Applied, 11*(3), 147–156. doi: 10.1037/1076-898X.11.3.147

Wells, G. L., Memon, A., & Penrod, S. D. (2006). Eyewitness evidence: Improving its probative value. *Psychological Science in the Public Interest*, 7(2), 45–75. doi:10.1111/j.15291006.2006.00027.x

Wiest, W. M. & Bell, B. (1985). Steven's exponent for psychophysical scaling of perceived, remembered and inferred distance. *Psychological Bulletin, 98*(3), 457–470. http://psycnet.apa.org/doi/10.1037/0033-2909.98.3.457

Wilford, M. M., Chan, J. C., & Tuhn, S. J. (2014). Retrieval enhances eyewitness suggestibility to misinformation in free and cued recall. *Journal of Experimental Psychology: Applied, 20*(1), 81–93. doi: 10.1037/xap0000001

Yuille, J. C. & Cutshall, J. L. (1986). A case study of eyewitness memory of a crime. *Journal of Applied Psychology, 71*(2), 291–201. doi: 10.1037/0021-9010.71.2.291

4

YOU LOOK LOST

Understanding Uncertainty and Representational Flexibility in Navigation

Tad T. Brunyé, Zach D. Haga, Lindsay A. Houck, and Holly A. Taylor

Building Flexible Spatial Mental Models

You have returned to your hometown after a 20-year absence. As you drive around, hoping to visit your old haunts, you tread the line between feelings of familiarity and novelty. Sometimes you know exactly where you are and what direction to turn to get to your next destination. Other times you question whether you took the correct turn because the environment only provides a few sparks of familiarity. Of course buildings have come up and down, businesses have changed names, and even roads have been re-routed in the last 20 years. As a result, your trip down memory lane presents some spatial memory challenges. To visit your former favorite places you must retrieve what memory you have, situate it within the current environment, likely updating your memory as a result, and then use this information to navigate. While you could simply serially input your destinations into your GPS, this would interfere with the nostalgia of this visit (Kun, Paek, Medenica, Memarović, & Palinko, 2009). Instead you set off, relying on your memory.

Most people can relate to this scenario, many with first-hand experience. However, the cohort of researchers exploring questions related to this common experience is relatively small. Barbara Tversky is among the researchers who raised consciousness about the cognitive challenges inherent in the activity of wayfinding, an activity we all engage in daily. Notably she focused the research field on how people build and use mental representations of environments. In our opening scenario, when what one sees in the environment matches one's mental representation nostalgia arises. On the flip side, when what one sees does not match, confusion ensues. Outcomes of using one's mental representation (including nostalgia or confusion) then motivate behavior, including updating one's mental representation. In this chapter, inspired by Barbara's focus on spatial mental representations, we explore navigational confusion and uncertainty, likely arising from an incomplete mental representation. More specifically, we examine a behavioral indicator of navigational confusion, tying it to wayfinding outcomes.

Although people successfully navigate through cities every day, the cognitive processes needed to do so are not simple (Wolbers & Hegarty, 2010). Success requires one to integrate different types of information over both time and space. Further, to be successful, one must also be prepared to use this information in both expected (following known route) and unexpected (finding detour) ways (Brunyé, Rapp, & Taylor, 2008; Taylor & Tversky, 1992) and to achieve different goals (Taylor, Naylor, & Chechile, 1999). Thus, success is enhanced by the ability to flexibly use environment knowledge. Such flexibility increases as one gets to know the environment better (Taylor & Tversky, 1992; Thorndyke & Hayes-Roth, 1982) and varies with how one learns an environment (Brunyé et al., 2008). However, because navigational aids tend to negatively impact environment memory (Gardony, Brunyé, Mahoney, & Taylor, 2013; Gardony, Brunyé, & Taylor, 2015; Waters & Winter, 2011), they may not be advised if developing a flexible spatial mental model is desired. What if instead your navigational system could sense when you felt lost and only provide information then?

Navigation aids, which come in hand-held, in-vehicle, and augmented-reality forms, provide precise guidance by detailing routes, turns, and landmarks along the way, resulting in efficient paths through even highly complex environments. Although they generally provide efficient paths, they are not without drawbacks, including distraction from driving or ambulation (Kun et al., 2009), complacency and over-reliance (Leshed, Velden, Rieger, Kot, & Sengers, 2008; Sheridan & Parasuraman, 2005), and interference with spatial memory development (Gardony et al., 2013; Gardony et al., 2015). Ideally, navigation aids could provide guidance and positively influence environment learning (Waters & Winter, 2011). One approach might be to provide guidance only as needed, either via explicit request or real-time monitoring for disorientation (Huang, Tsai, & Huang, 2012; Parasuraman & Rizzo, 2007). Anecdotally, if we see someone erratically looking around we might ask if the person is lost and needs assistance. However, other than explicitly asking, no validated methods for assessing disorientation in real-time exist. In this chapter, we discuss a potential method and proof-of-concept study for identifying disorientation.

Measuring Uncertainty

We propose that entropy in a user's heading direction may indicate transient disorientation. As conceptualized by Shannon and Weaver (1949), entropy is a probability-based construct assessing "*the degree of randomness, or shuffled-ness*" and the extent to which a physical system is "*less organized*". Theoretically, maximum entropy would be present with complete noise in a system, with all possible outcomes being identically probable over time; minimum entropy would be present with a single consistent signal (from the range of those possible) over time.

Entropy has been applied across a few domains in psychology. For instance, Friston's free-energy principle suggests that better prediction of sensory experience serves to reduce entropy and "surprisal," and maintain structure and order (Clark, 2013; Friston, 2010). Similarly, another extant theory explicitly links entropy with mental states, the *entropy model of uncertainty* (Hirsh, Mar, & Peterson, 2012). This model proposes a framework for understanding anxiety within inherently ambiguous situations and psychological entropy arises from uncertainty related to the conflict between perceptual inputs and behavioral outputs. While the concept of psychological entropy has been introduced, related behavioral measures have not been broadly quantified. This is unfortunate given that many behaviors may reflect (and possibly influence) mental states involved with uncertainty and/or failed prediction (Wilson, 2002). To our knowledge, behavioral entropy has only been comprehensively examined in the context of driver steering wheel inputs. In this research, the entropy of a driver's steering wheel movements predict cognitive workload in multi-tasking and distraction-based paradigms (Boer, 2000; Boer, Rakauskas, Ward, & Goodrich, 2005). When a user becomes lost they may similarly exhibit behaviors that indicate, and bi-directionally influence, their transient states of increased cognitive workload associated with disorientation. Again, anecdotally we can often tell if someone "looks lost."

How does someone behave when lost? To try to reorient, one often looks around, surveying the environment for familiar landmarks to inform the next navigation decision. Thus, entropy with respect to head direction may serve as a good behavioral indication of disorientation and information gathering for future decisions (Hirsh et al., 2012; Klein, 2008). Further, such behavior should be more evident at intersections, which are the primary decision points during navigation (Allen, 1981; Brunyé et al., 2015). If this suggestion is true, then heading entropy should predict the quality of navigation decisions, showing down-stream effects on navigation efficiency.

Exploring Heading Entropy in Navigation: An Empirical Study

To explore the utility of heading entropy, we asked participants to navigate a completely unfamiliar virtual urban environment in search of a series of 20 landmarks. While they navigated, we monitored their heading direction (yaw) and navigation efficiency. From the heading data we calculated two measures: heading entropy and heading variance (using circular statistics). If more changes in heading, similar to looking around, indicates disorientation, as we suggest, then one or both of these measures should predict navigation efficiency.

Methods

In the study, twenty-four Tufts University (M_{age} = 21.6, SD_{age} = 3.4, 14 male, 10 female) students participated for monetary compensation; 18 fully completed the navigation task (M_{age} = 21.9, SD_{age} = 3.7, 11 male, 7 female). This final sample size, compared against extant studies using virtual environments in both behavioral (Jansen-Osmann & Wiedenbauer, 2004) and neuroscientific (Cornwell, Johnson, Holroyd, Carver, & Grillon, 2008) contexts, should be sufficient to reveal relationships between heading change and navigation performance. Each participant completed questionnaires and then the virtual navigation task.

We used three questionnaires; the first asked for basic demographics, probing for participant age, sex, and handedness. Second, because we used a virtual environment, participants completed a video game experience questionnaire (VGE; Boot, Kramer, Simons, Fabiani, & Gratton, 2008) to probe for video game playing frequency, and finally the Santa Barbara Sense of Direction scale (SBSOD; Hegarty, Richardson, Montello, Lovelace, & Subbiah, 2002).

We developed a virtual urban environment using the Unity 3D gaming engine (Unity Technologies; San Francisco, CA, USA; see Fig. 4.1). The environment contained 553 buildings, 42 of them labeled (e.g., *Sweet Spot Candies*). Twenty-one of the labeled landmarks had facades that visually indicated the landmark's function (e.g., Pet Store); these landmarks served as goal destinations during navigation. The overall environment was approximately square, 1.29 km^2 in size. The Unity 3D software automatically tracked user location (in Cartesian space) and orientation (yaw, 1-360°) over time at 60Hz.

The experimental procedures were as follows. After consent, participants completed the three questionnaires. They were then guided through a brief practice virtual navigation session, in a small open environment, which involved navigating between six visible landmarks (e.g., *Car, Pool, Dog*). The practice session helped familiarize participants with the navigation controls and navigating between

FIGURE 4.1 Screen shot depicting a scene within the Unity virtual environment

successive landmarks. Participants held down the *W* key on a standard keyboard for forward movement/displacement, and they controlled heading by moving a standard computer mouse (i.e., left-right heading direction was linked to *x*-axis mouse movement). After navigation practice, participants received instructions for the primary experimental task. They were asked to find each of the 20 indicated destinations as quickly as possible. Importantly, they did not receive any information about the environment, either its layout or landmarks, leaving it completely unfamiliar to them. Participants began facing the first landmark (Laundromat) and were instructed to "*Find the Laundromat.*" Once a participant moved within one meter of a sign positioned in front of the Laundromat, the sequence of 20 successive landmark-to-landmark navigation trials began. Participants had three pieces of information available during navigation. The current objective always appeared in the upper left of the screen, a small compass indicating cardinal direction appeared in the upper right corner of the screen, and a trial counter was in the lower right. Trials were always in the same order (i.e., Trial 1: Laundromat to Pet Store; Trial 2: Pet Store to Gym, etc.). Each of the 21 landmarks served once as a destination (and then as the origin for the subsequent trial). Arrival at each destination (within one meter of a red and white sign; see Fig. 4.1) triggered the next trial ("*You have found the Pet Store. Now find the Gym.*"). The experiment ended after a participant found all 20 landmarks.

Data Scoring

For the VGE, we used dichotomous scoring to parse participants into self-reported gamers or non-gamers (Boot et al., 2008). To score the SBSOD, we used conventional procedures of reverse-scoring negatively stated items and averaging responses across all scale items (Hegarty et al., 2002).

To calculate *entropy* (*H*), we applied the following equation to raw heading (i.e., yaw; 1-360°) data: The equation involves summing the product of probabilities and normal-log probabilities. In this case, probabilities are calculated at each of 360° of yaw by counting the number of samples at each yaw value and dividing by the total number of trial samples. Note that because entropy uses a probability-based equation, it does not require the use of circular statistics.

To compare entropy to *heading variance* we calculated circular variance, *V*, after converting angles to circular statistics using the CIRCSTATS toolbox (Berens, 2009). To *calculate path efficiency* we related traveled trial-specific path lengths (denominator) to this path's optimal lengths (numerator), calculated using the A* pathfinding algorithm (Hart, Nilsson, & Raphael, 1968). Using this common technique (Brunyé, Gardony, Mahoney, & Taylor, 2012; Brunyé et al., 2014; Gardony, Brunyé, Mahoney, & Taylor, 2011) maximum path efficiency for a given trial was 1, and minimum path efficiency infinitely approached zero.

To differentiate periods of trial time when a participant was within versus outside of an intersection, we developed intersection bounding boxes extending between the four building corners outlining each intersection. Logged participant coordinates (x, y) were then dichotomously scored (1 = within, 0 = outside) based on whether they were located within or outside a bounding box.

Results

As discussed above, we calculated two potential markers of spatial uncertainty, *heading entropy* and *circular heading variance*, along with one measure of navigation success, *path efficiency*. Heading entropy and circular heading variance were highly correlated overall (Pearson's $r = .89$), though collinearity diagnoses using the variance inflation factor (VIF) never exceeded 2.75 in any regression analysis, well below the VIF > 5 and VIF > 10 thresholds proposed as indicating excessive or serious collinearity, respectively (Menard, 1995). Table 4.1 presents overall descriptive statistics for path efficiency, entropy, and circular heading variance.

Evidence of Environment Learning

Results clearly showed that participants learned the environment as the navigation trial proceeded. For path efficiency, a repeated-measures analysis of variance (ANOVA) demonstrated a main effect of Trial, $F(19, 323) = 5.04, p < .001, \eta^2 = .23$, showing that path efficiency increasing over the course of the 20 trials (linear regression: $\beta_{std} = .13$).

Further, if heading entropy indexes disorientation, then it should decrease as participants gain familiarity with the environment. For heading entropy, a repeated-measures ANOVA demonstrated a Trial main effect, $F(19, 323) = 8.20, p < .001, \eta^2 = .33$, with heading entropy decreasing over the 20 trials (linear regression: $\beta_{std} = -.19$). Limiting analyses to primary decision points (i.e., intersections) also showed decreased entropy over time. For heading entropy in intersections, there was a main effect of Trial, $F(19, 323) = 8.5, p < .001, \eta^2 = .33$, with heading entropy in intersections decreasing over time (linear regression: $\beta_{std} = -.19$). Environment learning more generally can be seen through heading entropy outside of intersections. Here, too, heading entropy decreased over time, showing a Trial main effect, $F(19, 323) = 5.49, p < .001, \eta^2 = .24$, with heading entropy decreasing over time/trials (linear regression: $\beta_{std} = -.14$).

TABLE 4.1 Mean, standard deviation, minimum, and maximum statistics for path efficiency, heading entropy, and circular (circ.) heading variance

	Path Efficiency	*Heading Entropy*	*Circ. Heading Variance*
Mean	.38	4.84	.68
SD	.29	0.61	.24
Minimum	.01	2.66	.11
Maximum	.99	5.69	.99

Our circular heading variance measure also indicated learning. A repeated-measures ANOVA using demonstrated an effect of Trial, $F(19, 323) = 5.3, p < .001, \eta^2 = .23$. Variance decreased over the 20 trials (linear regression: $\beta_{std} = -.10$). Looking in more detail, heading variance decreased both within, $F(19, 323) = 3.59, p < .001, \eta^2 = .17$ (linear regression: $\beta_{std} = -.09$), and outside of intersections, $F(19, 323) = 4.56, p < .001, \eta^2 = .21$ (linear regression: $\beta_{std} = -.09$).

In summary, path efficiency, heading entropy, and circular heading variance all indicated environmental learning in the form of increased efficiency, decreased entropy, and decreased variance over time. Note that heading entropy when participants were within intersections showed the overall strongest results, with the highest F statistic, effect size, and β value.

Predicting Path Efficiency

If disorientation measures have utility for next-generation navigational aids they would need to show a relationship to navigation success. In other words, disorientation should predict reduced navigation efficiency. Using the measures we identified here, we predicted that both heading entropy and variance would negatively relate to navigation decision quality, leading to down-stream effects on navigation efficiency.

To examine whether heading entropy and/or circular heading variance would predict path efficiency outcomes, we computed heading entropy and circular heading variance at different time intervals. For each trial, we calculated heading entropy and circular heading variance at 5%, 10%, 25%, and 50% into the trial duration. For instance, if a trial took 5 minutes to complete, heading entropy was calculated four times, once at 5% into the trial (15 seconds), once at 10% into the trial (30 seconds), once at 25% into the trial (75 seconds), and finally at 50% into the trial (150 seconds). This method allowed us to standardize across variable trial lengths and variable trial completion durations.

We conducted multiple regressions, one for each of the time intervals (5%, 10%, 25%, 50%), each with two predictors (heading entropy, circular heading variance). In the first set of analyses, we asked whether heading entropy and/or circular heading variance would predict path efficiency for the entire trial duration (i.e., overall path efficiency). In the second set of analyses, we asked whether heading entropy and/or circular heading variance would predict path efficiency for the *remainder* of a trial (i.e., subsequent path efficiency). The results of these regressions are detailed in Table 4.2.

Overall, heading entropy is a stronger and more reliable predictor of path efficiency relative to circular heading variance. In follow-up stepwise regressions, circular heading variance was consistently excluded in favor of a single-variable model with heading entropy alone. Even very early in a trial (5% of trial time), heading entropy could account for over 50% of path efficiency variability. Figure 4.2 depicts the relation between heading entropy and overall path efficiency at

TABLE 4.2 Results from multiple linear regression models testing predictions for overall trial versus remaining trial path efficiency outcomes at 5%, 10%, 25%, and 50% through individual trials

	Percentage Trial Time	*Overall ANOVA*	*Heading Entropy*	*Circ. Heading Variance*
Predicting Overall Path Efficiency	5%	$F(2, 342) = 186.53, p < .001, R^2 = .52$	$t(342) = 11.61, p < .001, \beta_{std} = -.62$ ($R^2 = .52$)	$t(342) = 2.64, p < .01, \beta_{std} = -.14$ ($R^2 = .33$)
	10%	$F(2, 355) = 201.55, p < .001, R^2 = .53$	$t(355) = 17.81, p < .001, \beta_{std} = -.81$ ($R^2 = .52$)	$t(355) = 3.13, p < .01, \beta_{std} = .14$ ($R^2 = .11$)
	25%	$F(2, 359) = 272.5, p < .001, R^2 = .60$	$t(359) = 17.91, p < .001, \beta_{std} = -.77$ ($R^2 = .60$)	$t(359) = 0.2, p = .84, \beta_{std} = -.01$ ($R^2 = .25$)
	50%	$F(2, 359) = 513.21, p < .001, R^2 = .74$	$t(359) = 13.76, p < .001, \beta_{std} = -.61$ ($R^2 = .71$)	$t(359) = 6.49, p < .001, \beta_{std} = -.29$ ($R^2 = .61$)
Predicting Remaining Path Efficiency	5%	$F(2, 342) = 186.58, p < .001, R^2 = .52$	$t(342) = 11.58, p < .001, \beta_{std} = -.62$ ($R^2 = .52$)	$t(342) = 2.67, p < .01, \beta_{std} = -.14$ ($R^2 = .34$)
	10%	$F(2, 355) = 206.44, p < .001, R^2 = .54$	$t(355) = 18.02, p < .001, \beta_{std} = -.81$ ($R^2 = .53$)	$t(355) = 3.17, p < .01, \beta_{std} = .14$ ($R^2 = .12$)
	25%	$F(2, 359) = 269.8, p < .001, R^2 = .60$	$t(359) = 17.78, p < .001, \beta_{std} = -.77$ ($R^2 = .60$)	$t(359) = 0.3, p = .79, \beta_{std} = -.01$ ($R^2 = .25$)
	50%	$F(2, 359) = 497.24, p < .001, R^2 = .74$	$t(359) = 13.25, p < .001, \beta_{std} = -.59$ ($R^2 = .70$)	$t(359) = 6.71, p < .001, \beta_{std} = -.30$ ($R^2 = .61$)

Note: Each regression model included both predictors, though parenthetical R^2 values are also provided for each predictor when entered independently into simple regression models.

50% through a trial. As trials progressed, its predictive value increased considerably, and halfway through a trial it accounted for over 70% of path efficiency variability. This was the case whether predicting overall path efficiency, or predicting path efficiency for the remainder of a trial.

While entropy levels overall impressively predicted path efficiency, we additionally explored whether a more fine-tuned model, taking into account the timing of navigation decisions (i.e., within intersections), might be similarly successful. Specifically, we tested whether heading entropy and circular heading variance within versus outside of intersections would differentially predict path efficiency. Given the consistent results for predicting overall path efficiency and path efficiency for the remainder of a trial, the following analysis only includes overall path efficiency data. During initial navigation phases (5%, 10%) this analysis was

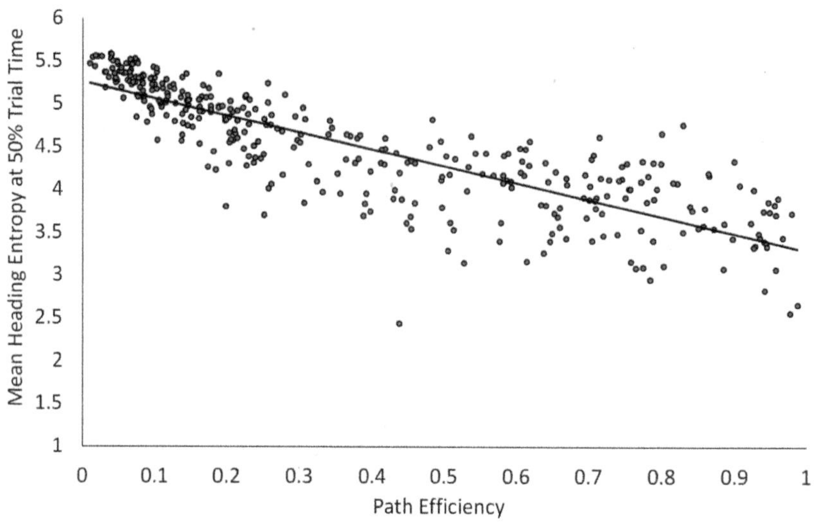

FIGURE 4.2 Scatterplot relating heading entropy values at 50% through a trial's time to overall path efficiency outcomes

TABLE 4.3 Multiple linear regression models testing whether heading entropy and/or circular heading variance predict path efficiency outcomes at 25% and 50% trial time

Intersection (in/out)	*Percentage Trial Time*	*Overall ANOVA*	*Heading Entropy*	*Circ. Heading Variance*
Within Intersections	25%	$F(2, 339) = 242.9$, $p < .001$, $R^2 = .59$	$t(339) = 9.42$, $p < .001$, $\beta_{std} = -.51$	$t(339) = 5.54$, $p < .001$, $\beta_{std} = -.30$
	50%	$F(2, 358) = 579.7$, $p < .001$, $R^2 = .77$	$t(358) = 13.68$, $p < .001$, $\beta_{std} = -.64$	$t(358) = 5.58$, $p < .001$, $\beta_{std} = -.26$
Outside Intersections	25%	$F(2, 355) = 161.5$, $p < .001$, $R^2 = .48$	$t(355) = 12.48$, $p < .001$, $\beta_{std} = -.66$	$t(355) = 0.96$, $p < .001$, $\beta_{std} = -.05$
	50%	$F(2, 358) = 394.56$, $p < .001$, $R^2 = .69$	$t(358) = 9.39$, $p < .001$, $\beta_{std} = -.46$	$t(358) = 8.33$, $p < .001$, $\beta_{std} = -.41$

Note: Results are categorized by whether participants were within versus outside of an intersection.

not possible given missing data points (51%, 33%, respectively; in many cases the participant had not yet moved through an intersection). Thus, we limit analyses to 25% (5.5% missing) and 50% (0.3% missing) trial time percentages (see Table 4.3). In the event of a missing entropy or variance data point, the trial was removed from analysis (as reflected in degrees of freedom).

Again, heading entropy was a stronger and more reliable predictor across trial time percentages, whether a participant was within or outside an intersection. The strongest predictive value came when measuring heading entropy within an intersection (accounting for 59% and 77% of path efficiency variation, for 25% and 50% of time, respectively). However, even outside intersections heading entropy strongly predicted path efficiency (accounting for 48% and 69% of path efficiency variation).

We conducted follow-up analyses to ensure that our standardization process did not significantly distort the data. Notably, a given trial time percentage (e.g., 5%) may contain more or fewer heading values for lower- and higher-efficiency trials, respectively. Specifically, 5% into a 3-minute trial likely results in fewer heading data points relative to 5% into a 10-minute trial. Thus, it is possible that lower-path-efficiency trials might be associated with higher entropy simply due to having more data points in the analysis.

To address this possibility, we reanalyzed our data to include the covariate elapsed time (in seconds) at each trial time percentage. The results of these analyses are detailed in Table 4.4. Overall, heading entropy remained a strong predictor at each percentage of trial time, even after adjustment. For instance, the adjusted R^2 value for heading entropy at 5% of trial time is .55, very similar to the unadjusted .52 value found in our original analyses. Furthermore, the increase in R^2 value from Model 1 to Model 2 (*F*-change) was significant across all time times. Thus, while elapsed time contributes predictive value, it does not meaningfully account for the overall data pattern.

TABLE 4.4 Multiple linear regression models using actual trial time as a covariate, predicting path efficiency at 5%, 10%, 25%, and 50% through individual trials

Percentage Trial Time	*Model 1 (covariate only)*	*Model 2 (covariate plus)*
5%	$F(1, 353) = 175.3, p < .001, R^2_{adj} = .33$	$F(1, 359) = 218.9, p < .001, R^2_{adj} = .55$
10%	$F(1, 357) = 178.7, p < .001, R^2_{adj} = .33$	$F(1, 359) = 218.8, p < .001, R^2_{adj} = .55$
25%	$F(1, 359) = 180.1, p < .001, R^2_{adj} = .33$	$F(1, 359) = 291.4, p < .001, R^2_{adj} = .62$
50%	$F(1, 359) = 180.1, p < .001, R^2_{adj} = .33$	$F(1, 359) = 454.6, p < .001, R^2_{adj} = .72$

Note: Two models were run for each trial time percentage: the first including only the covariate, and the second additionally including the two predictors (heading entropy, circular heading variance). All models were significant ($p < .001$), and the R^2 change always carried a significant F value ($p < .001$).

Individual Differences

To assess whether individual differences in VGE or SBSOD predicted performance on the navigation task, we conducted two multiple linear regressions. Both used VGE and SBSOD as predictors, with one using the slope of learning trends over time as an outcome, and the other using the intercept of learning trends over time as an outcome; none showed significant predictive value (all *p*'s > .19).

Path efficiency, heading entropy, and circular heading variance all varied widely across participants and trials, as detailed in Table 4.2. A series of multiple linear regressions with two predictors (VGE, SBSOD) were conducted for each of the three outcomes (path efficiency, heading entropy, and circular heading variance). None of the regressions reached significance (all *p*'s > .07). Thus, the predictive value of entropy, and to a lesser extent heading variance, were robust across participants and not predicted by video game experience or spatial sense of direction.

Discussion

We found that all of our measures, path efficiency, circular heading variance, and heading entropy reliably indicated environment learning, showing significant reductions with more experience within the environment. Comparing the measures, heading entropy showed the strongest learning effect and was particularly robust (with a 38% larger effect size) when measured while navigators were within versus outside intersections. Given the increased decision load associated with intersections (Allen, Kirasic, Siegel, & Herman, 1979; Brunyé et al., 2015), this pattern suggests that heading entropy is indeed indexing decision uncertainty. After all, it is primarily at intersections that decisions need to be made (Harvey, Coen, & Tank, 2012). Prior to arriving at an intersection, which itself signals the need for a decision, people likely consult their environment knowledge and potentially match it to what they see within the environment. More looking around may signal a poorer match between one's mental model and their current perception.

Second, we found evidence that heading entropy is a strong predictor of ultimate navigation outcomes. Heading entropy proved a more robust predictor than circular heading variance, accounting for very high proportions of path efficiency variation. Even during the very early phases of navigation time (i.e., 5–10%), heading entropy accounted for the majority ($R^2 > .50$) of path efficiency variation. This is particularly remarkable given that for 5%, the maximum amount of time was only approximately two minutes. To our knowledge, no other objective measure provides this predictive capability.

Theoretical and Real-World Implications

The present study carries implications for multiple theoretical and applied domains. First, heading entropy appears to reflect a relatively disorganized search for perceptual features that can reliably distinguish navigation options. This appears to be especially true when participants are in intersections and thus forced to make a decision on whether to continue straight or turn and if turning, which way. This result supports theory suggesting the importance of landmarks in distinguishing intersections and marking decision points (Brunyé et al., 2015; Klippel & Winter, 2005; Michon & Denis, 2001; Steck & Mallot, 2000). Navigators who are relatively indecisive at intersections likely show a less efficient and more disorganized search for visual landmarks to inform behavior or need more checks of the environment to match it to their environment knowledge. Second, heading entropy appears to provide a behavioral metric for states of psychological entropy as proposed by the *entropy model of uncertainty* (Hirsh et al., 2012). The present results demonstrate that the psychological entropy proposed by this theory can manifest in behavior; by inference, entropy of behavior likely reflects disorganized mental states that result from uncertainty at, or anticipation of, decision points. Finally, future navigation support systems may find value in monitoring heading entropy (e.g., via inertial measurement units) and using this information to strategically trigger navigation aids on an as-needed basis.

Entropy and Flexible Mental Models

Return again to that hometown you haven't visited in 20 years. Seeing familiar landmarks triggers fond memories and also your spatial mental model of the town. Yet after 20 years, not all landmarks (and maybe even roads) in town fit your mental model. When these landmarks do not match your mental model, you are more likely to take a second look. Anecdotally, erratic or more variable looking behavior can suggest that a navigator may be lost and need assistance. Such behavior triggers us to ask whether one needs directions somewhere.

Other than explicitly asking, there are no validated methods for assessing disorientation in real-time. Here, we demonstrated that even very early in a navigation task, heading entropy robustly predicts navigation path efficiency. By inference, we propose that heading entropy indicates transient states of disorientation and disorganized looking behavior in an attempt to gather the information needed to inform decisions. As one's mental representation gains accuracy and fidelity, evidence of disorientation decreases. This overall finding carries implications for the design and development of smart GPS systems that can monitor, predict, and optimize human navigation performance. Would a smart GPS systems allow users to develop flexible mental models that could be used to identify detours without the GPS once an environment has been learned? Currently GPS use is often associated with reduced environment learning (Gardony et al., 2013, 2015). If a machine can serve as your mental model, the need to develop one diminishes.

How do we define "optimized human navigation performance"? We argue that navigation performance is optimized when environment knowledge allows one to effectively problem solve within a known environment. Effective problem solving involves flexible use of one's spatial mental model. This point was clearly evident in Barbara Tversky's earlier spatial mental representation research (e.g., Taylor & Tversky, 1992). While we cannot stem the rising tide of navigational aid use as this technology becomes integrated in a host of our other tools (cars, smart phones, wearable technology, etc.), next-generation GPS development can consider spatial cognition. GPS developments rooted in spatial cognitive ideas may lead to systems that promote, rather than impair, development of flexible spatial representations.

Author Note

Research reported in this chapter was supported by a grant awarded to H.A.T. from the U.S. Army Natick Soldier Research, Development, and Engineering Center (W911QY-13-C-0012). Permission was granted by the U.S. Army to publish this material. The views expressed in this article are solely those of the authors and do not reflect the official policies or positions of the Department of the Army, the Department of Defense, or any other department or agency of the U.S. government. We wish to thank Mr. Brian Westgate for programming the computerized navigation tasks. We have no conflicts of interest to declare.

References

Allen, G. L. (1981). A developmental perspective on the effects of "subdividing" macrospatial experience. *Journal of Experimental Psychology: Human Learning & Memory, 7*, 120–132.

Allen, G. L., Kirasic, K. C., Siegel, A. W., & Herman, J. F. (1979). Developmental issues in cognitive mapping: The selection and utilization of environmental landmarks. *Child Development, 50*, 1062–1070.

Berens, P. (2009). CircStat: A MATLAB toolbox for circular statistics. *Journal of Statistical Software, 31*, 1–21. doi: 10.1002/wics.10

Boer, E. R. (2000). *Behavioral entropy as an index of workload.* Paper presented at the Human Factors and Ergonomics Society, San Diego.

Boer, E. R., Rakauskas, M., Ward, N. J., & Goodrich, M. A. (2005). *Steering entropy revisited.* Paper presented at the 3rd International Driving Symposium on Human Factors in Driver Assessment, Training and Vehicle Design, Rockport, ME.

Boot, W. R., Kramer, A. F., Simons, D. J., Fabiani, M., & Gratton, G. (2008). The effects of video game playing on attention, memory, and executive control. *Acta Psychologica, 129*, 387–398. doi: 10.1016/j.actpsy.2008.09.005

Brunyé, T. T., Gagnon, S. A., Gardony, A. L., Gopal, N., Holmes, A., Taylor, H. A., & Tenbrink, T. (2015). Where did it come from, where do you go? Direction sources influence navigation decisions during spatial uncertainty. *Quarterly Journal of Experimental Psychology 68*, 585–607. doi: 10.1080/17470218.2014.963131

Brunyé, T. T., Gardony, A. L., Mahoney, C. R., & Taylor, H. A. (2012). Going to town: Visualized perspectives and navigation through virtual environments. *Computers in Human Behavior, 28*, 257–266.

Brunyé, T. T., Holmes, A., Cantelon, J., Eddy, M. D., Gardony, A. L., Mahoney, C. R., & Taylor, H. A. (2014). Direct current brain stimulation enhances navigation efficiency in individuals with low sense of direction. *Neuroreport, 25*, 1175–1179.

Brunyé, T. T., Rapp, D. N., & Taylor, H. A. (2008). Representational flexibility and specificity following spatial descriptions of real-world environments. *Cognition, 108*, 418–443. doi: 10.1016/j.cognition.2008.03.005

Clark, A. (2013). Whatever next? Predictive brains, situated agents, and the future of cognitive science. *Behavioral and Brain Sciences, 36*(3), 181–204.

Cornwell, B. R., Johnson, L. L., Holroyd, T., Carver, F. W., & Grillon, C. (2008). Human hippocampal and parahippocampal theta during goal-directed spatial navigation predicts performance on a virtual Morris water maze. *The Journal of Neuroscience, 28*, 5983–5990.

Friston, K. (2010). The free-energy principle: A unified theory? *Nature Reviews Neuroscience, 11*, 127–138.

Gardony, A. L., Brunyé, T. T., Mahoney, C. R., & Taylor, H. A. (2011). Affective states influence spatial cue utilization during navigation. *Presence: Teleoperators and Virtual Environments, 20*, 223–240.

Gardony, A. L., Brunyé, T. T., Mahoney, C. R., & Taylor, H. A. (2013). How navigational aids impair spatial memory: Evidence for divided attention. *Spatial Cognition & Computation, 13*, 319–350. doi: 10.1080/13875868.2013.792821

Gardony, A. L., Brunyé, T. T., & Taylor, H. A. (2015). Navigational aids and spatial memory impairment: the role of divided attention. *Spatial Cognition & Computation.*

Hart, P. E., Nilsson, N. J., & Raphael, B. (1968). A formal basis for the heuristic determination of minimum cost paths. *IEEE Transactions on Systems Science and Cybernetics, 4*, 100–107. doi: 10.1109/TSSC.1968.300136

Harvey, C. D., Coen, P., & Tank, D. W. (2012). Choice-specific sequences in parietal cortex during a virtual-navigation decision task. *Nature, 484*, 62–68.

Hegarty, M., Richardson, A. E., Montello, D. R., Lovelace, K., & Subbiah, I. (2002). Development of a self-report measure of environmental spatial ability. *Intelligence, 30*, 425–447.

Hirsh, J. B., Mar, R. A., & Peterson, J. B. (2012). Psychological entropy: a framework for understanding uncertainty-related anxiety. *Psychological Review, 119*, 304–320. doi: 10.1037/a0026767

Huang, J. Y., Tsai, C. H., & Huang, S. T. (2012). The next generation of GPS navigation systems. *Communications of the ACM, 55*, 84. doi: 10.1145/2093548.2093570

Jansen-Osmann, P. & Wiedenbauer, G. (2004). Distance cognition in virtual environmental space: Further investigations to clarify the route-angularity effect. *Psychological Research Psychologische Forschung, 70*, 43–51. doi: 10.1007/s00426-004-0183-8

Klein, G. (2008). Naturalistic decision making. *Human Factors, 50*, 456–460.

Klippel, A. & Winter, S. (2005). Structural salience of landmarks for route directions. *Proceeedings of the International Conference, COSIT.* Ellicottville, NY: Springer Berlin Heidelberg.

Kun, A. L., Paek, T., Medenica, Ž., Memarović, N., & Palinko, O. (2009). Glancing at personal navigation devices can affect driving. *Proceedings of the 1st International Conference on Automotive User Interfaces and Interactive Vehicular Applications - AutomotiveUI '09.* New York, New York, USA: ACM Press.

Leshed, G., Velden, T., Rieger, O., Kot, B., & Sengers, P. (2008). In-car GPS navigation: Engagement with and disengagement from the environment. *Proceedings of the Twenty-Sixth Annual CHI Conference on Human factors in computing systems - CHI '08.* New York, USA: ACM Press.

Menard, S. (1995). *Applied Logistic Regression Analysis.* Thousand Oaks, CA: Sage.

Michon, P.-E. & Denis, M. (2001). When and why are visual landmarks used in giving directions? *Proceedings of the Foundations of Geographic Information Science International Conference, COSIT*. Morro Bay, CA: Springer Berlin Heidelberg.

Parasuraman, R. & Rizzo, M. (2007). *Neuroergonomics: The Brain at Work*. New York: Oxford University Press, 430.

Shannon, C. E. & Weaver, W. (1949). *The Mathematical Theory of Communication*, Urbana: University of Illinois Press.

Sheridan, T. B. & Parasuraman, R. (2005). Human-automation interaction. *Reviews of Human Factors and Ergonomics, 1*, 89–129. doi: 10.1518/155723405783703082

Steck, S. D. & Mallot, H. A. (2000). The role of global and local landmarks in virtual environment navigation. *Presence: Teleoperators and Virtual Environments, 9*, 69–83. doi: 10.1162/105474600566628

Taylor, H. A. & Tversky, B. (1992). Spatial mental models derived from survey and route descriptions. *Journal of Memory and Language, 31*(2), 261–292.

Taylor, H. A., Naylor, S. J., & Chechile, N. A. (1999). Goal-specific influences on the representation of spatial perspective. *Memory & Cognition, 27*, 309–319.

Thorndyke, P. W. & Hayes-Roth, B. (1982). Differences in spatial knowledge acquired from maps and navigation. *Cognitive Psychology, 14*, 560–589.

Waters, W. & Winter, S. (2011). A wayfinding aid to increase navigator independence. *Journal of Spatial Information Science, 2011*(3), 103–122.

Weaver, W. (1953). Recent contributions to the mathematical theory of communication. *ETC: A Review of General Semantics*, 261–281.

Wilson, M. (2002). Six views of embodied cognition. *Psychonomic Bulletin & Review, 9*, 625–636. doi: 10.3758/BF03196322

Wolbers, T. & Hegarty, M. (2010). What determines our navigational abilities? *Trends in Cognitive Sciences, 14*, 138–146. doi: 10.1016/j.tics.2010.01.001

Representations in World

5

EXPLAINING DIAGRAMS

Jane Nisselson

Writing a paper based on a movie based on a paper about visual cognition is meta. My introduction to Barbara Tversky's work was a seminar lecture on diagrams at a Gordon Conference in Oxford in 2009. With slide after slide of arrows, colliding comic book frames and Steinberg illustrations, clearly her topic had cinematic potential.

What came next was a grant to make a three-minute pilot for a long-format documentary about diagrams and their role in visual thinking and communication. A draft of "Visualizing Thought" is the paper that became the basis for this movie short, called "Explaining Diagrams: A Short Introduction."

I'd lectured on the "essay film" and made films on molecules and fragrance (invisible), so this topic was catnip. The first challenge was how to fillet the right parts out of a 35-page academic paper which was, as Tversky wrote at the ending of this unpublished draft, "a whirlwind tour of the nature of graphic inventions, their meanings, their use, and their design."

The second, self-imposed, challenge was to make the film a visual essay – no talking head, no voice-over, no talking whatsoever. The only words would be titles selected from the precise prose that (pardon the diagrammatic verb) delineates, over 35 pages, thought visualized. This makes Pat Irwin's soundtrack, scored for the movie, essential.

Figure 5.1 shows still pictures from "Explaining Diagrams." The core of the movie is built from Tversky's (2011) observation:

> What are the tools of depictions, especially diagrams? How do they communicate? The components of visual communication are simple: Typically, a flat surface, prototypically, a page (or something analogous to a page like a computer screen) and marks or forms placed on it. Each of these, place

> and form, represent meanings that are literal and metaphoric, concrete and abstract. The interpretations depend on content and context, on Gestalt or mathematical properties of the marks in space, on the place of the marks on the page, as well as the information processing capacities and proclivities of the mind. [Passage has been lightly edited.]

The first half of the movie builds a Powers of Ten catalogue of the marks – point, line, arrow, circle, and box. From there, these elements build into a toolkit. At this point, halfway through, when the movie pivots to the network, some title

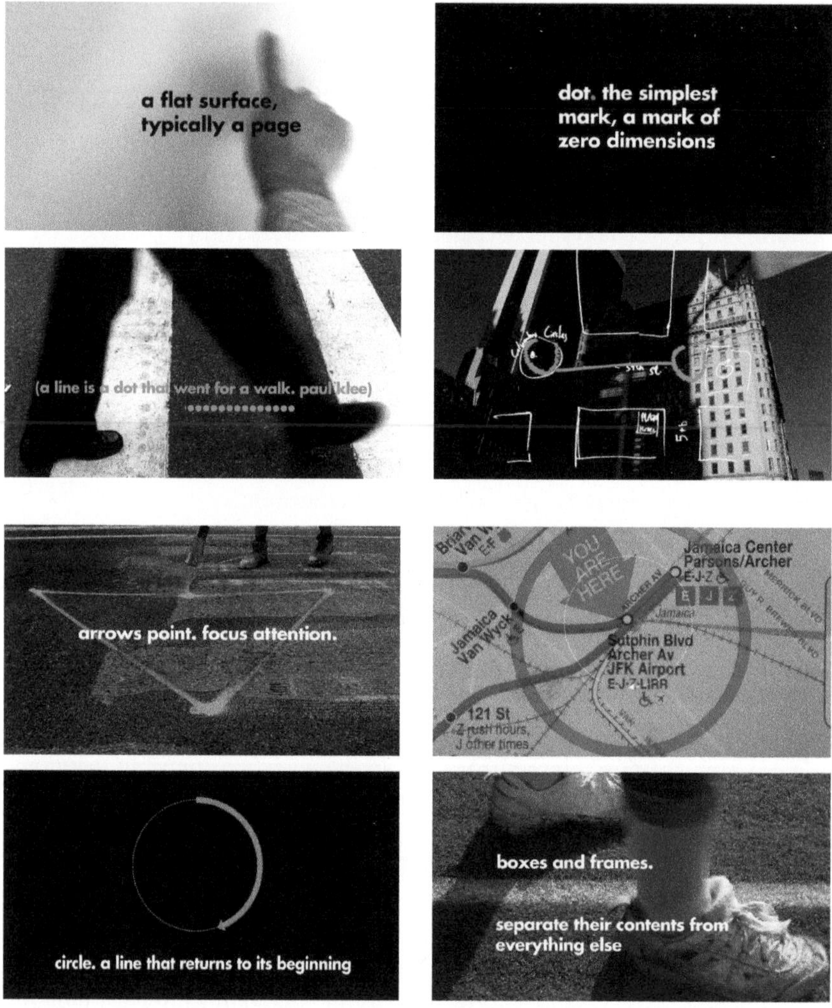

FIGURE 5.1 Still pictures from the video "Explaining Diagrams: A Short Introduction" show the components of visual communication and their application

improvisation took place but always in tandem with Tversky, in conversations, meetings, and emails. If the activity in the video hasn't sunk in, the four words "pattern. sequence. structure. action" telegraph the paper's insights into how we tack visually between the world and marks on the page.

The movie happens over time. It's primarily an urban journey. The surface is often the city, the scale of marking from a cityscape to a tennis court. The published paper sums up the film: "The designed world is a diagram."

Link to the film: https://vimeo.com/50810215

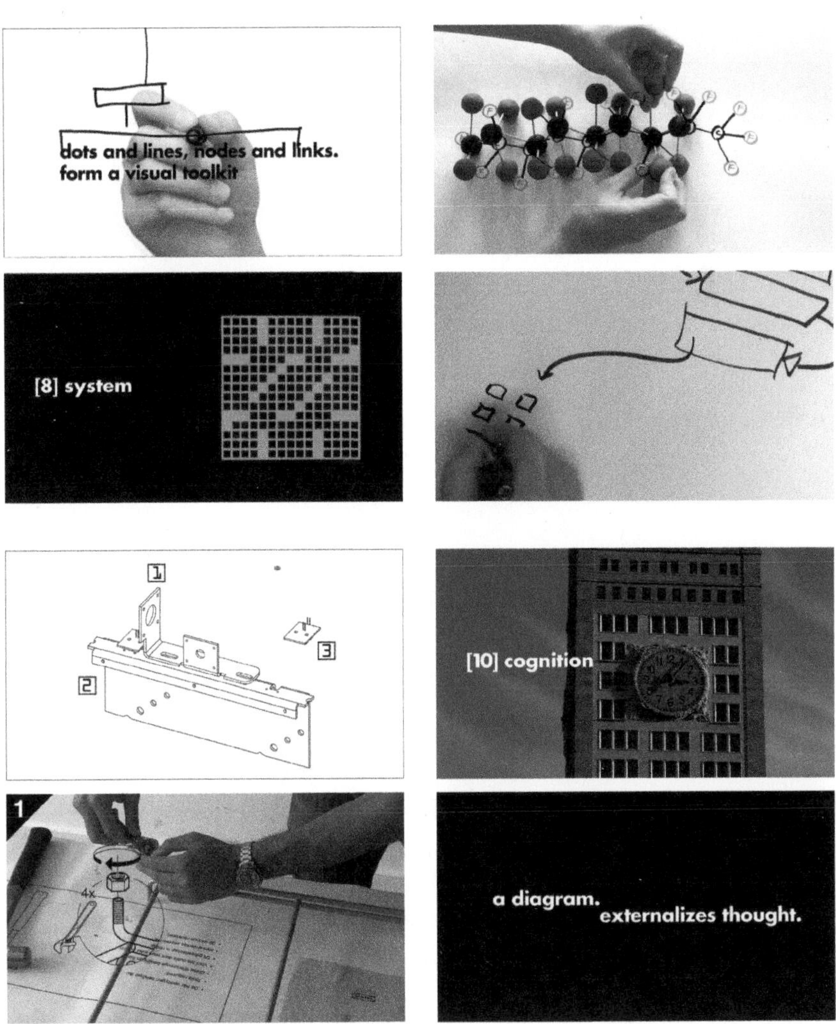

FIGURE 5.1 *continued*

Reference

Tversky, B. (2011). Visualizing thought. *Topics in Cognitive Science*, *3*(3), 499–535.

6

ARROWS IN DIAGRAMMATIC AND NAVIGATIONAL SPACES

Michel Denis

It is a peculiar feature of a great scientist not only to produce high-quality and well-regarded research but also to offer to the scientific community a broad view of a field, by designing a large-size theoretical framework and then navigating through it to attack every specific facet of the area in turn. This exactly draws the portrait of Barbara Tversky, as demonstrated by a prolific and creative scientific career. Her contributions are amply recognized in the broad areas of cognition, memory, and human communication.

More specifically, Barbara's domain encompasses every aspect of visual and spatial thinking, a wide area that has offered her the opportunity to develop a variety of approaches to visual perception, spatial reasoning, spatial language, and to widen her research area through fruitful contacts with the worlds of architecture, design, the visual arts, and the conception of diagrams, up to the design of comics. I do not know if there has been any intentional "plan" subtending Barbara's widely varying excursions through the broad domain of visual cognition. Whether such a plan existed or not, I take it as a positive feature for a scientist to be on the lookout for so many facets of a domain, by entertaining an "opportunistic" attitude (in the most positive sense of the word) and by taking advantage of every encounter with other people and other disciplines. The art of mentally traveling and seizing ideas to nurture the broad domain of visual and spatial cognition has created around Barbara an attraction that has continually made her work inspiring and respected in a wide international community.

In the present chapter, I will recount how my scientific journey crossed Barbara's own exploration of human visuo-spatial cognition. In particular, I will emphasize our efforts to assess the value of various navigational aids, with a particular focus on directional arrows and their role in wayfinding. This will lead me to recall how arrow-like patterns are helpful in the study of other cognitive functions, such as visual attention.

Crossroads

Researchers are travelers. Each follows his or her own route, but their paths are bound to meet at some point. Scientific encounters offer opportunities for confronting ideas and coming up with new questions. This has been precisely the case every time I had the opportunity to cross Barbara's route. I am indebted to her for having approached subjects of special theoretical and societal significance. While conducting our research programs independently, we soon realized that we were exploring a set of common topics, and that exchanges would provide more coherence and validity to our knowledge of human cognitive functions.

In the 1990s, Barbara and I conducted parallel research on various aspects of spatial cognition, and more specifically on how spatial knowledge is expressed through language. These years were marked by experimental programs dedicated to understanding how language renders the perspective taken by a speaker/writer on a described environment. On the listener/reader side, the question focused on the processes by which the conveyed perspective would "shape" his/her representation. This approach was the starting point for implementing a conceptual framework to account for the contrast between survey and route perspectives. A survey perspective is provided by a bird's-eye view of an environment, whereas a succession of views taken while one is traveling through an environment generates a route perspective. Not only were these two perspectives shown to elicit quite distinct patterns of verbal descriptions (involving either allocentric or egocentric language, respectively), but the major question was about the cognitive impact of the two kinds of discourse. Would they result in the construction of functionally distinct mental representations on the part of people listening to such descriptions?

The first attempts to answer this question provided results in favor of the existence of such differences both during the processing of the descriptions and later on in the processing of the representations stored in memory (cf. Perrig & Kintsch, 1985). Along with Holly Taylor, Barbara challenged this view and set the target of identifying the commonalities of representations constructed from these two types of descriptions. They eventually collected evidence for this hypothesis. In particular, they demonstrated that the verification of inferences following the reading of descriptions was as fast and correct regardless of the perspective imposed by the description and the perspective of the to-be-judged spatial relation statement (cf. Taylor & Tversky, 1992). These findings suggested that the mental models constructed from both types of descriptions were abstract and schematic enough to encode spatial relations described from whichever perspective. Later on, the supposed equivalence between representations resulting from the two sorts of descriptions was put under scrutiny. Schneider and Taylor (1999) showed that when readers of a spatial description were asked to recall it, those who read survey descriptions more frequently drew sketch maps than those who read route descriptions, thus attesting to their capacity to maintain an integrated representation of the transmitted spatial information. Further indications were collected to confirm the special value of survey descriptions, which were found to help construct more fine-grained representations, where metric information is more accurately encoded, and from which a perspective change is easier to implement (cf. Brunyé, Rapp, & Taylor, 2008; Noordzij & Postma, 2005; Péruch, Chabanne, Nesa, Thinus-Blanc, & Denis, 2006).

Parallel to this set of studies, a great deal of effort was developed in the same period to account for a specific type of spatial discourse, namely, route directions (cf. Allen, 1997; Couclelis, 1996; Golding, Graesser, & Hauselt, 1996). To some extent, verbal route directions may be seen as a special case of route descriptions, if one considers the fact that they typically adopt an egocentric perspective on an environment. But they do more than that since their objective is to provide instructions to *execute* a sequence of actions that will bring a person to a target place, and consequently they include a critical *procedural* component. Route directions include components that are usually present in route descriptions, but they are constrained by a strong temporal organization, namely, the sequence of the spatial course to be completed. To generate this type of discourse, the describer typically adopts a frontal egocentric view on the environment to describe. Another feature of route directions in natural language is the frequent mention of visual landmarks available along the route, used as reference points to guide the traveler's actions.

Our approach was based on the analysis of route instructions collected in various contexts from a variety of informants (cf. Denis, 1997). First, our findings revealed that most route directions can be reduced to a basic iterative structure: progressing along a segment; reaching a reorientation point, typically signaled by referring to a visual landmark; reorienting and progressing along the new segment. Second, the reference to landmarks is of major value, providing the receivers with an opportunity to build in advance a visual model of the environment that they will traverse. Third, there are considerable differences between the descriptions of a single itinerary given by different speakers. However, they share the same "leading thread". The cognitive value of this underlying structure, or "skeletal description" (to some extent comparable to the concept of macrostructure in text analysis), has been illustrated in further research in both lab and field experiments (cf. Daniel & Denis, 2004; Daniel, Tom, Manghi, & Denis, 2003; Denis, Pazzaglia, Cornoldi, & Bertolo, 1999; Fontaine & Denis, 1999).

The concept of skeletal description, as the core structure assumed to underlie a set of diverse individual descriptions, was implemented through a straightforward method that consisted in compiling the statements available in all individual protocols to generate a "megadescription" and implementing a statistical selection of the statements whose frequency is above a set threshold. As a result, the subset of statements that form the skeletal description provide an informational package with particular structure and content. Skeletal descriptions are saturated with statements that tightly associate a landmark and the action to be executed when this landmark is attained.

Individual protocols were thus approached as variants generated from a core structure that combines a set of links and nodes. This skeletal version is easier to process than more complex ones structured with unnecessary specifications and details, and it is eventually the most efficient in actual on-site navigation. Importantly, our 1997 study showed that the individual protocols that received the highest ratings were those that shared the most similar contents with the skeletal description of the corresponding itinerary. A "good describer" adjusts his/her sequence of instructions to an iterative structure of progressions and reorientations. Fifteen years later, I was grateful to Barbara for having proposed a thoughtful reformulation of the structure of route directions as outlined in my first paper on this subject (cf. Tversky, 2012).

Through the years, this view of the structure and function of route directions developed and a number of exchanges took place between our respective research groups. A significant interface took place when Barbara developed her own research program on the transmission of directional information based on a figural support. Along with Paul Lee, she collected route sketches that she analyzed in order to compare their structure to that of route directions (cf. Tversky & Lee, 1998, 1999). In this context, the conception that route maps share similar features with verbal directions emerged. Not only can both route maps and route directions be divided into segments, but they also similarly refer to the landmarks that mark starting and ending points of a route, as well as reorientation points along the route. In both cases, a route is summarized in the form of an ordered succession of segments that connect intermediate points where orientation changes must be executed. Furthermore, there appears to be no difference between the semantics attached to the elements that compose route maps and verbal directions. The results, indeed, showed similar structure and similar semantic content for the descriptions and depictions generated to assist navigational performance, providing strong suggestion that the same underlying mental representations are used to produce either verbal or pictorial forms of navigational assistance and that "route depictions and descriptions schematiz[e] the real world information in similar ways" (Tversky & Lee, 1999). Route maps and verbal directions can thus be considered as externalizations of a common underlying conceptual structure.

After establishing the concept of a skeletal structure underlying verbal route directions, a further challenge involved extending the concept from the domain where it had been elaborated originally to the domain of depictions and sketch maps. The opportunity to examine the validity of this extension was provided by a collaboration involving a Canadian team dedicated to geomatics (cf. Fontaine, Edwards, Tversky, & Denis, 2005). In this study, we collected sketch maps of the Plains of Abraham, a park well known by every inhabitant of Quebec City. The maps were submitted for evaluation to a group of judges, either expert and non-experts in geomatics. We hypothesized that if people have some metacognitive knowledge of what is a good cartographic representation, they might produce consistent judgments about the quality of a set of maps. It turned out that experts and non-expert evaluators alike agreed in their evaluations and rankings, indicating that they shared a similar concept of what constitutes a "good" map. Another way to test this idea was to check whether judges would also agree in a task that consisted of selecting from sketch maps only those elements deemed essential. To this purpose, we built a "megamap" containing all information provided by all the participants in the previous experiment. The judges were asked to review each item present in the megamap (buildings, paths, roads, monuments, etc.) and to judge on a rating scale whether it was to be kept in an ideal map expected to be useful for navigating. Again, the expectation was that a kind of common implicit knowledge might be operating for most evaluators. Indeed, a high level of consensus emerged regarding the classification of items of primary value for guidance or navigation purposes (thus recommended to be maintained in the ideal map) and those items of secondary importance (to be eliminated). By taking these judgments into account, we constructed a "skeletal map" containing only items recognized as important (main roads and most significant landmarks). Returning to the initially collected sketch maps, we found that those that were judged the best contained the greatest proportion of elements from the skeletal map. (Not surprisingly, these maps had been generated mainly by experts in geomatics.) When carefully analyzed, the sketch maps reveal the mental representations of their producers, just as was the case with verbal route directions in our previous experiments. When evaluated by others for goodness and essential information, both maps and verbal directions prove to be useful to elaborate principles for designing effective navigational aids.

Barbara and I had another occasion to think together about such design principles, working on a set of experiments run by Ariane Tom in Orsay and Stanford. These experiments were designed to document further the role of landmarks in route directions. Not only did the majority of describers spontaneously include numerous references to visual landmarks in their descriptions, but the users of these descriptions reported that such references were useful to them. The privileged cognitive status of landmarks likely reflects the fact that they help users create a visual model that includes the critical aspects of the to-be-traversed environment, and prepares them to make adequate decisions at ambiguous points in the environment. The information conveyed by landmarks may even be preferred to the information about the streets to take. Our experiments revealed that pedestrians had better navigational performance when they received a set of instructions referring to the upcoming landmarks than when they only used the list of streets that they would take. Furthermore, processing of route directions exclusively centered on the streets was more time-consuming than processing of directions focusing on landmarks. Street-based directions were also more difficult to memorize than landmark-based directions. This effect was explained by the vividness or distinctiveness of information attached to landmarks (cf. Tom & Denis, 2003, 2004; Tom & Tversky, 2012). Further work in our research group provided evidence for the significance of landmarks in memory for spatial information collected through spatial discourse as well as during navigation (cf. Denis & Fernandez, 2013; Denis, Mores, Gras, Gyselinck, & Daniel, 2014).

Thus, the paths followed by Barbara and myself crossed each other several times, obviously not by chance, but for good scientific reasons, thus contributing to an exceptional context for a longstanding intellectual friendship. Incidentally, as everyone knows, crossroads are locations in an environment where people typically come across traffic signs and directional arrows. These particular artifacts, which are expected to be of value for every navigator, form the main subject of the rest of this chapter.

Arrows

Barbara and I have always shared the same interest in spatial knowledge and the conditions in which navigators exploit all available information to accomplish safe and efficient progress to their destination. Although my own research mainly focused on the challenging situation in which language is the main – or even sole – vehicle to provide navigational assistance to a traveler, I have cultivated my curiosity for the vast range of devices designed to deliver directional information.

In strong contrast to linguistic devices, arrows are analog, intuitive, non-verbal sources of navigational assistance. After all, they are just *lines*, but lines of a very special kind. The curiosity elicited by arrows is perhaps related to the fact that beyond the frequent circumstances where they prove to be useful, they are sometimes at the

FIGURE 6.1 Inconsistent directional information (Frelighsburg, Quebec, Canada). Photo credit: G. Cotteret

origin of troublesome situations, such as when a traveler is confronted with vague, ambiguous, or inconsistent directional information (Figure 6.1).

From traffic signage to teaching media and flowcharts to route maps and diagrams, arrows are universal and ubiquitous devices used in a variety of contexts, a good number of which are not directly relevant to navigation proper. Because arrows elicit or assist people's behavior in a variety of daily circumstances, a psychologist can only be intrigued by the fact that although they obviously call for cognitive processing, the processes underlying their perception and comprehension have been left implicit and scarcely documented by psychological research. Some authors have pointed to the variety of the functions served by arrows in various domains, in particular science, where they are recognized as "one of the most commonly used graphical devices in scientific figures" (Wong, 2011). Because they seem particularly suited to show or suggest logical and temporal dependencies, they are used to make concepts, processes, and theories easier to understand than purely discursive descriptions (Figure 6.2). Beyond scientific communication, arrows are used to assist communication in a variety of areas, thus necessitating the need to formulate principles to enhance their functional value (cf. Frankel & DePace, 2012; Horn, 1998; Mollerup, 2013).

Every cognitive scientist interested in comprehending the significance of arrows will refer to the seminal contribution of Barbara and her collaborators at the turn of the millennium (cf. Tversky, Zacks, Lee, & Heiser, 2000). In their paper, the authors outlined a framework to account for a large family of graphic devices, namely, "lines, blobs, crosses, and arrows". This enumeration was intended to encompass those schematic figures that can be used as graphical primitives and eventually contribute to make diagram-based communication an efficient process. Those figures have in common the goal to "convey certain specific concepts, where the forms themselves suggest meanings". They "bear resemblance to the things they convey", and by this very fact, they "appear to convey meaning less arbitrarily than symbols". It is not a surprise to realize that these schematic figures constitute the core elements of route depictions, as documented by the previously mentioned work by Tversky and Lee (1998, 1999).

Tversky et al. (2000) focused particularly on functional or causal arrows, those used to suggest direction of movement, temporal direction, and causality (or implication). They pointed out the fact that the use of these figures, although "well designed to indicate direction in space, time, and causality", is not restricted to such directional meanings. They may also be used metaphorically, for instance to suggest increases (or decreases) of physical quantities or even more abstract values.

In diagrams, arrows are commonly used to suggest directions in space and in time. Interestingly, they frequently appear in diagrams with a plurality of meanings. For instance, in a set of illustrations used to teach electricity concepts the same plain arrow shape may serve to indicate either the movement of bodies that are attracting each other or the transition from one state of affairs to a further one (Figure 6.3) (cf. Gyselinck, Cornoldi, Dubois, De Beni, & Ehrlich, 2002). This

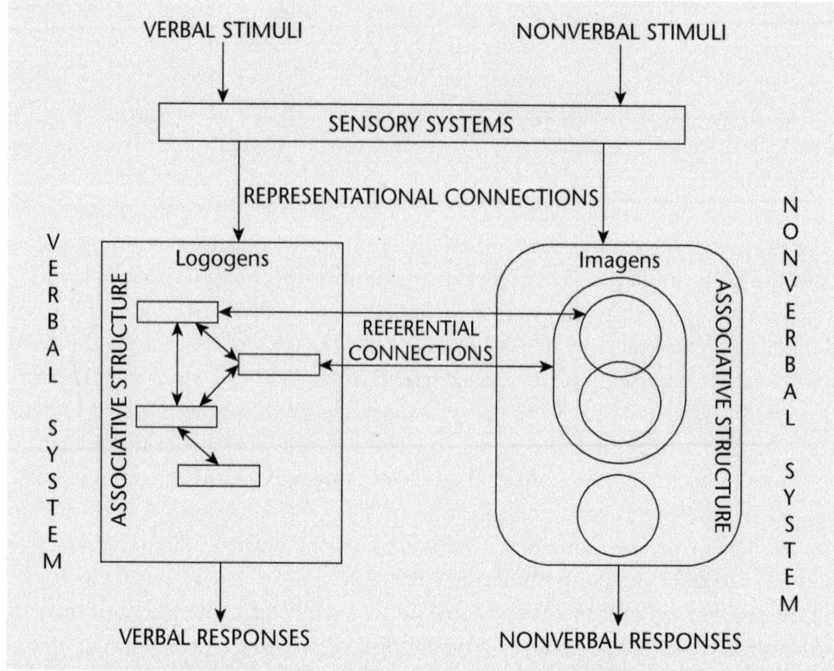

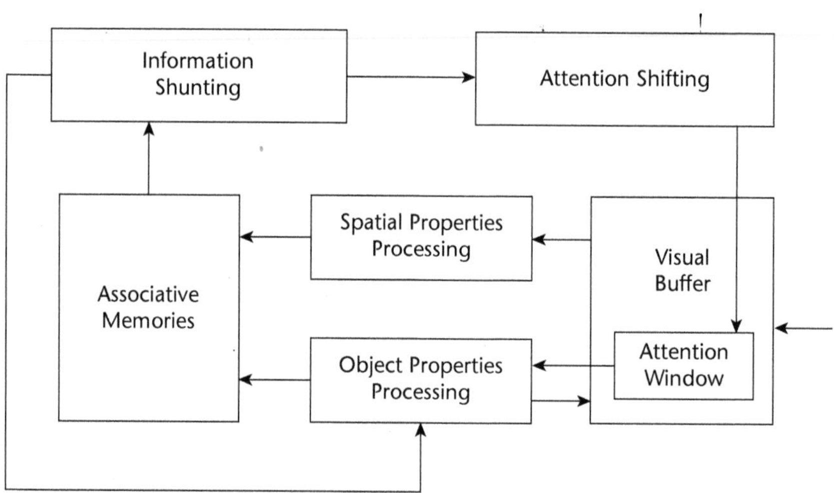

FIGURE 6.2 Arrows are inherent to diagrams intended to make explicit psychological theories. The examples shown here summarize Paivio's dual coding theory (top) and Kosslyn's model of imagery processing (bottom). Reproduced from *Mental representations: A dual coding approach*, by A. Paivio (1986), and *The case for mental imagery*, by S. M. Kosslyn, W. L. Thompson, and G. Ganis (2006)

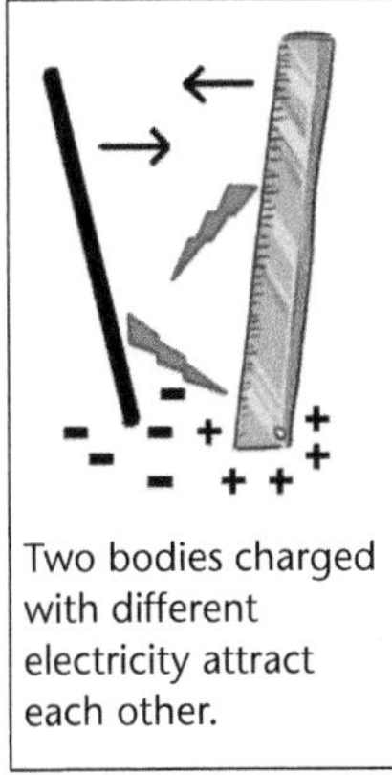

Two bodies charged with different electricity attract each other.

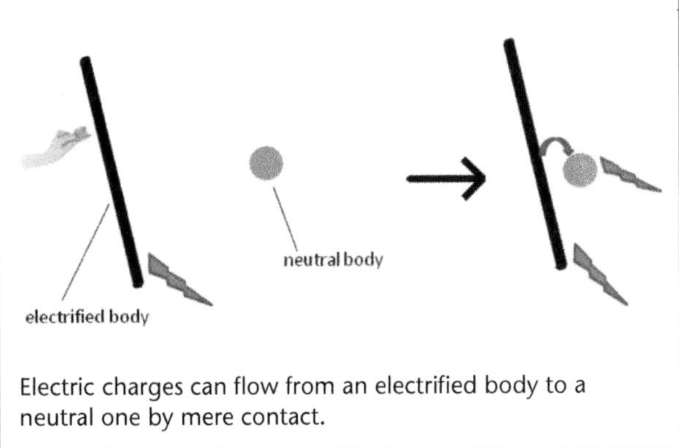

neutral body
electrified body
Electric charges can flow from an electrified body to a neutral one by mere contact.

FIGURE 6.3 Arrows in illustrations used to teach electricity concepts. Figures designed and generously provided by V. Gyselinck

forces the researcher to recognize the cognitive flexibility of those people who effortlessly process distinct meanings of the same symbol at the same time.

A special value of diagrammatic arrows appears when they are used to help make inferences about a complex process and develop adequate reasoning from diagrams showing mechanical systems (like pulleys; e.g., Hegarty, 1992). Of course, many students will demonstrate their ability to perform a "mental animation process", which involves "decomposing the representation of [the] system into smaller units corresponding to the machine components and animating these components in a sequence corresponding to the causal sequence of events in the machine's operation" (Hegarty, 1992; see also Hegarty, 2004).

As pointed out by Tversky et al. (2000), in such diagrams, "the arrows function to show the route and sequence of events in the operation of the system". In the absence of arrows, only the structure of the system will be made visible. If arrows are included, the temporal sequence of events becomes apparent, even if it is conveyed through a static diagram (Figure 6.4). The presence of arrows should thus be expected to encourage a functional interpretation of the diagram.

This was precisely the hypothesis that was tested by Heiser and Tversky (2006). In their study, participants were presented with pictures illustrating a mechanical phenomenon, such as the functioning of a car brake. In one version of the material, the diagram included arrows indicating the temporal sequence of the system. In another version, the diagram simply did not include arrows. The participants were invited to write a description of the system depicted by the diagram. The results showed that people who were presented with diagrams containing arrows generated descriptions that included more units conveying functional information (such as the description of the operations and their causal consequences, the function of the individual parts of the system and how they work together) than the participants who did not see arrows. On the other hand, people who described

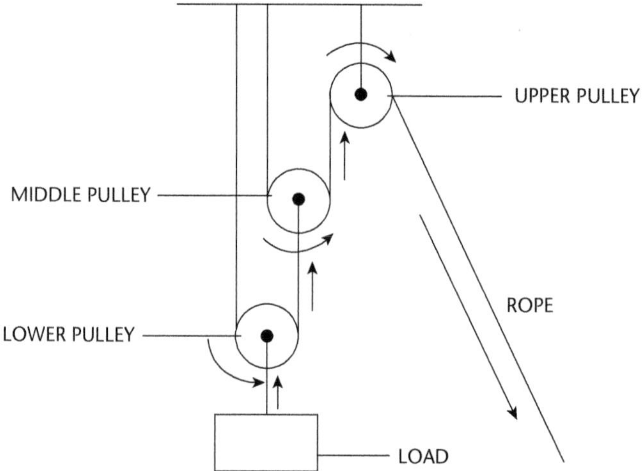

FIGURE 6.4 Diagram of a pulley system with arrows. Reproduced from "Lines, blobs, crosses and arrows: Diagrammatic communication with schematic figures", by B. Tversky, J. Zacks, P. Lee, and J. Heiser, in *Theory and application of diagrams (Proceedings of Diagrams 2000)*, with the kind permission of J. Heiser and Springer

diagrams without arrows produced more structural units (description of the components of the system, their shape, etc.) than those exposed to diagrams including arrows. In another experiment, the participants were invited to read descriptions of the system and construct a diagram of what they thought the description was intended to convey. People who read functional descriptions depicted them by spontaneously using arrows, whereas structural descriptions resulted in the drawing of diagrams with much lower use of arrows.

Not only do arrows encourage causal or functional interpretations of the systems depicted, but diagrams generated from causal or functional descriptions are more likely to contain arrows than diagrams of structural descriptions of the same systems. Considering these results altogether, Tversky and her colleagues were well founded to claim that arrows belong to "the class of diagrammatic forms that readily convey a restricted set of meanings in context" (Tversky et al., 2000; see also Tversky, Heiser, Lee, & Daniel, 2009).

Arrows in Space

Arrows have obviously special significance with respect to space. Not only are they spatially extended, but they are used to say something about space; more specifically, about the relation between a human agent and a temporarily non-visible target in an environment. In the present analysis, I focus on the function of arrows that are designed to assist a navigating agent who lacks full information about an environment. Sometimes, arrows succeed in this function. Sometimes, they fail to do so, especially if there is some mismatch between the information that they convey and the context in which it is delivered. In such cases, arrows may prove that they are not always friendly cognitive aids.

Arrows are graphic, non-verbal assisting devices, but their non-verbal nature does not mean that they have no semantic content. The precise meaning of an arrow is established by a person in a particular context. Beyond the typical context of navigation, arrows focus or direct someone's attention to a piece of information that is not yet at the center of the person's attentional field, but is potentially relevant. If a process of attention shifting to a point of interest is unlikely to occur spontaneously, a pointing device (such as an arrow) will ensure that the addressee's attention is effectively drawn to this critical point. Arrows can be used as reminders or pointers to specific parts of written material, to posted instructions, or to objects or places that might be neglected and create a dangerous situation (Figure 6.5).

It is generally recognized that the use of arrows is a particular case of pointing. Digital pointing is a universal, quite early human capacity, which appears as early as the infant's first year (Butterworth, Franco, McKenzie, Graupner, & Todd, 2002; Tomasello, Carpenter, & Liszkowski, 2007). Like pointing, arrows *direct* someone's attention to a relevant target. At least, the target is perceived as relevant by the pointing person in a given context. The expectation of the pointing person is to have another one (or more) share his/her perceptual experience.

Arrows are also typically used to trigger someone's *physical movement* toward a target. The intent is to help someone reduce the distance between him/her and some remote entity or place to reach, either visually or cognitively or by physical translation. The operation is successful if the intended contact is eventually achieved (eye contact, cognitive contact, physical contact in shared space).

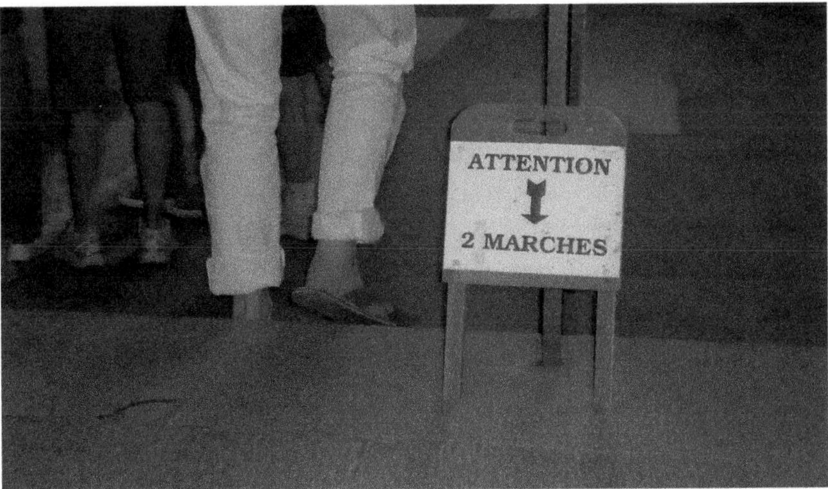

FIGURE 6.5 "Mind the steps!"

An intriguing question is to understand why this "distance-reducing function" is typically implemented in the particular form of an *arrow*. Let's remember that arrows are human-made artifacts that have very specific functional properties. They are weapons. As weapons, they are of course not intended to elicit someone's movement, or to direct a person's attention to a point of interest. Arrows are projectiles that are intended to traverse space along some distance, reach an object or location, and get fixed or attached to it.

Arrows are used in a variety of contexts, cultures, and environments. They are composed of three parts: an arrowhead, a shaft, and a fletching, each of which has a specific contribution to serve the function and ballistic properties of the arrow. Symbolic directional arrows inherit these features from arrows/weapons. However, fletching is most frequently left aside. Shafts may also be deleted, without hindering the validity of the directional information conveyed by the symbol.

The arrowhead is the essential component of arrows. Its geometrical shape (sharpened tip) is critical, although many variants can be found. This is true as well of symbolic directional arrows. There are many variants of their fine geometry and visual appearance. But the essential pattern (beyond the variants) is the angular structure of the arrowhead, namely a sharpened tip defined by two converging lines. Whatever the angle of the arrowhead, the bisecting line provides the directional information in a purely analog way. You just have to align your movement (or your sight) to the direction given by the bisecting line, and by following this direction, you must reach the target.

The visual appearance of arrows is extraordinarily variable. Beyond the variants, the meaning remains the same. The essence of the semantics of arrows resides in both their asymmetry and their directionality (cf. Tversky, 2001; Tversky et al., 2000). The informational value of arrows basically consists in giving a direction to a movement to be accomplished by a moving agent aimed at a target.

In some cases, a clever designer will opt for the formula that consists of drawing the arrow on the ground, in such a way that direct matching is ensured between the displayed direction and the effective sequence of steps to be executed. This is quite a reliable mode of navigational assistance (Figure 6.6). Another well-known example of this is the Freedom Trail, a four-kilometer red line to be followed by the visitors of Boston to visit every major historical spot of the city[1]. More unexpected is the procedure that consists of displaying directional arrows on the ceiling of a building, but its functional value is not called in question (Figure 6.7).

The semantics conveyed by a directional arrow ("Proceed in the direction that the arrowhead is pointing to") is quite transparent at first sight. However, the supposedly "analog" meaning conveyed by arrows cannot be always taken literally. Take for instance the case of arrows that are pointing upwards, in places where they are not intended to suggest that an ascending movement should be implemented. They are to be interpreted as the frontal-plane repositioning of an arrow which, on the ground, would invite a walking person to go forward. More subtle cases are found in which an upward oriented arrow ("Go forward") is combined with a

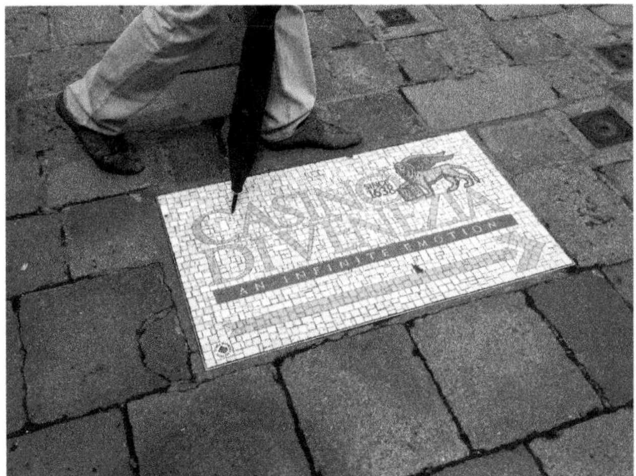

FIGURE 6.6 Arrows on the ground in the city of Venice

FIGURE 6.7 Arrows on the ceiling (Osnabrück University ofApplied Science, Germany). Reproduced from the book by P. Mollerup, *Wayshowing>Wayfinding: Basic and interactive* (2013), with the kind permission of P. Mollerup

downward-oriented one, which basically conveys the same directional instruction and also acts as a pointer to indicate the place where the navigator should place his/her steps (Figure 6.8). The fact that most people are not troubled when they process these two distinct arrows to integrate them in the form of an effective single action is a good illustration of the capacity of people to adapt cognitively to such situations.

FIGURE 6.8 Upward and downward arrows intended to deliver similar instructions

An arrow displayed alone, without any additional information, is hardly meaningful. The only exception is when the navigator has contextual knowledge about the implicit message conveyed by the arrow, as is the case with those universally used arrows on a green background that signal the way to move to the exit of a building in case of emergency. Excepting such cases, typically, every sign involving a directional arrow conveys information regarding the object or the place that the arrow signals to the navigator's attention. This additional information may be expressed in the form of a symbol easy to recognize or, quite frequently, of a verbal label that designates the target (the name of a monument, of a city, etc.).

The design of directional arrows is subject to principles that are supposed to ensure adequate delivery of the informational content of the sign (cf. Mollerup, 2013). Some spatial proximity must be ensured between the arrow and the name of the target. Beyond a critical distance between them, there is a risk that the navigator will mistake the intended information, or at least be momentarily confused (Figure 6.9).

Another relevant issue is that of the spatial relationship between the target's name and the body of the arrow. In practice, the target's name, in addition to being displayed in a reasonable proximity with the arrow, typically appears above or

FIGURE 6.9 Different distances separating an arrow and the corresponding building number. The above case is canonical, while the one below looks rather unusual

FIGURE 6.10 Canonical vs. unexpected location of an arrow relatively to a target's name

below the arrow. When it is displayed in alignment with the axis of the shaft, the canonical position of the name is somewhere by the tail of the arrow, in such a way that the arrow is posited between the target (to which it points) and the symbolic designation of the target (attached to the tail of the arrow). Unexpected are the arrows that are designed in such a way that they point simultaneously to both the target and its name (Figure 6.10).

Among the principles that are likely to govern the generation of arrows in an ergonomic fashion, a principle of parsimony is certainly in order, as is the case for other forms of symbolic signage. Twenty arrows are not supposed to say more than a single one, unless a designer intends to create a striking visual effect for the users of the sign (Figure 6.11).

FIGURE 6.11 One arrow is enough!

Arrows in Psychological Research

Distinct from directional arrows considered in studies of spatial and environmental cognition, arrow-like patterns have been sporadically investigated in psychological research as figures likely to elicit special cognitive processing. In particular, they have been used for their singular geometric characteristics, mainly their asymmetric structure, in the study of visual attention.

The most famous arrow since the early days of scientific psychology is the figure that revealed the Müller-Lyer illusion (cf. Müller-Lyer, 1889). We know, however, that the illusory effect can be generated by other geometric patterns than arrowheads. One should note also that in the canonical version of the illusory situation, the figure cannot really be said to be an arrow, if only because it displays a symmetric pattern, with *two* diverging arrowheads at the respective ends of a straight line.

The Eriksen Flanker Task is a test of people's capacity to inhibit responses to a given item in spite of the pressure exercised by other contextual items. It has been widely used in psychological research for decades (cf. Eriksen & Eriksen, 1974). In the canonical version, a target is flanked by non-targets which either call for the same response as the target or for another response. The original test used upper-case letters, but it was extended to other materials, of which arrows are probably the most interesting (Figure 6.12). The variant of the task with arrows provided evidence for their particularly compelling effect on the production of motor responses (e.g., Kopp, Mattler, & Rist, 1994).

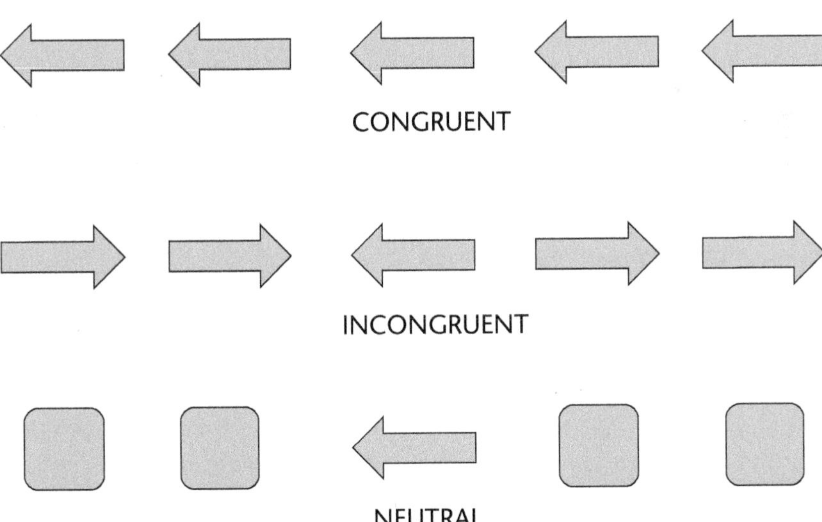

FIGURE 6.12 Congruent, incongruent, and neutral flankers. The target is the arrow at the center of each line

Another valuable use of arrows was illustrated by Posner and Cohen (1984), with the objective of providing cues for particular locations in a visual field. In their studies of visual orienting, they used arrows as cues to indicate where to attend a target. When the target appeared in the part of the visual field pointed to by the arrow, the detection of the target was facilitated (with faster responses). When it appeared on the other side, responses were delayed. The Posner and Cohen studies showed that attention can be affected by the directional characteristics attached to an arrow used as a visual cue. Later on, in cued-attention experiments where peripheral attention is caused by an arrow that is predictive or not of the target location, attentional shift was shown to involve a left parieto-frontal network (cf. Kato, Matsuo, Matsuzawa, Moriya, Glover, & Nakai, 2001).

In a visuo-spatial orienting task, where arrow cues are known to trigger automatic orienting, response times are typically faster when the arrows point toward the target location, as compared with the case where they point away from it. This pattern of results appears even when participants have been informed that the arrows do not predict where the target would appear (cf. Tipples, 2002, 2008). As a matter of fact, arrow-like patterns include geometric features that are typically those of predictive cues. Note, however, that the interesting thing about arrows is that they sometimes produce cuing even when they are not predictive (cf. Friesen, Ristic, & Kingstone, 2004; Ristic, Friesen, & Kingstone, 2002).

Other potentially interesting experiments could be imagined to assess the attentional value attached to arrows in information processing. For instance, would it be possible to profit from arrows as cognitive pointers to parts of complex materials that are important or particularly relevant? Suppose that a person is presented with a set of objects or a list of words to memorize. Would any memory advantage be conferred to items indicated by an arrow? Of course, some controls would be needed in such an investigation to compare the effect of arrows, if any, with the effect of other devices or pointers intended to single out particular items. In the case where an arrow effect would be detected, would this effect be modulated by the distance separating the arrow and the item? Straightforward experiments could be implemented to establish whether this putative arrow effect is real or not.

In all the examples discussed above, arrows are used to generate an attentional orientation toward a stimulus, and the detection or memory of the stimulus benefits of this manipulation. In other experimental contexts, arrows may be investigated by considering their proper semantics, in particular in navigation tasks, where they can be compared to other forms of directional assistance. For instance, in urban environments, similar assistance is expected to be provided by verbal directions and by the display of arrow signs. A wide field of environmental studies might be developed to compare the ergonomic value of verbal and graphic devices in assisting a navigator in search of particular targets in urban or countryside contexts (cf. Mollerup, 2013).

Toward a Cognitive Science of Arrows?

At the crossroads where psychology, geomatics and artificial intelligence meet, special attempts are being developed to analyze the mechanisms by which arrows ensure their cognitive functions, in particular in contexts of communication between human beings and artificial systems. The challenge is to test whether a system will understand the semantics attached to an arrow in a particular context. As pointed out by Kurata and Egenhofer (2005, 2008), a reason for the popularity of arrows is that with their simple shape, they capture a large variety of semantics. Humans cope pretty well with this polysemy, but the task is likely to be more difficult for computers. Kurata and Egenhofer have developed a systematic classification of the possible interpretations of arrow diagrams: express a direction, illustrate a spatial movement (both path and direction), suggest spatial interaction, express a temporal order, express a conditional relation or a causal relation, label a symbol by assigning a description (or simply a name) to an element present in a diagram or a map. The key feature in all those cases is that the relations that are expressed by an arrow are *directed* relations.

There is certainly much to be gained by developing the capacity of computers to correctly interpret the arrows displayed in diagrams. When humans express some of their knowledge in the form of arrow symbols, they hope for more intuitive interaction between them and machines. In short, the objective would be to transfer to artificial systems the capacity of interpreting arrows in diagrams describing a system.

Accounting for the functional value of arrows in the comprehension of complex systems is one of the challenges to be taken up by scientists open to interdisciplinary endeavors. Barbara is definitely one of them, and an authoritative leader in this area. She has opened avenues of research for scholars in cognitive psychology and neuroscience, but also in those disciplines dedicated to the expression of spatial information, be it in the domains of architecture, visual arts, or the design of navigational systems. Her research has been, and continues to be, an invaluable input and motivation for generations of cognitive scientists.

Note

1 Although the Freedom Trail does not display any explicit arrow-like pattern, arrows are virtually present for a pedestrian since the line passes by 16 locations in a strictly ordered sequence, from the starting point (the Boston Common) to the final site (the Bunker Hill Monument).

References

Allen, G. L. (1997). From knowledge to words to wayfinding: Issues in the production and comprehension of route directions. In S. C. Hirtle & A. U. Frank (Eds.), *Spatial information theory: A theoretical basis for GIS (Proceedings of COSIT 1997)* (pp. 363–372). Berlin: Springer.

Brunyé, T. T., Rapp, D. N., & Taylor, H. A. (2008). Representational flexibility and specificity following spatial descriptions of real-world environments. *Cognition, 108*, 418–443.

Butterworth, G., Franco, F., McKenzie, B., Graupner, L., & Todd, B. (2002). Dynamic aspects of visual event perception and the production of pointing by human infants. *British Journal of Developmental Psychology, 20*, 1–24.

Couclelis, H. (1996). Verbal directions for way-finding: Space, cognition, and language. In J. Portugali (Ed.), *The construction of cognitive maps* (pp. 133–153). Dordrecht, The Netherlands: Kluwer.

Daniel, M.-P. & Denis, M. (2004). The production of route directions: Investigating conditions that favour conciseness in spatial discourse. *Applied Cognitive Psychology, 18*, 57–75.

Daniel, M.-P., Tom, A., Manghi, E., & Denis, M. (2003). Testing the value of route directions through navigational performance. *Spatial Cognition and Computation, 3*, 269–289.

Denis, M. (1997). The description of routes: A cognitive approach to the production of spatial discourse. *Current Psychology of Cognition, 16*, 409–458.

Denis, M. & Fernandez, G. (2013). The processing of landmarks in route directions. In T. Tenbrink, J. Wiener, & C. Claramunt (Eds.), *Representing space in cognition: Interrelations of behaviour, language, and formal models* (pp. 42–55). Oxford, UK: Oxford University Press.

Denis, M., Mores, C., Gras, D., Gyselinck, V., & Daniel, M.-P. (2014). Is memory for routes enhanced by an environment's richness in visual landmarks? *Spatial Cognition and Computation, 14*, 284–305.

Denis, M., Pazzaglia, F., Cornoldi, C., & Bertolo, L. (1999). Spatial discourse and navigation: An analysis of route directions in the city of Venice. *Applied Cognitive Psychology, 13*, 145–174.

Eriksen, B. A. & Eriksen, C. W. (1974). Effects of noise letters upon the identification of a target letter in a nonsearch task. *Perception and Psychophysics, 16*, 143–149.

Fontaine, S. & Denis, M. (1999). The production of route instructions in underground and urban environments. In C. Freksa & D. M. Mark (Eds.), *Spatial information theory: Cognitive and computational foundations of geographic information science (Proceedings of COSIT 1999)* (pp. 83–94). Berlin: Springer.

Fontaine, S., Edwards, G., Tversky, B., & Denis, M. (2005). Expert and non-expert knowledge of loosely structured environments. In A. G. Cohn & D. M. Mark (Eds.), *Spatial information theory (Proceedings of COSIT 2005)* (pp. 363–378). Berlin: Springer.

Frankel, F. C. & DePace, A. H. (2012). *Visual strategies: A practical guide to graphics for scientists and engineers*. New Haven, CT: Yale University Press.

Friesen, C. K., Ristic, J., & Kingstone, A. (2004). Attentional effects of counterpredictive gaze and arrow cues. *Journal of Experimental Psychology: Human Perception and Performance, 30*, 319–329.

Golding, J. M., Graesser, A. C., & Hauselt, J. (1996). The process of answering direction-giving questions when someone is lost on a university campus: The role of pragmatics. *Applied Cognitive Psychology, 10*, 23–39.

Gyselinck, V., Cornoldi, C., Dubois, V., De Beni, R., & Ehrlich, M.-F. (2002). Visuospatial memory and phonological loop in learning from multimedia. *Applied Cognitive Psychology, 16*, 665–685.

Hegarty, M. (1992). Mental animation: Inferring motion from static displays of mechanical systems. *Journal of Experimental Psychology: Learning, Memory, and Cognition, 18*, 1084–1102.

Hegarty, M. (2004). Mechanical reasoning by mental simulation. *Trends in Cognitive Sciences, 8*, 280–285.

Heiser, J. & Tversky, B. (2006). Arrows in comprehending and producing mechanical diagrams. *Cognitive Science, 30*, 581–592.

Horn, R. E. (1998). *Visual language: Global communication for the 21st century*. Bainbridge Island, WA: MacroVU.

Kato, C., Matsuo, K., Matsuzawa, M., Moriya, T., Glover, G. H., & Nakai, T. (2001). Activation during endogenous orienting of visual attention using symbolic pointers in the human parietal and frontal cortices: A functional magnetic resonance imaging study. *Neuroscience Letters, 314*, 5–8.

Kopp, B., Mattler, U., & Rist, F. (1994). Selective attention and response competition in schizophrenic patients. *Psychiatric Research, 53*, 129–139.

Kosslyn, S. M., Thompson, W. L., & Ganis, G. (2006). *The case for mental imagery*. New York: Oxford University Press.

Kurata, Y. & Egenhofer, M. J. (2005). Structure and semantics of arrow diagrams. In A. G. Cohn & D. M. Mark (Eds.), *Spatial information theory (Proceedings of COSIT 2005)* (pp. 232–250). Berlin: Springer.

Kurata, Y. & Egenhofer, M. J. (2008). The Arrow-Semantics Interpreter. *Spatial Cognition and Computation*, 8, 306–332.

Mollerup, P. (2013). *Wayshowing>Wayfinding: Basic and interactive*. Amsterdam: BIS.

Müller-Lyer, F. C. (1889). Optische Urteilstäuschungen. *Archiv für Anatomie und Physiologie, Physiologische Abteilung, 2*, 263–270.

Noordzij, M. L. & Postma, A. (2005). Categorical and metric distance information in mental representations derived from route and survey descriptions. *Psychological Research, 69*, 221–232.

Paivio, A. (1986). *Mental representations: A dual coding approach*. New York: Oxford University Press.

Perrig, W. & Kintsch, W. (1985). Propositional and situational representations of text. *Journal of Memory and Language, 24*, 503–518.

Péruch, P., Chabanne, V., Nesa, M.-P., Thinus-Blanc, C., & Denis, M. (2006). Comparing distances in mental images constructed from visual experience or verbal descriptions: The impact of survey versus route perspective. *Quarterly Journal of Experimental Psychology, 59*, 1950–1967.

Posner, M. I. & Cohen, Y. (1984). Components of visual orienting. In H. Bouma & D. Bouwhuis (Eds.), *Attention and performance X* (pp. 531–556). Hillsdale, NJ: Lawrence Erlbaum Associates.

Ristic, J., Friesen, C. K., & Kingstone, A. (2002). Are eyes special? It depends on how you look at it. *Psychonomic Bulletin and Review, 9*, 507–513.

Schneider, L. F. & Taylor, H. A. (1999). How do you get there from here? Mental representations of route descriptions. *Applied Cognitive Psychology*, 13, 415–441.

Taylor, H. A. & Tversky, B. (1992). Spatial mental models derived from survey and route descriptions. *Journal of Memory and Language, 31*, 261–292.

Tipples, J. (2002). Eye gaze is not unique: Automatic orienting in response to uninformative arrows. *Psychonomic Bulletin and Review, 9*, 314–318.

Tipples, J. (2008). Orienting to counterpredictive gaze and arrow cues. *Perception and Psychophysics, 70*, 77–87.

Tom, A. & Denis, M. (2003). Referring to landmark or street information in route directions: What difference does it make? In W. Kuhn, M. F. Worboys, & S. Timpf (Eds.), *Spatial information theory: Foundations of geographic information science (Proceedings of COSIT 2003)* (pp. 384–397). Berlin: Springer.

Tom, A. & Denis, M. (2004). Language and spatial cognition: Comparing the roles of landmarks and street names in route instructions. *Applied Cognitive Psychology, 18*, 1213–1230.

Tom, A. C. & Tversky, B. (2012). Remembering routes: Streets and landmarks. *Applied Cognitive Psychology, 26*, 182–193.

Tomasello, M., Carpenter, M., & Liszkowski, U. (2007). A new look at infant pointing. *Child Development, 78*, 705–722.

Tversky, B. (2001). Spatial schemas in depictions. In M. Gattis (Ed.), *Spatial schemas and abstract thought* (pp. 79–111). Cambridge, MA: The MIT Press.

Tversky, B. (2012). Telling tales, or journeys. In V. Gyselinck & F. Pazzaglia (Eds.), *From mental imagery to spatial cognition and language: Essays in honour of Michel Denis* (pp. 3–15). Hove, UK: Psychology Press.

Tversky, B., Heiser, J., Lee, P., & Daniel, M.-P. (2009). Explanations in gesture, diagram, and word. In K. R. Coventry, T. Tenbrink, & J. Bateman (Eds.), *Spatial language and dialogue* (pp. 119–131). Oxford, UK: Oxford University Press.

Tversky, B. & Lee, P. U. (1998). How space structures language. In C. Freksa, C. Habel, & K. F. Wender (Eds.), *Spatial cognition: An interdisciplinary approach to representing and processing spatial knowledge* (pp. 157–175). Berlin: Springer.

Tversky, B. & Lee, P. U. (1999). Pictorial and verbal tools for conveying routes. In C. Freksa & D. M. Mark (Eds.), *Spatial information theory: Cognitive and computational foundations of geographic information science (Proceedings of COSIT 1999)* (pp. 51–64). Berlin: Springer.

Tversky, B., Zacks, J., Lee, P., & Heiser, J. (2000). Lines, blobs, crosses and arrows: Diagrammatic communication with schematic figures. In M. Anderson, P. Cheng, & V. Haarslev (Eds.), *Theory and application of diagrams (Proceedings of Diagrams 2000)* (pp. 221–230). Berlin: Springer.

Wong, B. (2011). Arrows. *Nature Methods, 8*, 701.

7

COMPUTER ANIMATION AND THE MENTAL REPRESENTATION OF CHANGE OVER TIME

Mireille Bétrancourt

Instructional Animation: Assumptions and Empirical Findings

Computer animation began to be widely used in instructional documents in the 1990s, when the processing capacity of personal computers made it possible to display graphic visualizations changing rapidly enough for the human visual system to perceive it as a continuous change and not a series of static frames. Intuitively, animation seems ideally suited to convey dynamic information because it directly depicts change over time that needs only to be viewed rather than being inferred by mental simulation. In this respect, animation holds a "computational advantage" (Larkin & Simon, 1987) over static graphics because the cognitive process required to mentally represent change over time should be facilitated. In addition, animated graphics can disambiguate dynamic information compared to a series of static graphics, such as intermediary positions or trajectories of moving objects. Thus, just as graphics are seen as being more expressive than text (Stenning & Oberlander, 1995), animation can be considered to be more expressive than static graphics with regard to dynamic information. For all these reasons, animation is expected to be beneficial for novice learners who are unable to infer the *microsteps* of a complex dynamic phenomenon (as in meteorology, mechanics, biology) because the microchanges are directly depicted in animation contrary to static pictures (Tversky, Bétrancourt, and Bauer-Morrison, 2002). From a cognitive perspective, this should facilitate or even enable novice learners' constructions of a mental representation of the dynamic system (Schnotz, 2002).

When I arrived as a post-doc in Barbara Tversky's lab in 1996, I was quite convinced that computer animation would support comprehension of content changing over time, but Barbara, with her deep knowledge about graphics and the human mind, wisely advised to conduct a review of literature comparing static and animated visualizations. This work, revealing a more contrasting picture as summarized in the next section, shaped a large part of the subsequent research in the field of animated instruction.

Animation: Can It Facilitate?

Researchers began to investigate whether animation really makes a difference compared to static visualizations as early as the 1980s, before animation became widely used, as in the Baek and Layne (1988) study featuring a "Pong-like"[1] minimal interface to explain Newton's laws of motion. Before the turn of the century, most of the instructional research on animation was conducted with a focus on computer-assisted learning and human-computer interaction and with much less of a focus on the cognitive processing of graphics. As a consequence, the theoretical rationales underlying the use of animation and the paradigms used in the studies varied significantly, precluding the possibility of comparison and generalization of the results. Even the concrete features of animation (e.g., user control, computer-generated or video, schematic vs. realistic visualizations) were extremely diverse. For a clearer picture, Bétrancourt and Tversky (2000) conducted a systematic literature review on the effects of computer animation on learning. They proposed a definition that could encompass all types of computer animation encountered in the research: "Computer animation refers to any application which generates a series of frames, so that each frame appears as an alteration of the previous one, and where the sequence of frames is determined either by the designer or the user" (p. 313).

Among the 21 studies reviewed by Bétrancourt and Tversky (2000), 5 compared a class using computer-assisted learning with a regular class, 4 examined the factors that might affect the effectiveness of computer animation, and 12 actually compared static and animated displays (of them, 2 compared static text vs. animated graphics explaining software procedures). Of these 12 studies, 7 found a beneficial effect of animation on at least one learning outcome, and 5 found no difference at all. The two studies comparing static text and animated graphics found a beneficial effect of animated graphics over text during training but not in the test phase. In addition to the fact that the studies could not easily be compared due to the variety of the animations used and the type of knowledge targeted by instruction (factual, conceptual, or procedural), Tversky, Bétrancourt, and Bauer-Morrison (2002) noticed that in many cases, the conditions were not equivalent with respect to factors other than visualization per se. First, the amount and type of information provided in both conditions was sometimes not equivalent. For example, the static graphics used by Rieber (1991) to explain Newton's laws of motion did not include the fact that initial force should be applied to trigger or stop the object's motion, information fundamental to understanding inertia, which is a main concept in Newton's laws. Second, in many cases, the animated condition involved interactivity (e.g., simple control over the pace of animation), whereas the static condition did not; thus, the benefit of animation can actually come from interactivity itself (Mayer & Chandler, 2001).

The Contribution of Meta-Analyses

The research conducted at the turn of the century revealed a shift from asking whether animation was more effective than static visualization to when and why animation would make a difference and for whom. A lively body of research contributed to deepen the theoretical foundation of the expected effect of animation (Lowe, 2003; Narayanan & Hegarty, 2002; Lowe & Boucheix, 2008) and identified a set of factors that moderate the effect of animation, as will be developed in the next section of this chapter. The research then was careful to control or manipulate the effect of the factors that were not inherently linked to the visualization itself so that any effect on learning outcomes could be attributed to the animation factor. Höffler and Leutner's (2007) meta-analysis using the results of 26 studies covering the period from 1973–2003 revealed a medium-sized overall advantage of instructional animations over static pictures. However, a closer look at the results shows that animation was indeed superior to the static condition in 21 comparisons (27.6%), whereas two (2.6%) were in favor of static graphics and the majority (53 comparisons, 69.7%) did not find any difference. In addition, the meta-analysis identified significant effects of several moderators, such as the type of information depicted (procedural-motor, declarative, or problem-solving) and level of realism. Taken together, the findings led to the conclusion that realistic, video-based animations that target procedural learning objectives were more likely to be beneficial but did not provide additional cues to explain that, in many cases, animation was not more effective than static graphics for learning about conceptual dynamic phenomena. More recently, Berney and Bétrancourt (2016) conducted a meta-analysis of 61 studies comparing static and animated visualization conducted between 1976 and 2013, selecting only studies using computer-based (not video-based) and expository (not decorative) animations that measured knowledge acquisition. The meta-analysis found a significant effect size of small magnitude in favor of animation, which is in agreement with the results of Höffler and Leutner (2007). A detailed analysis of the 140 pairwise comparisons showed that animations were superior to static graphics displays in 43 comparisons (30.7%), whereas 14 (10%) were in favor of static illustrations; furthermore, once again, the majority (83 comparisons, 59.3%) found no significant difference between these two presentation formats. The fact that publications mention non-significant difference between conditions is a sign of safe practice in research, but it questions the original assumption of the inherent superiority of animation for understanding dynamic information. In recent decades, many authors have proposed tentative explanations that fall into three main approaches: 1. explanations linked to the semiotic diversity of the external representation, that postulate that a global theory of animation will necessarily miss the subtleties of the different types of animation; 2. explanations related to delivery or instructional factors that hold the basic assumption that animation is potentially effective but that other factors can pre-empt this potential; and 3. explanations linked to the way humans conceive of dynamic concept and change over time. These three approaches will be discussed in the following sections.

First Approach: The Diverse Nature of Animation

Animations That Depict Motor Procedures and Human Movement

Instructional animation appears in a variety of forms and for a variety of learning purposes (Ainsworth, 2008). The oldest use is the representation of human movements to learn motor procedures (e.g., assembly procedures in Baggett (1987); tying knots in Schwan and Riempp (2004); origami in Wong et al. (2009); first-aid procedures in Arguel and Jamet (2009)). Such instructional use of animation appears to be generally effective (Höffler & Leutner, 2007), one explanation being that visualizing human movements triggers motor cortex neuronal activity (Iacoboni et al., 1999), thus facilitating subsequent reproduction.

Animations That Represent Conceptual Models

Another "natural" use of animation is to represent phenomena that are not easily perceived by the human visual system due to their size, temporal scale, or practical reasons (e.g., planet relative trajectories in Rebetez, Sangin, Bétrancourt, & Dillenbourg (2010); fish locomotion in Scheiter, Gerjets, Huk, Imhof, & Kammerer (2009); kangaroo jumps in Lowe, Schnotz, & Rasch, (2011)). It should be noted that most animations representing dynamic phenomena are not a strict reproduction of the phenomenon on another time or space scale but rather graphically represent *models* of the phenomenon. In that category, we can find models of scientific concepts as in meteorology (Lowe, 2003; Mayer, & Chandler, 2001), biology (the human circulatory system in de Koning, Tabbers, Rikers, and Paas (2010)), and mechanics (e.g., the bicycle pump in Mayer and Sims (1994); pulley systems in Boucheix and Schneider, (2009); the pendulum clock in Fischer and Schwan (2010)). It may very well be that the fragile beneficial effect of animation is due to the learner's difficulty in understanding the underlying conceptual model more than their inability to perceive or process information correctly. The use of visualization in science education (e.g., Gilbert, 2005) is investigated using a lively multidisciplinary research community that is well aware of the necessity of combining didactics, cognitive principles, and empirical studies to gain insights on how to design better instructional displays (Hegarty, 2011). Finally, animation can be used to represent phenomena that are not inherently spatial but in which space is used to convey functional or symbolic relationships (computer algorithms in Catrambone and Fleming Seay (2002); stages in a statistical procedure in Scheiter, Gerjets, and Catrambone (2006)). In that case, the effect of animation is not easily disentangled from the instructional strategy adopted to explain the phenomenon and can be seen as a way to reinforce memorization for the story to understand the concept (Wolfe & Mienko, 2007).

As Ainsworth (2008) claimed, it is very likely that the type of representation will trigger different cognitive processes and lead to various learning outcomes, thus preempting the generalization of findings across types of animation. However, the opposite relativist attitude stating that it depends on so many factors that nothing can be concluded overall is neither constructive nor true. Leading a thorough categorization of the animations used in the literature, Ploetzner and Lowe (2012) proposed a framework to describe animation consisting of four dimensions (presentation, user control, scaffolding, and configuration), of which the first dimension linked to the nature of the representation offers five features. The authors suggested that researchers use the framework both to pay more attention to the design of instructional animation and to lead systematic investigations of their educational effectiveness.

Second Approach: Tuning Interface and Instructional Factors

The lack of the beneficial effect of animation over static graphics has often been attributed to factors external to the representation itself, but related to the way the animation was delivered to the learners. As Tversky et al. (2002) identified, animations are by definition continuously changing over time and are transient; contrary to static graphics, they do not allow for comparisons between different steps of the process, should be reinspected sequentially, and are always in motion, thus imposing a considerable visual memory load. In addition, *event segmentation theory* states that people spontaneously segment ongoing activity into meaningful events during perception (Zacks et al., 2007), with evidence from experiments with videos or computer-generated visualizations of events (for a review, see Zacks & Tversky, 2001). As individual differences in mental segmentation can lead to differences in learning outcomes (Koopman & Newtson, 1981), it is important to provide learners with aids such as control over the pace and pre-segmentation of the animation to support the extraction of significant steps in the instructional material (Spanjers, van Gog, & van Merriënboer, 2010).

User Control and Segmentation: Two Factors That Are Not Easily Disentangled

User control over the pace of the animation was one of the first factors investigated in the literature. Using instructional material explaining lightning formation, Mayer and Chandler (2001) showed that learners performed better in transfer but not in retention tests if they received the animation segmented with a simple "resume" interaction rather than a non-interactive animation. Schwan and Riempp (2004) showed that learners who received an interactive animation with full control over the pace learned more efficiently how to tie nautical knots than learners with system-paced animation. These two studies provide evidence that user-controlled pacing gives learners the possibility to allocate the time they need to integrate information into their mental model before proceeding to the next segment of animation. Berney and Bétrancourt's (2016) meta-analysis showed that pacing control was a significant moderator of the effect of animation, with, surprisingly, animation being significantly superior to static graphics only for studies in which the animation was system-paced and not for studies using user-controlled pacing. One explanation is that in many studies providing user control, the animation was also segmented in meaningful chunks. Spanjers, van Gog, Wouters, and van Merriënboer (2012) used either visual segmentation (a darkened screen between segments) or temporal segmentation (two-second pauses, non-interactive) as factors. They found that temporal segmentation increased post-test performance and did not affect perceived mental effort, whereas visual segmentation decreased perceived mental effort without affecting performance. The authors concluded that temporal segmentation gave learners additional time to process the content after each segment, in agreement with previous literature. In contrast, visual segmentation supported the natural process of extracting meaningful events, thus decreasing cognitive load during perception. In this study, however, pauses also support the segmentation process so that the two effects, time for integration and segmentation support, cannot be disentangled. In addition, Tabbers and De Koeijer (2010) found that control over the pace can interact with other delivery factors, such as the sensory modality of the commentary (audio vs. written). Whereas it has been repeatedly evidenced that with animation, the commentary should be delivered in audio rather than written modality (see the meta-analysis conducted by Ginns, 2005), Tabbers (2002) showed that when the animation was user paced, the effect of modality was no longer significant because the learners could allocate sufficient time to mentally process the verbal and graphic information.

Adding Static Frames to Support Segmentation

Another technique to support the conception of the different important steps in an animation is to provide these steps as static graphics along the animation. Using videos explaining first-aid procedures, Arguel and Jamet (2009) found that presenting static pictures with the video (Figure 7.1a) was superior to presenting video alone or static graphics alone. However, the next question is how many static graphics to provide. Using a computer animation explaining plate tectonics, Rebetez et al. (2010) presented 12 static graphics corresponding to the 12 sequences of the animation (Figure 7.1b) and found no beneficial effect of providing the snapshots for learning. An explanation of this lack of benefit may be found in Arguel and Jamet's (2009) study showing that using fewer static graphics was better (three or four rather than six or eight), most likely because then, the static graphics become memory cues for the main steps and do not create undesirable difficulties such as split attention or memory overload.

a.

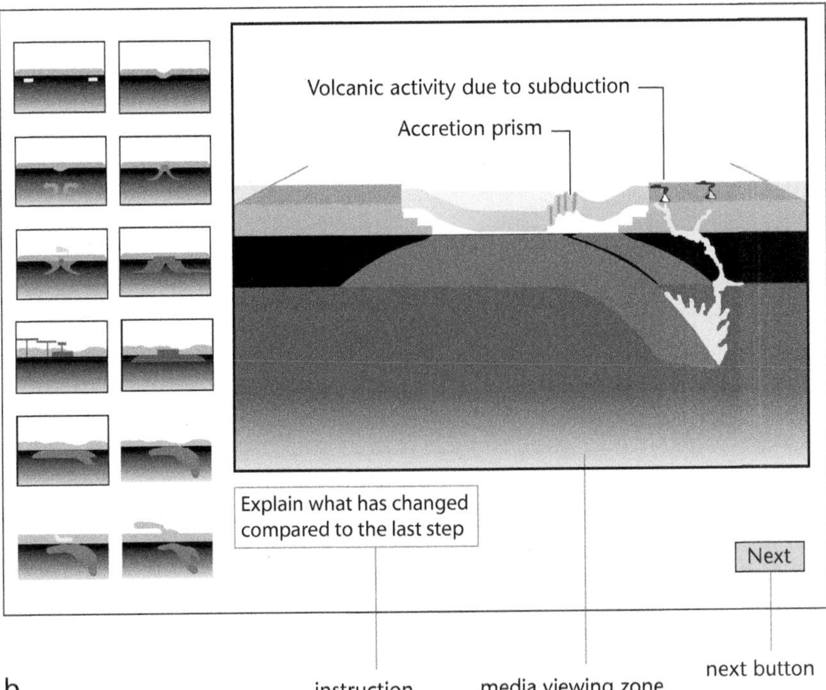

b.

FIGURE 7.1 a) Screenshot of the material used by Arguel and Jamet (2009), and b) Translated example of the material used by Rebetez et al. (2010)

Fostering Cognitive Engagement

Another hypothesis commonly advanced in the literature to explain the failure of animation to produce benefits is the fact that learners tend to watch the animation passively without engaging cognitively because the direct visualization provokes an illusion of understanding—what Lowe (2003) called the "underwhelming effect" of animation. The instructional design should thus force learners to engage in deep processing, prompting them to extract the relevant information and understand and memorize the causal chain rather than only the temporal sequence of events. For example, Hegarty, Narayanan, and Freitas (2002) showed that asking people to mentally animate a mechanical system presented in static graphics before seeing the animation improved comprehension. Visual cueing (e.g., highlighting, arrows, color change) is also a way to attract attention to the right place at the right time (de Koning et al., 2010) but this solution does not always lead to the expected effect because cueing can counteract spontaneous exploration and add extraneous visual information (Boucheix, Lowe, Putri, & Groff, 2013).

Over the past two decades, many factors related to the way the animation is delivered were investigated, leading to a series of principles for designing cognitively effective multimedia documents (Moreno & Mayer, 1999; Mayer, 2009). However, exploration of the factors that can impact the instructional effectiveness of animation is potentially infinite unless guided by a cognitive model of how we build a mental representation from animation, such as the one Narayanan and Hegarty (2002) and Lowe and Boucheix (2008) proposed.

Third Approach: Considering How Change Over Time Is Perceived and Represented in the Mind

The aforementioned literature in the first two approaches holds the assumption that animation is fundamentally adequate to represent dynamic phenomena, but that learners should be provided with an interface or instructional support to overcome the obstacle of processing fleeting information. Surprisingly, the question of the content that is represented and that we want the learners to understand and memorize is often relegated to a position of secondary importance. On the contrary, the third approach considers that this question should guide the design of instructional animations.

Apprehension and Congruence Principles

More than a decade ago, Tversky et al. (2002) defined two principles. The *apprehension principle* states that learners should directly perceive and apprehend the characteristics of the external representation. In other words, the graphic design of the objects depicted in the animation should follow the graphic representation conventions in the domain (assuming that learners know them). This principle also recommends that any additional cosmetic feature that is not directly useful for understanding should be banished from animation and, more generally, any graphical element that is not related to the content to be understood. Tversky (2010) noted that "features and forms that have been invented and reinvented across cultures and time are likely to be effective" (p. 3). In other words, good graphic design should be inspired from this natural user testing over centuries and consider the usual association between visuospatial features and the meanings they intend to convey. Tversky, Kugelmass, and Winter (1991) investigated how children and adults spontaneously represented several dimensions of time. Across different cultures, adults mapped order in time on a virtual horizontal line, using spatial proximity to convey temporal intervals from the ages of 11 to 12. They noted that preschool children used a line to represent time earlier than other dimensions, such as quantity and preference. Then, space can be used to represent time quite effectively, which would explain the numerous studies in which static graphics were equivalent to animation. Thus, animation should be proposed only when visuospatial information cannot be used, or when visuospatial information in itself is important or microchanges cannot be inferred from the comparison of static graphics, as Tversky et al. (2002) stated.

Second, the *congruence principle* states that changes in animation should map changes in the conceptual model rather than changes in the behavior of the phenomenon. A simple example is the functioning of mechanical systems in which successive events in the causal chain (e.g., opening the valve that causes the air to come in) are actually occurring simultaneously in time. A first consequence is that animation is better suited to convey the conceptual model in which change over time is a main feature. This assumption was confirmed in Höffler and Leutner's (2007) meta-analysis, in which they found that the beneficial effect of animation was maximal for sensory-motor procedures that essentially change over time (no causal chain to infer) and for videos, in which there is a direct mapping between what is depicted and the conceptual model to be developed. A second consequence is that the realism of the depicted phenomenon can be distorted if it helps in understanding the conceptual model, such as the cause-effect relationships between events of dynamic phenomena presented in the example above. In that sense, the congruence principle is similar to the *representational correspondence principles* that Chabris and Kosslyn (2005) described; they mentioned caricatures as an example of diagrams that conveyed the features of the desired model better than the features of the real person and yet were very recognizable. Following these principles, the animated visualization should thus be easily apprehended and map the desired conceptual representation of the phenomenon, assuming the research already possesses enough information about the perception of dynamic information and the internal representation of events occurring over time.

Perception and Conception of Dynamic Information

Beyond pure visual perception occurring below consciousness, little is known about the way we make sense of objects that change in shape or location over time. For example, *inattentional blindness* is a counterintuitive phenomenon in which we are unaware of certain changes in the environment, even visually salient changes, if our attention is attracted to other elements (Simons & Chabris, 1999). The phenomenon is well known as the famous "invisible gorilla" video experiment, in which viewers who have to count the number of passes between basketball players are completely unaware that a gorilla is dancing in the middle of the visual scene. Even without disruption or distraction, we do not easily perceive subtle changes in a visual scene, and memory for events occurring naturally is scarce or even completely false (Davis & Loftus, 2009). Inattentional blindness illustrates the fact that we actually grasp much less of a visual scene than we think we do (Chabris & Kosslyn, 2005). Consequently, what do learners really grasp from an instructional animation? To investigate this question, Rebetez and Bétrancourt (2009) presented participants with five animated sequences or six static graphics representing a biological process (meiosis) and asked them to describe all of the elements and changes they saw in the material. The animated sequences and static graphics were presented simultaneously (see Figure 7.2, Rebetez, 2009) without commentary. The five animated segments ran automatically in loops of the same duration so that they ended and began at the same time without user control. The types of changes reported by the participants were coded according to Lowe's (2004) classification of changes in animation: transformation (change in the visual properties of one of the graphic entities), translation (change in the position over time of the graphic entities), and transition (disappearance and appearance of the graphic entities). The results show that participants in the animated condition reported more transformation changes than their static counterpart (but not translation and transition changes). More surprisingly, they also recalled more descriptive information that was not inherently dynamic (like the visual appearance of the objects) than participants in the static condition. This suggests that animation conveys supplementary dynamic information to learners, especially subtle changes that are difficult to infer from static graphics, such as transformations. In addition, animation could also make some visual static information more salient, as text accompanying static graphics can make configuration information more salient in mental representation (Hegarty & Just, 1993).

Researchers still need to investigate how dynamic information is extracted from external animated graphics and the individual factors that impact this processing, such as prior knowledge and visuospatial abilities. To this end, Hegarty, Kriz, and Cate (2003) postulated that learning dynamic systems was related to the ability to perform mental simulation because participants with higher visuospatial abilities had higher performance. In addition, some studies provided evidence that there may be specific abilities for processing dynamic visualizations (Hunt et al., 1988) that would affect the ability to learn from instructional animation (Sanchez

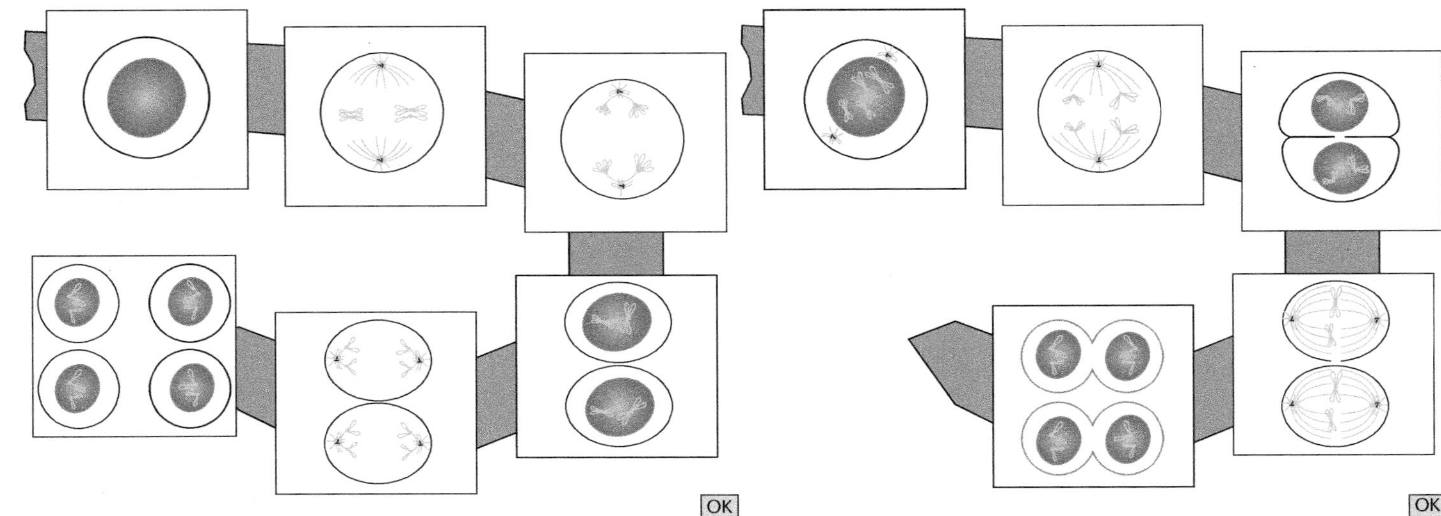

FIGURE 7.2 Screenshots of the learning material in the static condition (left) and in the dynamic condition (right) (from Rebetez (2009), p. 183)

& Wiley, 2014). Similarly, the existence of such a dynamic visuospatial ability would have both theoretical and practical implications and is worthy of further investigation.

The fundamental assumption for using animation is that a continuous visualization of change over time is the most direct mapping for the mental representation of dynamic information. However, the literature provides evidence that contradicts this assumption. In her 1992 paper, using the novel eye-tracking technique, Mary Hegarty found evidence that participants mentally animate a pulley system in a piecemeal way in the order of the causal chain of events and not all at once. In addition, inference of motion does not always require mental simulation and can also be based on reasoning or prior knowledge (Narayanan & Hegarty, 1998). Regarding the way we conceive of events, this chapter has already mentioned *event segmentation theory*, which proposes that people conceive activities as sequences of discrete events organized hierarchically (Zacks & Tversky, 2001; Zacks et al., 2007). Zacks and Tversky (2003) further concluded that animation may not be the best way to convey change over time unless the instruction is structured with small sequences organized in larger meaningful units to facilitate the mapping with the conceptual model.

On this basis, the two principles, *apprehension* and *congruence*, could be completed by a third *parsimony principle*: use animation when the dynamic information is inherently continuous (e.g., gestures, complex patterns of trajectories) and when it cannot be conveyed through static visuospatial information. To comply with the congruence principle, it is important to provide structure emphasizing the main steps with static images or linguistic organizers.

Conclusion

With nearly three decades of research, the literature on instructional animation now represents a considerable body of research. The empirical questioning evolved from a pure effectiveness issue (is animation superior to static graphics?) to identifying the conditions under which animation may be beneficial for learning. Until now, most research has dealt with understanding animation, and it may be time to focus on understanding *from* animation. In other words, we should pay attention to the type of content to be learned in relation to the type of mental representation upon which we wish the learners to elaborate. As a consequence, it is necessary to better describe the characteristics of the external representation. In their meta-analysis, Berney and Bétrancourt (2016) noted that many studies provided only a scarce description of the material, sometimes not even including a visual illustration. Now that scientific journals offer the possibility to provide links to the actual material, hopefully the research will seize the opportunity to discuss more in depth the design properties of their material. Furthermore, as Ainsworth (2008) suggested, the research should deeply investigate the nature of the representation elaborated by learners using qualitative methods along with quantitative data such as online measurement (e.g., eye-movement tracking) and verbal protocols (through retrospective verbalization, self-explanation, and dyad discussion).

As a final word, I would like to heartily thank Barbara Tversky, who is still an inspiration to me, not only because her knowledge on spatial cognition is immense, not only because her research goes beyond the surface and is not trapped within the narrow walls of disciplinarity, but also because she knows how to help her young colleagues to find their own path.

Note

1 This is a reference to one of the first video games to reach mainstream popularity and be disseminated in a home version by Atari.

References

Ainsworth, S. (2008). How do animations influence learning? In D. Robinson & G. Schraw (Eds.), *Current Perspectives on Cognition, Learning, and Instruction: Recent Innovations in Educational Technology that Facilitate Student Learning* (pp. 37–67). Information Age Publishing.

Arguel, A. & Jamet, E. (2009). Using video and static pictures to improve learning of procedural contents. *Computers in Human Behavior, 25*(2), 354–359.

Baek, Y. K. & Layne, B. H. (1988). Color, graphics, and animation in a computer-assisted learning tutorial lesson. *Journal of Computer-Based Instruction, 15*, 131–135.

Baggett, P. (1987). Learning a procedure from multimedia instructions: the effects of film and practice. *Applied Cognitive Psychology, 1*, 183–195.

Berney, S. & Bétrancourt, M. (2016). Does animation enhance learning? A meta-analysis. *Computers in Education. 101*(1), 150–167.

Bétrancourt, M. & Tversky, B. (2000). Effect of computer animation on users' performance: a review. *Le travail Humain, 63*, 311–330.

Boucheix, J. M. & Schneider, E. (2009). Static and animated presentations in learning dynamic mechanical systems. *Learning and Instruction, 19*(2), 112–127.

Boucheix, J. M., Lowe, R. K., Putri, D. K., & Groff, J. (2013). Cueing animations: Dynamic signaling aids information extraction and comprehension. *Learning and Instruction, 25*, 71–84.

Catrambone, R. and Fleming Seay, A. (2002). Using animation to help students learn computer algorithms. *Human Factors*, 44, 495–511.

Davis, D. & Loftus, E. F. (2009). Expectancies, emotion and memory reports of visual events. In J.R. Brockmole (Ed.), *The Visual World in Memory*. Hove & NY: Psychology Press, p. 178–214.

de Koning, B. B., Tabbers, H. K., Rikers, R. M. J. P., & Paas, F. (2010). Attention guidance in learning from a complex animation: Seeing is understanding? *Learning and Instruction, 20*(2), 111–122.

Chabris, C. F. & Kosslyn, S. M. (2005). Representational Correspondence as a Basic Principle of Diagram Design. In S.-O. Tergan & T. Keller (Eds.), *Knowledge and Information Visualization, LNCS 3426* (pp. 36–57). Berlin: Springer Verlag.

Fischer, S. & Schwan, S. (2010). Comprehending animations: Effects of spatial cueing versus temporal scaling. *Learning and Instruction, 20*, 465–475.

Gilbert, J. K. (Ed.) (2005). *Visualization in Science and Education*. Dordrecht, The Netherlands: Kluwer Academic Publishers.

Ginns, P. (2005). Meta-analysis of the modality effect. *Learning and Instruction, 15*(4), 313–331.

Hegarty, M. (1992). Mental animation: Inferring motion from static displays of mechanical systems. *Journal of Experimental Psychology: Learning, Memory and Cognition, 18*(5), 1084–1102.

Hegarty, M. (2011). The Cognitive Science of Visual-Spatial Displays: Implications for Design. *Topics in Cognitive Science, 3*(3), 446–474.

Hegarty, M. & Just, A. M. (1993). Constructing mental models of machines from text and diagrams, *Journal of Memory and Language, 32*(6), 717–742.

Hegarty, M., Kriz, S., & Cate, C. (2003). The roles of mental animations and external animations in understanding mechanical systems. *Cognition and Instruction, 2*, 325–360.

Hegarty, M., Narayanan, N. H., & Freitas, P. (2002). Understanding machines from multimedia and hypermedia presentations. In J. Otero, J. A. Leon & A. Graesser, Eds. *The Psychology of Science Text Comprehension* (pp. 357–384). Hillsdale, NJ: Lawrence Erlbaum.

Höffler, T. N. & Leutner, D. (2007). Instructional animation versus static pictures: A meta-analysis. *Learning and Instruction, 17*(6), 722–738.

Hunt, E., Pellegrino, J., Frick, R., Farr, S., & Alderton, D. (1988). The ability to reason about movement in the visual field. *Intelligence, 100*, 77–100.

Iacoboni, M., Woods, R., Brass, M., Bekkering, H., Mazziotta, J., & Rizzolatti, G. (1999). Cortical mechanisms of human imitation. *Science, 286*, 2526–2528.

Koopman, C. & Newtson, D. (1981). Level of analysis in the perception of ongoing instruction: An exploratory study. *Journal of Education & Psychology, 73*, 212–223.

Larkin, J. H. & Simon, H. A. (1987). Why a diagram is (sometimes) worth 10000 words. *Cognitive Science, 11*(1), 65–99.

Lowe, R. K. (2003). Animation and learning: selective processing of information in dynamic graphics. *Learning and Instruction, 13*, 247–262.

Lowe, R. (2004). Interrogation of a dynamic visualization during learning. *Learning and Instruction, 14*(3), 257–274.

Lowe, R. & Boucheix, J.-M. (2008). Learning from animated diagrams: How are mental models built? In G. Stapleton, J. Howse, & J. Lee (Eds.), *Diagrammatic representations and inference – Proceedings of the fifth international conference diagrams 2008* (pp. 266–281). Berlin: Springer Publishers.

Lowe, R., Schnotz, W., & Rasch, T. (2011). Aligning affordances of graphics with learning task requirements. *Applied Cognitive Psychology*, 25, 452–459.

Mayer, R. E. & Chandler, P. (2001). When learning is just a click away: Does simple interaction foster deeper understanding of multimedia messages? *Journal of Educational Psychology, 93*, 390–397.

Mayer, R. E. (2009). *Multimedia Learning* (2nd ed.). New York: Cambridge University Press.

Mayer, R. E. & Sims, K. (1994). For whom is a picture worth a thousand words? Extensions of a dual-coding theory of multi-media learning. *Journal of Educational Psychology, 86*, 389–401.

Moreno, R. & Mayer, R. E. (1999). Cognitive principles of multimedia learning: The role of modality and contiguity. *Journal of Educational Psychology, 91*(2), 358–268.

Narayanan, N. H. & Hegarty, M. (1998). On designing comprehensible hypermedia manuals. *International Journal of Human-Computer Studies, 48*, 267–301.

Narayanan, N. H. & Hegarty, M. (2002). Multimedia design for communication of dynamic information. International *Journal of Human-Computer Studies, 57*, 279–315.

Ploetzner, R. & Lowe, R. (2012). A systematic characterisation of expository animations. *Computers in Human Behavior, 28*(3), 781–794.

Rebetez, C. (2009). *Learning from animations: control, collaboration and learners' exploration.* Unpublished PhD dissertation, University of Geneva (Switzerland), June 2009.

Rebetez, C. & Bétrancourt, M. (2009). Simultaneous static or animated graphics in the construction of a dynamic mental model. *Proceedings of the Biennial Conference of the European Association for Learning and Instruction*, 27–31 August 2009, Budapest (Hungary).

Rebetez, C., Sangin, M., Bétrancourt, M., & Dillenbourg, P. (2010). Learning from animation enabled by collaboration. *Instructional Science, 38*, 471–485.

Rieber, L. P. (1991). Animation, incidental learning and continuing motivation. *Journal of Educational Psychology, 83*, 318–328.

Sanchez, C. A. & Wiley, J. (2014). The role of dynamic spatial ability in geoscience text comprehension. *Learning and Instruction, 31*, 33–45.

Scheiter, K., Gerjets, P., & Catrambone, R. (2006). Making the abstract concrete: Visualizing mathematical solution procedures. *Computers in Human Behavior, 22*(1), 9–25.

Scheiter, K., Gerjets, P., Huk, T., Imhof, B., & Kammerer, Y. (2009). The effects of realism in learning with dynamic visualizations. *Learning and Instruction, 19*(6), 481–494.

Schnotz, W. (2002). Enabling, Facilitating, and Inhibiting Effects in Learning from Animated Pictures. Paper presented at the Dynamic Visualizations workshop, Knowledge Media Research Centre, Tübingen.

Schwan, S. & Riempp, R. (2004). The cognitive benefits of interactive videos: learning to tie nautical knots. *Learning and Instruction, 14*, 293–305.

Simons, D. J. & Chabris, C. F. (1999). Gorillas in our midst: sustained inattentional blindness for dynamic events. *Perception, 28*, 1059–1074.

Spanjers, I. A. E., van Gog, T., & van Merriënboer, J. J. G. (2010). A theoretical analysis of how segmentation of dynamic visualizations optimizes students' learning. *Educational Psychology Review, 22*(4), 411–423.

Spanjers, I. A. E., van Gog, T., Wouters, P., & van Merriënboer, J. J. G. (2012). Explaining the segmentation effect in learning from animations: The role of pausing and temporal cueing. *Computers & Education*, 59(2), 274–280.

Stenning, K. & Oberlander, J. (1995). A cognitive theory of graphical and linguistic reasoning: logic and implementation. *Cognitive Science, 19*, 97–140.

Tabbers, H. K. (2002). *The modality of text in multimedia instructions: refining the design guidelines.* Unpublished doctoral dissertation, Open University of the Netherlands, Heerlen.

Tabbers, H. K. & De Koeijer, B. (2010). Learner control in animated multimedia instructions. *Instructional Science, 38*, 441–453.

Tversky, B. (2010). Visualizing Thought. *Topics in Cognitive Science, 3*, 499–535.

Tversky, B., Bauer-Morrison, J., & Bétrancourt, M. (2002). Animation: Can it facilitate? *International Journal of Human-Computer Studies, 57*, 247–262.

Tversky, B., Kugelmass, S., & Winter, A. (1991). Cross-cultural and developmental trends in graphic productions. *Cognitive Psychology, 23*, 515–557.

Wolfe, M. B. & Mienko, J. A. (2007). Learning and memory of factual content from narrative and expository text. *British Journal of Educational Psychology*, 77(3), 541–64.

Wong, A., Marcus, N., Ayres, P., Smith, L., Cooper, G. A., Paas, F., & Sweller, J. (2009). Instructional animations can be superior to statics when learning human motor skills. *Computers in Human Behavior, 25*(2), 339–347.

Zacks, J. M. & Tversky, B. (2001). Event structure in perception and cognition. *Psychological Bulletin, 127*(1), 3–21.

Zacks, J. M. & Tversky, B. (2003). Structuring Information Interfaces For Procedural Learning. *Journal of Experimental Psychology: Applied, 9*, 88–100.

Zacks, J. M., Tversky, B., & Iyer, G. (2001). Perceiving, remembering, and communicating structure in events. *Journal of Experimental Psychology: General, 130*, 29–58.

Zacks, J. M., Speer, N. K., Swallow, K. M., Braver, T. S., & Reynolds, J. R. (2007). Event perception: A mind–brain perspective. *Psychological Bulletin, 133*, 273–293.

8

DIAGRAMS IN DESIGN

Jeffrey V. Nickerson

Introduction

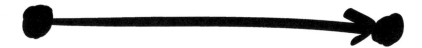

FIGURE 8.1 Connection

> "Please bring examples of sketches, especially space and time; I'm excited to see them. Russell Sage is a sleek modern building on the south side of 64th, closer to Park than to Lexington."

This email from Barbara Tversky invited me to a lunch in January of 2005. This was the first time I met her, although we had been trading emails and grant proposal ideas for a while. I brought sketches from my business school students who were drawing information systems diagrams. The two sentences of her email succinctly set the agenda for the lunch and described perfectly the spatial location for the meeting; Barbara was a visiting scholar at Russell Sage at the time, right before joining Teachers College Columbia University.

I realized part way into the conversation that Barbara understood diagrams in a much different way than I did. She saw them as some of many ways of communicating with oneself and others. While I thought of diagrams as a kind of sign that could be optimized, she understood that diagrams would display our minds' occasional brilliance and persistent biases. To her they were manifestations of cognitive processes.

My view of diagrams was not rooted in psychology. As an undergraduate, I studied Visual Design at Berkeley, and then Graphic Design as a master's student at Rhode Island School of Design. I worked as a designer and a programmer, and, while working, I completed a Ph.D. in computer science. As a graphic design student I had been taught that diagrams were indexical, that they were like pointers, that they were traces of things in space and time (Peirce, 1974). From my training, I had the belief that diagrams could perfectly represent information, and in order to do so the designer needed to pay attention to syntax, stripping away anything unnecessary. But the diagrams I saw in the information literature mixed their metaphors: arrows and nodes were overloaded with many meanings, even in the same diagram. Control flow, data flow, type-of relations, part-of relations, causality, system modularity: all of these things were represented in a hodgepodge manner. The extent of this problem became clear when I looked at all the diagrams in the proceedings of a large information systems conference and cataloged problems related to one aspect of diagrams, the arrows. When I met Barbara I had just returned from Hawaii after presenting that paper (Nickerson, 2005). My attitude about the information systems diagrams was incredulous: how could the diagrams be so universally badly designed, so muddled and confusing?

Barbara had written not only about arrows, but also lines and bars and blobs (Tversky et al., 2000; Zacks & Tversky, 1999). She did not share my indignation over diagrams; she wanted to look at student diagrams, in order to figure out what the students were doing. I saw bad diagrams as design failures; she saw them as data that might help us understand cognition better. Because of this attitude, she described diagrams in a more nuanced way. She understood their physicality, their capturing of gesture. She could point out the universal characteristics of a diagram, and the culturally specific aspects; she could predict when some things would be shown above or below, left or right. She understood the physical pages on which figures were drawn as constraints, and she understood that constraints could sometimes cause errors and other times activate creativity.

This is what I sensed in our first conversation. What I received was just a glimpse, but one striking enough to motivate me to learn more. We worked together on two National Science Foundation-funded projects over a six-year span, together with James Corter at Columbia Teachers College and many students and postdocs. Our projects were focused on diagrams used in designing and understanding information systems. These are diagrams about computer and software systems. They are complex, abstract, domain specific, and, to the honest, obtuse. Psychologists generally don't study them. Practitioners, including systems analysts, consultants, and programmers, take them for granted. They assume that the conventions of the diagrams are consistent, that people understand them, that they can make correct inferences from them. We found that these assumptions are often untrue.

For me, this area is worth studying. I research information systems. I teach in a business school. Students have worked for banks, hedge funds, government agencies, pharmaceutical companies, consulting companies, video game companies, and startups. Many end up designing systems. It is especially important that such designers understand the representations of past and present systems. Just as we hope architects can read a floor plan, we hope systems architects can read a network diagram. Moreover, the better a designer understands the diagrams the more likely the designer will come up with a better system, one that does what is needed, that is reliable and flexible. While the set of people designing systems as a profession is a small one, increasingly consumers buy multiple complex networked devices such as wireless routers and printers, and increasingly they are expected to generate web-based content and configure cloud-based applications; a basic literacy in systems architecture is handy.

For Barbara, the motivations were different. She had already studied sketches, maps, graphs, comic books, instruction manuals and animations (Suwa & Tversky, 1996, 2003; Tversky et al., 2002; Tversky et al., 2000; Zacks & Tversky, 1999). Here was a different domain, a new challenge.

Connections

Diagrams can be used to portray computer networks. What matters to the engineer are the connections. In most applications of computer networks, the distances between elements don't matter very much, because electrical signals travel very fast. There are some exceptions: the designer of a high-frequency trading system needs to consider the distance between the computer and the stock exchange. But the designer of a typical company's information system does not need to focus on distance, because there is no discernable difference in performance in the printing of a spreadsheet if the file server is in the same room as the printer or is in a closet at the end of the hallway: for all intents and purposes the signals travel at roughly the speed of light, and as humans we are unlikely to detect a hundred-mile, never mind a hundred-foot difference.

In most configurations, when local area networks are put in place, at the logical level, everything connects to everything else. When everything connects to everything, topologically we have what is called a complete graph, as shown in Figure 8.2. The graph rightly implies that we can send information directly between any pair of these five connected computers: we say these computers are part of the same broadcast domain.

But network designers don't draw graphs like Figure 8.2. For one thing, it would imply to them that a lot of unnecessary cable was run. For another, the diagram takes too long to draw for larger networks: for a network of 100 machines, one would need to draw 100× 99/2, or 4950 lines. Clearly that is not efficient. While there are many ways to draw the network, one typical diagram of such a system as drawn by a network designer looks like Figure 8.3.

The reason for the shape of the diagram is partly historical: computers were at one point wired almost exclusively through Ethernet cables. The cables were thick. As more computers were bought, new machines would actually be attached to the

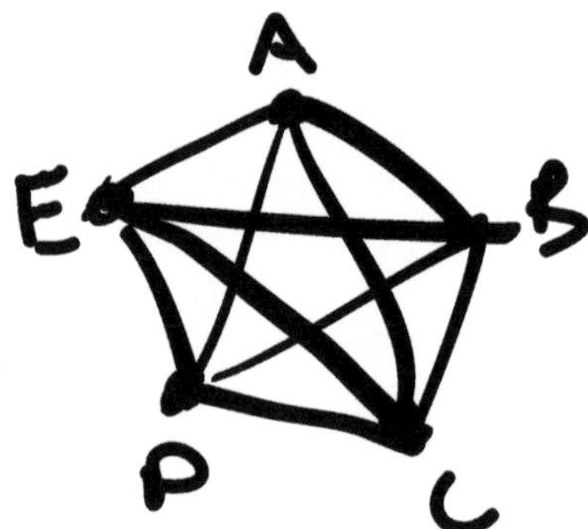

FIGURE 8.2 A complete graph

FIGURE 8.3 A network diagram

wire using what was called a vampire tap. I remember installing such a tap; one had to hammer down a sharp pick in order to splice into the thick Ethernet wire. The machine shown on the top of Figure 8.3 would often be a server of some sort, and the machines on the bottom would be clients. So the diagrams, which are meant to represent local area networks, look a lot like organizational diagrams. Today, network wiring is very different: usually each location has a wire running back to a network closet on a floor where a switch or hub handles communications between machines on the same broadcast domain. Or a wireless access point is used for the same purpose. But the diagram convention persists.

When I showed Barbara what the network diagrams look like, she wondered if in fact novice systems designers actually understood them. I thought to myself that of course they did, but I agreed to do a test. Why did I think they would understand them? Because this type of diagram (called a *LAN diagram*) is ubiquitous in information systems textbooks and in industry. Most of our students had worked in companies in positions where they would be looking at and making inferences from these diagrams. So of course they would understand them. But many didn't. A common error was interpreting the diagram to indicate the machines were chained together: that a message going from B to E passed through C and D. In general, most of the errors can be attributed to students interpreting these connection-based diagrams as spatial diagrams. Because your eyes move through C and D on a journey from B to E, you conclude that a message must also move through C and D.

In other words, systems design diagrams are topological; all that matters is connection. Line length doesn't matter, just as cable length doesn't matter. But often we understand the diagrams as if they are maps of a physical location where distance and neighborhoods matter.

Barbara wasn't surprised by this result, but I was. How could such a basic diagram be misunderstood by students? To me, it was an important experience in teaching. I had taken for granted knowledge that, in retrospect, I should have tested for. In particular, I thought that these diagrams had a clear semantics that students would understand. But they didn't. It is really uncommon to see the semantics of a diagram explained in detail in textbooks. The initial motivation for these diagrams, old-fashioned Ethernet cabling techniques, is no longer practiced. So designers or authors of a certain generation use diagrams that they understand, and simply presume the technicians or readers will also. The confusions can happen because of the many layers of abstraction present in networks. In older technologies, wires were shared, and created an obvious broadcast domain: a message broadcast on the wire could be heard by anyone, like someone shouting in a room. With the newer technologies of hubs and switches, individual wires, the spokes, are connected to the hub or switch, but the effect is the same: when someone shouts, the shout is so quickly sent to everyone in the broadcast domain that they all hear the message simultaneously. So even though the physical topology is a hub and spoke, the logical topology is a complete graph: everyone can see everyone inside the broadcast domain.

Knowing that there could be confusion, it was not hard to correct the problem: in the classroom we can explain that a network diagram like that of Figure 8.3, or a hub and spoke diagram with hubs or switches in the middle, can be replaced at the logical level with a complete graph, a graph in which each node can connect directly to every other node, as in Figure 8.2. That is, replacing the physical-level diagram with the logical-level diagram leads to proper inferences on how communication will happen in a system. For example, it helps in understanding which machines will see a network broadcast. When we tested this intervention it worked (Corter et al., 2009).

While diagrams are ubiquitous in systems design, the absence of explicit semantics makes misinterpretation possible. In the case of information systems, it is easy to let Euclidean concepts – that two things are similar if they are close to each other – override topological concepts: two things are similar if they are connected to each other (no matter what the distance). Indeed, I think this is a common cause for confusion when encountering problems with computer systems. It is easy to misattribute the location of a technical problem, because it is often difficult to know where certain activities are taking place: locally on a phone? Up in a satellite? In a store? On a server in Silicon Valley? Time (as perceived by people) doesn't give useful clues, because most connections are practically instant when they are working. When connections appear to slow down, it doesn't mean that the distances have increased: it probably means something has broken somewhere along the path, and queues are building. In the Euclidean space of street grids, we know that traffic delays will eventually lift, but in the topological space of computer systems, we learn that sometimes our transactions are permanently stalled: we need to stop, terminate processes, reboot, and reinitiate.

Diagrams can be important because they give us a sense of how things connect, and how to diagnose what is going wrong. With respect to design, diagrams are important because they help us reason through how users may experience complex systems, and where functions should be located to maximize speed and minimize interruption.

Diagrams always are embedded in Euclidean space. For topological diagrams, this can cause confusion. But the space can also be used to express important features of a design. That is, distance can be thought of as a feature of a diagram that can be used to intentionally express something.

We found this out by looking at the diagrams of more experienced students, those who had built software systems before. We found that they were more likely than novice students to use distance to express an important aspect of any design: hierarchy. Most design activity involves breaking things down into smaller elements: Simon (1969) said that most systems are nearly decomposable, and design activity is about finding the ways to break things apart at the right places, so that the within-subsystem communication is much higher than the between-subsystem communication.

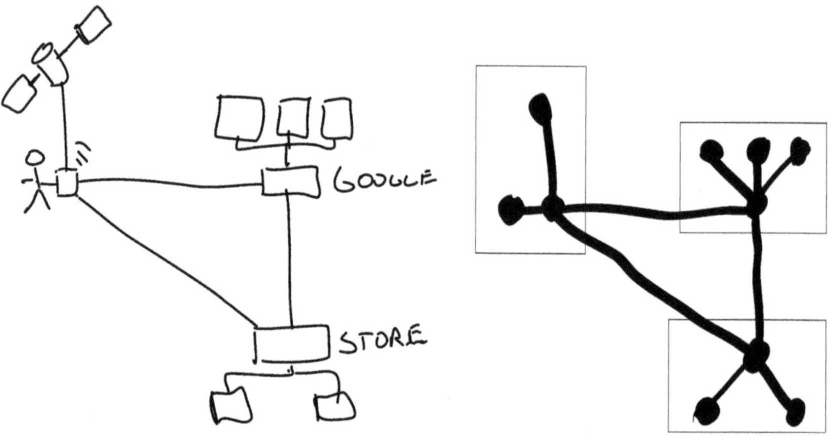

FIGURE 8.4 On the left, a diagram for a mobile system: students were asked to design an app that would detect someone searching for books in the vicinity of a bookstore and would offer them a coupon redeemable at the cash register. On the right, the same diagram abstracted into a graph and clustered based on distance

Experienced designers do this naturally. Even though all nodes could be drawn equidistant from each other, some are drawn closer to each other. They form natural subsystems on the page. On the left of Figure 8.4 is a typical diagram, modeled after a diagram from a student. On the right of Figure 8.4 is the same diagram abstracted. Notice that the components that form subsystems have been drawn close to each other: they naturally cluster. We noticed that many designers did this, and we analyzed the distances: they did indeed cluster into logical subsystems. Designers use Euclidean distance to decompose a complex system into subsystems. Barbara noticed something else. The satellite was almost always drawn at the top of the page. The phone was almost always to the right of the person. The store was almost always down, and Google was almost always up. Left-right seemed to correspond to the order of the actors in the problem scenarios. Up-down seemed to have cultural connotations. Stores are heavy: they are brick and mortar, so they are shown low. Google is light: it is in the cloud, so it is shown high (Nickerson et al., 2013). I would never have noticed this particular consistency across the different diagrams; by contrast, Barbara has a talent for seeing such phenomena in diagrams and sketches (Nickerson et al., 2008; Tversky, 2005, 2011).

Distance, Thickness, Containment

We also noticed that some designers used other conventions besides distance to indicate subsystems. They would draw an enclosure around the subsystem, as in Figure 8.5 in the center. Or they would thicken a line in order to indicate the strength of a relationship as on the left. By contrast, on the right, they use only distance to indicate relationships.

We observed these three different conventions for representing the strength of relationships. For inference tasks, which is better? As I learned from Barbara, most cognitive phenomena are sensitive to the problem domain. As I understood it from our conversations, Barbara's intuition is that we have many different kinds of cognitive facilities we can bring to bear on problems, and the problems themselves may

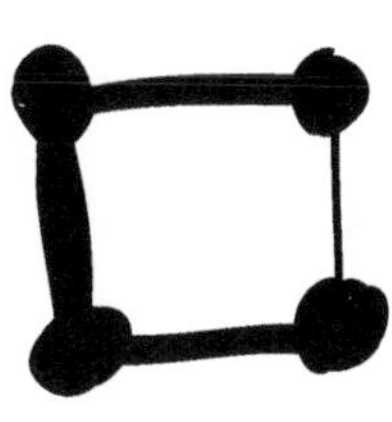

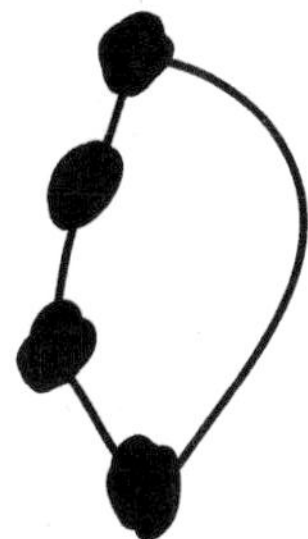

FIGURE 8.5 Three alternative ways of representing strength of a relationship: line thickness, containment, and distance

trigger one facility over another. I will contrast this with another assumption: that a phenomenon observed in one setting will work in others. When findings aren't general they are considered less applicable, and so some research just presumes generality. Barbara is also interested in generality, but she assumes from the start there will be differences by domains, and she finds this interesting and worthy of investigation. So we assumed that the effectiveness of the diagram would depend on the type of problem presented. We wanted to know which diagrams worked better.

We created two tasks, one about the frequency of communication between computers, one about security. The tasks were isomorphic to each other. Given a particular diagram, we either asked which path would be the fastest or which path would be the most secure; because of the way we defined the problem the solutions would be the same.

The frequency question (Along which pathway will the message arrive first?) was answered better by line thickness and distance. The grouping question (Which pathway is the most secure?) was answered better by containment and line thickness. Barbara pointed out that the results illustrate a more general principle of visualization, congruence. Frequency is continuous, and so line thickness and distance are congruent representations. Grouping is categorical, and so containment conventions aid inference. So does line thickness. Why? Line thickness is a very flexible convention. We can think of it as representing flow, in which case it is continuous. We can also think of it as a binary signal: we are used to diagrams in which two line weights are used: light lines represent possible paths and dark lines represent the path to be taken (Tversky et al., 2012).

The Gestural

Designers work in offices on white boards. Or in bars on napkins. Or in subways drawing in the air. Barbara points out how important gestures are for our own thinking processes, as well as for our communication processes with others (Emmorey et al., 2000; Lozano & Tversky, 2006). I didn't truly understand the importance of gesture in design until I had the opportunity to analyze videos as part of a National Science Foundation-sponsored workshop. The workshop was fascinating: Andre Van Der Hoek and Marian Petre at UC Irvine had made videos of professional software designers, teams of two, each team given the same problem (Van Der Hoek & Petre, 2014). The videos were transcribed, and the videos and transcriptions distributed for analysis by a number of different research teams; we all met and reported our results. Some of the software designers, the stars of the videos, participated in the workshop. Barbara synthesizes many of the ideas of the workshop in the first chapter of Andre and Marian's book (Tversky, 2014).

I noticed for the first time that gestures are not just diagrammatic; they can also be *about* diagrams. Designers would draw something on the white board, and then point at what they had drawn, point at each other, and through the pointing lift the conversation out of detail about a design space into a meta conversation

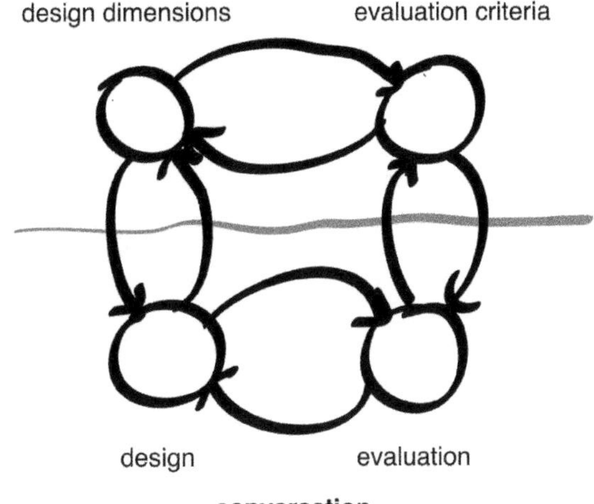

FIGURE 8.6 Meta conversation

about design criteria (Nickerson & Yu, 2014). From looking at the videos we can extract a model of design conversation, as in Figure 8.6.

This idea of meta conversation is useful in many design contexts. For example, Wikipedia talk pages are where editors have meta conversations about what they are writing in the article pages (Ozturk & Nickerson, 2015). When I was a software design consultant, I learned that I needed to have conversations with clients at the meta level to discuss how the design was going to be evaluated. I also would have conversations at the meta level about design options: was it important as a general principle, for example, to be able to roll back transactions as if they never happened, or was it enough to allow a compensating transaction that would nullify the effect of a first one? This would affect a whole range of options in the design space.

Design Space

The analysis of design discussions from videos, and the interactions at the workshop with Fred Brooks (Brooks, 2010) and Mary Shaw (Shaw, 2014), cemented something in my own mind. Designers talk about design space. And in many instances it really is a space, meaning that designers make decisions along a set of independent and continuous design decisions. For example, the designer of a cardboard cereal container of a certain volume really confronts a design space of length and width. From the choices of these two, the depth follows.

But design decisions often also have categorical variables. For example, the designer of a cereal container may need to decide first if the container will be a box, or instead a bag. This is a binary decision. Moreover, once this decision is

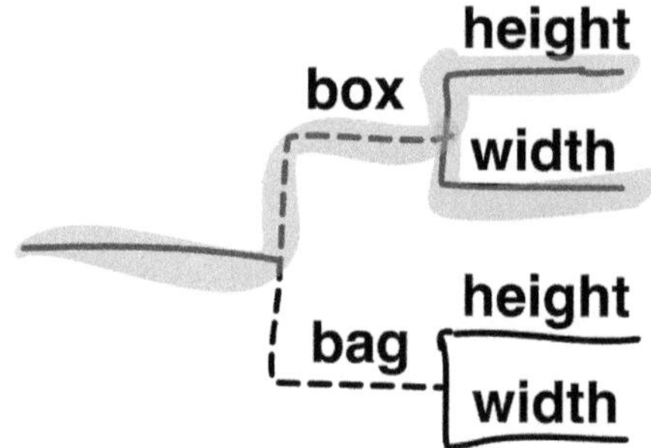

FIGURE 8.7 Design space

made, other decisions may be contingent on it. For example, the material of a box is most likely cardboard, and that of a bag, either plastic or paper.

Brooks uses a graphical notation like that shown in Figure 8.7 (Brooks Jr, 2010).

He points out that some decisions are mutually exclusive: the design is either a box or bag. Other decisions, such as those relating to height and width, are independent, and both decisions need to be made.

When all dimensions are continuous and independent, then a design can be thought of as a point in an N dimensional space, one dimension for each independent decision. But when there are categorical decisions, and then choices need to be made contingent on those decisions, a design is a set of sequential decisions, which can be thought of as a tree, the paths taken through the overall decision tree; this is shown as the lightly colored thick line in Figure 8.7.

Design is complex. In designing a house, a computer application, a book, hundreds of decisions are likely made, and many of these will then change the options available at the next stage. Ideally, we try to decompose a problem so that we are confronted at every instant with a small number of decisions. We try to reduce the dimensionality of the problem.

How can we do so? One way is to start with an exemplar, a design that worked before, and then vary one thing at a time. But the exemplar and its variants may not reach our design goals. In design, there is a back and forth between function and form. The function is what we expect something to do. One of our criteria for a design will always be whether it reaches a goal (Kan & Gero, 2014).

Time

In information systems, a large number of problems are related to parallelization: how to get multiple machines to efficiently work at the same time. It is much like a management delegation problem: by handing off tasks to others, one can make sure that several people are working in parallel. Students have a hard time understanding when and how to parallelize a system, just as new managers have a hard time understanding how to delegate tasks to direct reports. We came up with a simple challenge to test the relationship between problem solving and representation: parallelizing a call tree. Imagine having to notify a set of people of an impending organization change. You want all communication to be done face to face. You can ask others to pass on the news. Given five people in an organization, what is the shortest way to arrange the meetings? If you meet with all four people, your elapsed time will be 4. If each of you passes the information to one other person, the elapsed time will be 4 (Figure 8.8). But if you meet with two people, and the first person meets with at least one other person, the elapsed time will be 3 (Figure 8.9). The natural way to represent the problem is with a tree.

Some trees are more helpful than others: if you use the vertical dimension to represent time, you can easily see the relative merits of different arrangements, as in the right side of Figure 8.9. For example, the person at the top of the chain talks to one person. One time period elapses. Then the top person talks to someone else. That conversation will end at time period two. On the left-hand side of Figure 8.9, if one thinks of the tree as descending in time, it appears as if the top person's conversations both finish at the same time. On the right-hand side it is clearer that the second conversation finishes after the first. Moreover, once the convention is understood, it is clear that the entire tree will not complete until the second conversation of the second person, at time step 3.

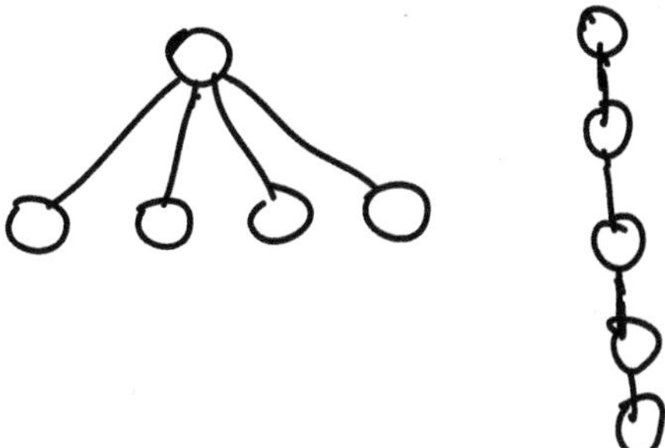

FIGURE 8.8 Extreme time trees

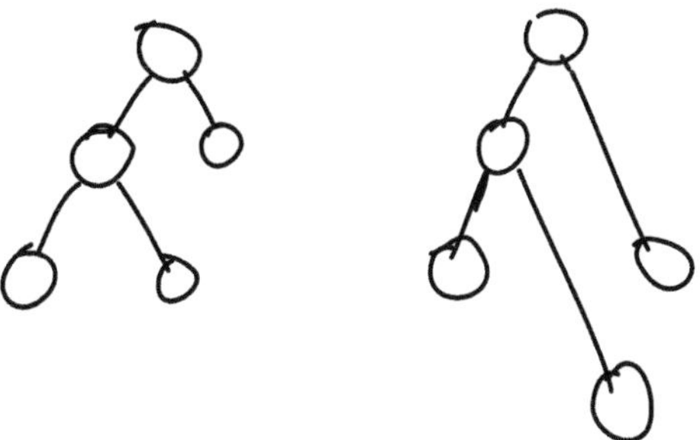

FIGURE 8.9 Two representations of the same optimal time tree

In our experiments, those who discovered on their own the time tree convention did better at finding the optimal tree (Nickerson et al., 2010). We couldn't tell for sure if the discovery of the convention helped, or if some other skill drove both the discovery of the convention and the ability to solve such problems. Cuing people with the time tree convention helped somewhat. Cuing may not be enough: as in other pedagogy situations, very explicit instruction may be necessary.

Barbara pointed out that mixed conventions are hard. Once we use links to indicate connection, and once we recognize the convention of a drawn tree, it may be difficult to imagine using one dimension of the diagram to represent time, which may seem far afield from the spatial structure of nodes and links. Thus, diagrams can help us think through problems, but they present constraints of their own. We may discover ways of mapping abstract concepts to physical dimensions, but we may not. Hints may not be enough: if we really want people to use specific representations, we need to very explicitly train them on the syntax and semantics rather than trust to transfer of learning. On the other hand, there are many problems that occur where we don't truly know what representations will work: is there a general way of thinking about the mapping of dimensions?

Dimension Reduction

Designers of systems often confront the issue of how to take complex ideas and relations and embed them on paper or screens. In many cases, it is possible to acquire or generate a distance matrix between all the components of a system. This matrix may be based on the similarity between computer components, the frequency of interactions between people or computers, or user's preferences for particular applications. The challenge is that the distance matrix has as many dimensions as there are elements. We have a hard time reasoning about high-dimensional space, and reducing down the number of dimensions is often difficult.

I had little exposure to the psychological literature on dimension reduction until I worked with James Corter while visiting for a semester at Columbia Teachers College as part of a National Science Foundation-funded project. Jim was teaching a course on multidimensional scaling, and I sat in. I learned about metric and non-metric spaces, the ways that similarity can be measured, the ways distance matrices can be transformed. Jim had worked on tree-based representations of space with Amos Tversky (Corter & Tversky, 1986) and is the author of a book on tree representations (Corter, 1996). Collaborating on the NSF project was fun because as investigators we formed an interesting triangle of different skills and interests: Barbara told us she stayed away from the algorithmic techniques of dimension reduction, because she always considered them to be Amos's territory. Jim knew the territory, Barbara had the uncannily accurate intuitions about what we would find, and I had a problem domain.

Research on dimension reduction is still active: there are many different ways to do the mapping from high to low dimensions. For example, Maneesh Agrawala, who I also met through Barbara, has automatically created maps that mimic hand-drawn local event maps, exaggerating local features that are important for getting to and from an event (Grabler et al., 2008). More generally, maps can be improved by using distance to represent not just route distance, but time, complexity, salience, and other aspects of journeys (Agrawala & Stolte, 2001). Recently, work on neural networks has argued that autoencoding, a process of compression that uses neural networks, can discover more clever ways to reduce dimensionality (Hinton & Salakhutdinov, 2006; Yumer et al., 2015). An autoencoder is trained to reproduce its inputs on its outputs, and autoencoders perform dimension reduction by forcing the path from input to output to go through a reduced-dimensionality intermediate representation. Because a multilayered neural network can perform arbitrarily complex computations, this form of compression can potentially uncover structure that other forms of reduction would miss: this is one reason for the current interest in deep learning networks.

Dimension reduction can have an impact on design activity. Design spaces are large, and many design applications require a designer to manipulate hundreds of variables. I imagine a designer controlling a machine with hundreds of dials and levers. In some cases, the problem is even more complex, because the designer is manipulating growth processes. For example, imagine designing artificial trees that will disguise cell towers. A dimension that is being manipulated, like the rate of growth, interacts with other dimensions like the number of branches at each juncture, and it can be hard to control the interactions to achieve a desired end product. By using autoencoding, it is possible to collapse hundreds of controls into a small number, presenting a more intuitive interface. Yumer et al. (2015) found empirically that the right number was three. The issue is surely more complex: less dimensions arguably reduce cognitive load, but also reduce the accessibility of at least some design options. Autoencoding will find a particular set of dimensions that optimize matching a set of standard exemplars, but a different set of dimensions might lead to the discovery of more unusual shapes. This doesn't negate the main claim of the research: by discovering structure and reducing dimensionality, we may, through these calculated constraints, encourage a more productive exploration of design space. But this idea might be informed by one of Barbara's thoughts on representation: that in design activity we use the gestural in our manipulations of form and function. Are the slider bars in three dimensions presenting a kind of gestural interface in which we can locate designs in space? Or, by optimizing for efficiency by predefining the dimensions are we losing the flexibility that the ambiguity and malleability of gesture give us?

The Performative

Barbara also led me to appreciate the performative nature of diagrams. We perform when we create diagrams: they are traces of our gestural mark making. We also perform when we interpret them: we need to reverse the compression of the diagram, unfolding its dimensions. The page has affordances, as Barbara so eloquently put it in one of our papers (Nickerson et al., 2013). We use these affordances when we create a diagram. We map different concepts to different aspects of the page, especially distance and connection. When we look at a diagram we reverse this process, guessing at how to map back from the 2D spatial representations to the higher-dimensional concepts being represented. We have a conversation with ourselves as we do this. If we are with other people, we talk with them as we draw and interpret diagrams.

There are writers who distinguish the representative from the performative (Pickering, 2010). There are good reasons to make this distinction. But a more cognitive perspective holds that representational processes are themselves performative. We have to gesture to make signs. We follow our noses in creating sketches, each line informed by the line we have just drawn. And interpreting the representations is also performative: we map from physical space into other kinds of conceptual space. In doing so, we can make all sorts of mistakes. When we look at sketches, even our own, the ambiguity of the sketches allows us to misinterpret them (Suwa & Tversky, 1996). That is, we see them in a different way than was intended. This difference generates variation. And this variation leads to invention.

Future Design

How will new technologies and processes affect the use of diagrams in design? Here I consider one emerging technology, augmented reality, and one new design process, designing with crowds and online communities.

Unlike virtual reality technology, which presents self-contained environments, augmented reality superimposes text, diagrams, maps and photos over the real world. Given our experiences with the cognitive impairment of cell-phone-absorbed pedestrians and drivers, augmented reality applications should ideally respond not just to geography but also to the user's situation. Indeed, the debut of the augmented reality game Pokémon Go illustrates the problem: players became so involved with finding imaginary creatures that they ignored real threats (Serino et al., 2016). Barbara has been working with Steven Feiner on augmented reality (Sukan et al., 2012; Sukan et al., 2014). The technology is still in its early stages: in time, clunky goggles and gloves may give way to light field and ultrasound interfaces that are tightly integrated with our bodies (Sandor et al., 2015).

Regardless of the kind of interface, we will want to better understand when the augmentation is optional or essential, distracting or helpful. While the technology is now oriented toward individual experience, the most interesting applications may be in the creation of environments, in which both the physical and virtual realities are shared and manipulable by a set of people (Perlin, 2016; Royston et al., 2016; Sandor et al., 2015).

This might provide ways of generating diagrams with others: not on whiteboards, but in the air. That is, we can gesture, and have the traces of our gestures persist. I think Barbara might say we can already do these things: we can generate diagrams, draw in the air, and maintain in our mind's eye images. However, these images fade, and the augmented reality images persist. This may be not desirable: Barbara's work on architectural drawing showed the advantages of trace paper: it slightly blurs one's previous version, allowing for new interpretations, a kind of temporal and conceptual fading (Suwa & Tversky, 2003). So perhaps the hyper-real crystalline lines of today's augmented reality systems will eventually soften into more pencil-like marks.

These interfaces are designed for individuals or small groups, sharing diagrammatic representations in conversations. But these technologies are also interesting when we consider collectives, sets of people that may not know each other well, but have common goals. At one extreme are crowds, where no one knows each other and the work is short-term. At the other extreme are online communities that usually contain a core of active participants who learn to work with each other over the years. In between are many varieties of organization structure. A big part of what makes these crowds and communities work is knowledge reuse. That is, individuals create artifacts, such as designs, and others reuse them, sometimes as is, but often by modifying them, or recombining them with other things. Language itself is perhaps our best example of reuse: we create concepts that get condensed into words that allow us through recombination to express even more complex concepts (O'Donnell, 2015). Online environments allow the sharing not just of text but also of designs, which are a very explicit form of knowledge that can also be recombined.

This sharing can result in innovation, because many people can simultaneously search a design space, picking up where others left off. It can be forced by a system (Yu & Nickerson, 2011), it can happen naturally (Han & Nickerson, 2015; Kyriakou et al., 2017; Kyriakou et al., 2017; Ozturk & Nickerson, 2015), or it can be nudged through recommendation (Ozturk & Han, 2014). One of the open questions with such collectives is how we help members navigate the constantly growing knowledge base. As knowledge grows, it becomes impossible to search it all. And to see an example may be destructive: once we are exposed to a design, we may become unable to generate alternative ideas that are substantially different: we fixate on the example.

As part of our project with Barbara, we studied fixation in design processes (Zahner et al., 2010). One possible way to counteract fixation is abstraction. Showing exemplars may not be the best way to encourage collective creativity. On the other hand, if we can measure the contributions of all members of a community and their similarity to each other we can see in an overview how different the designs are. We noticed in one experiment that when people generated several ideas in a constrained design space, at least some of their ideas were likely to be close to someone else's idea. That is, each designer generates a lot of variation, and the overall design space is constrained. If we think of the three variations from a single designer as defining the points of a triangular territory in a two-dimensional design space, then we will notice that the territories of different designers intersect. You might think that all of your ideas are closely related, but in fact the closest idea to your first idea might be someone else's first idea (Nickerson et al., 2013). As a designer, it may be useful to know when you are exploring a territory that has already been explored by others, and when you are the first explorer.

In some recent experiments, we have measured distance in design space, specifically by measuring differences in shape (Kyriakou & Nickerson, 2013; Kyriakou et al., 2017). In order to understand the method, imagine a vase. How many tennis balls would fit inside it? Then how many ping pong balls? Then how many marbles? The counts provide a signature for a shape that is invariant to rotation, and can be made invariant to scale; this and similar techniques are used in computer graphics to compute distance measures (Kazhdan et al., 2003). Alternatively, if one can infer latent variables that generate shapes, the Euclidean distance between the latent variables can be used to calculate shape distance (Huang et al., 2015).

In addition to shape distance, we can also measure semantic distance using textual descriptions of shapes, in particular tags. For example, when the same words tag two objects, we can assume that the objects are semantically similar. In order to take into account different but synonymous words, we can use Latent Semantic Analysis or Latent Dirichlet Analysis, which will provide a more nuanced measure of semantic distance (Hofmann, 2004).

The differences in the semantics of tags appear to reflect differences in function. For many designers, the most intriguing aspect of design is the tie between form and function. It works in two directions. Large changes in form will often change function. Large changes in functional requirements often call for changes in design space. But where to look in design space? This is the type of problem where Barbara's insights will be useful, because it will involve insights into verbal expression, visual representation, and performance, while taking into account the different features of human cognition and machine processing.

Concluding Thoughts

Many of Barbara's insights into design come from her belief that we use a wide range of different cognitive models. While there are many dichotomous competing models in cognitive psychology – visual vs. propositional, exemplar vs. prototype, and connectionist vs. representational – most probably all these models apply, either always activated or activated in response to particular situations. If we make that assumption, then we are looking for the theories that work in particular situations, and perhaps meta-theories that help us understand when certain strategies are activated and when they are more effective.

These theories can help us understand how design works, how to better train designers, and how to build better tools to support them. We don't have one language, we have many, and designers in particular can benefit by making use of the different affordances of different media, the potentials of expressing ideas in speech, in diagrams, in illustrations, in gesture, and all in combination. Design is a special kind of exploration through a landscape we not only navigate but also shape: our constraints, our previous designs, our interactions with other designers, our languages, and our choice of tools all let us constitute fragments of our future.

Acknowledgments

This material is based upon work supported by the National Science Foundation under grants IIS-0968561, IIS-1211084, IIS-1422066, CCF-1442840.

References

Agrawala, M. & Stolte, C. (2001). *Rendering effective route maps: improving usability through generalization*. Paper presented at the Proceedings of the 28th annual conference on computer graphics and interactive techniques.

Brooks Jr, F. P. (2010). *The design of design: essays from a computer scientist*. Pearson Education.

Corter, J. E. (1996). *Tree models of similarity and association* (Vol. 7). Sage.

Corter, J. E. & Tversky, A. (1986). Extended similarity trees. *Psychometrika, 51*(3), 429–451.

Corter, J. E., Rho, Y. J., Zahner, D., Nickerson, J. V., & Tversky, B. (2009). Bugs and biases: Diagnosing misconceptions in the understanding of diagrams. *Proceedings of the Cognitive Science Society*. Mahwah, NJ.

Emmorey, K., Tversky, B., & Taylor, H. A. (2000). Using space to describe space: Perspective in speech, sign, and gesture. *Spatial Cognition and Computation, 2*(3), 157–180.

Grabler, F., Agrawala, M., Sumner, R. W., & Pauly, M. (2008). *Automatic generation of tourist maps* (Vol. 27). ACM.

Han, Y. & Nickerson, J. V. (2015). Exploring design space through remixing. *Collective Intelligence*.

Hinton, G. E. & Salakhutdinov, R. R. (2006). Reducing the dimensionality of data with neural networks. *Science, 313*(5786), 504–507.

Hofmann, T. (2004). Latent semantic models for collaborative filtering. *ACM Transactions on Information Systems (TOIS), 22*(1), 89–115.

Huang, H., Kalogerakis, E., & Marlin, B. (2015). *Analysis and synthesis of 3D shape families via deep-learned generative models of surfaces*. Paper presented at the Computer Graphics Forum.

Kan, J. W. T. & Gero, J. (2014). Studying software design cognition. In A. Van Der Hoek & M. Petre (Eds.), *Software designers in action* (pp. 61–77): CRC Press.

Kazhdan, M., Funkhouser, T., & Rusinkiewicz, S. (2003). *Rotation Invariant Spherical Harmonic Representation of 3D Shape Descriptors*, Symposium on Geometry Processing, 156–164.

Kyriakou, H. & Nickerson, J. V. (2013). *Idea inheritance, originality, and collective innovation*. Paper presented at the Workshop on Information in Networks.

Kyriakou, H., Nickerson, J. V., & Sabnis, G. (2017). Knowledge reuse for customization: Metamodels in an open design community for 3D printing. *MIS Quarterly, 41*(1), 315–332.

Lozano, S. C. & Tversky, B. (2006). Communicative gestures facilitate problem solving for both communicators and recipients. *Journal of Memory and Language, 55*(1), 47–63.

Nickerson, J. V. & Yu, L. (2014). Going meta: design space and evaluation space in software design. In A. Van Der Hoek & M. Petre (Eds.), *Software designers in action* (pp. 323–343): CRC Press.

Nickerson, J., Corter, J., Tversky, B., Zahner, D., & Rho, Y. (2008). *The spatial nature of thought.* Paper presented at the Proceedings of the 29th International Conference on Information Systems. Association for Information Systems, Paris, France.
Nickerson, J. V. (2005). *The meaning of arrows: Diagrams and other facets in system sciences literature.* Paper presented at the Proceedings of the 38th Annual Hawaii International Conference on System Sciences, 2005. HICSS'05.
Nickerson, J.V., Corter, J. E., Tversky, B., Rho, Y.-J., Zahner, D., & Yu, L. (2013). Cognitive tools shape thought: diagrams in design. *Cognitive processing, 14*(3), 255–272.
Nickerson, J.V., Tversky, B., Corter, J. E., Yu, L., & Mason, D. (2010). *Thinking with networks.* Paper presented at the Proceedings of the 32nd Annual Conference of the Cognitive Science Society.
O'Donnell, T. J. (2015). *Productivity and reuse in language: A theory of linguistic computation and storage.* MIT Press.
Ozturk, P. & Han, Y. (2014). Similar, yet diverse: a recommender system. *Collective Intelligence.*
Ozturk, P. & Nickerson, J. (2015). *Paths from talk to action.* Paper presented at the International Conference on Information Systems.
Peirce, C. S. (1974). *Collected papers of Charles Sanders Peirce* (Vol. 5). Harvard University Press.
Perlin, K. (2016). Future reality: how emerging technologies will change language itself. *IEEE Computer Graphics and Applications, 36*(3), 84–89.
Pickering, A. (2010). *The mangle of practice: Time, agency, and science.* University of Chicago Press.
Royston, S., DeFanti, C., & Perlin, K. (2016). A collaborative untethered virtual reality environment for interactive social network visualization. *arXiv preprint arXiv:1604.08239.*
Sandor, C., Fuchs, M., Cassinelli, A., Li, H., Newcombe, R., Yamamoto, G., & Feiner, S. (2015). Breaking the barriers to true augmented reality. *arXiv preprint arXiv:1512.05471.*
Serino, M., Cordrey, K., McLaughlin, L., & Milanaik, R. L. (2016). Pokémon Go and augmented virtual reality games: a cautionary commentary for parents and pediatricians. *Current opinion in pediatrics, 28*(5), 673–677.
Shaw, M. (2014). Role of design spaces in guiding a software design. In A. Van Der Hoek & M. Petre (Eds.), *Software Designers in Action* (pp. 31–46): CRC Press.
Sukan, M., Elvezio, C., Oda, O., Feiner, S., & Tversky, B. (2014). *ParaFrustum: visualization techniques for guiding a user to a constrained set of viewing positions and orientations.* Paper presented at the Proceedings of the 27th Annual ACM Symposium on User Interface Software and Technology.
Sukan, M., Feiner, S., Tversky, B., & Energin, S. (2012). *Quick viewpoint switching for manipulating virtual objects in hand-held augmented reality using stored snapshots.* Paper presented at the Mixed and Augmented Reality (ISMAR), 2012 IEEE International Symposium.
Suwa, M. & Tversky, B. (1996). *What architects see in their sketches: Implications for design tools.* Paper presented at the Conference Companion on Human Factors in Computing Systems.
Suwa, M. & Tversky, B. (2003). *Constructive perception: A metacognitive skill for coordinating perception and conception.* Paper presented at the Proceedings of the Annual Conference of the Cognitive Science Society, Boston.
Tversky, B. (2005). Functional significance of visuospatial representations. In P. Shah & A. Miyake (Eds.) *Handbook of Higher-Level Visuospatial Thinking* (pp. 1–34): Cambridge: Cambridge University Press.
Tversky, B. (2011). Visualizing thought. *Topics in Cognitive Science, 3*(3), 499–535.
Tversky, B. (2014). Designing designs, or designs on designs. In A. Van Der Hoek & M. Petre (Eds.), *Software Designers in Action* (pp. 3–9): CRC Press.

Tversky, B., Corter, J. E., Yu, L., Mason, D. L., & Nickerson, J. V. (2012). Representing category and continuum: Visualizing thought. In P. Rodgers, P. Cox and B. Plimmer (Eds.), *Diagrammatic representation and inference* (pp. 23–34): Springer.

Tversky, B., Morrison, J. B., & Bétrancourt, M. (2002). Animation: can it facilitate? *International journal of human-computer studies, 57*(4), 247–262.

Tversky, B., Zacks, J., Lee, P., & Heiser, J. (2000). Lines, blobs, crosses and arrows: Diagrammatic communication with schematic figures. In M. Anderson, P. Cheng, and V. Haarslev (Eds.), *Theory and application of diagrams* (pp. 221–230): Springer.

Van Der Hoek, A. & Petre, M. (2014). *Software designers in action: a human-centric look at design work*: CRC Press.

Yu, L. & Nickerson, J. V. (2011). *Cooks or cobblers?: crowd creativity through combination.* Paper presented at the SIGCHI conference on human factors in computing systems.

Yumer, M. E., Asente, P., Mech, R., & Kara, L. B. (2015). *Procedural modeling using autoencoder networks.* Paper presented at the Proceedings of the 28th Annual ACM Symposium on User Interface Software and Technology.

Zacks, J. & Tversky, B. (1999). Bars and lines: A study of graphic communication. *Memory & Cognition, 27*(6), 1073–1079.

Zahner, D., Nickerson, J. V., Tversky, B., Corter, J. E., & Ma, J. (2010). A fix for fixation? Rerepresenting and abstracting as creative processes in the design of information systems. *Artificial Intelligence for Engineering Design, Analysis and Manufacturing, 24*(2), 231–244.

9

ACQUIRING SPATIAL KNOWLEDGE FROM DIFFERENT SOURCES AND PERSPECTIVES

Abilities, Strategies and Representations

Francesca Pazzaglia and Chiara Meneghetti

Introduction

In recent years our Memory and Learning lab at the University of Padua has conducted research projects, many of them inspired by Barbara Tversky's work, to investigate the interactions between individual and environmental variables affecting performance in several spatial tasks: navigation, short-cut finding, map learning, and spatial text comprehension. A variety of methods and tools have been used to do so, from self-reports (questionnaires on sense of direction [SOD], strategies and preferences in spatial representations) to objective measures of spatial abilities and visuospatial working memory (VSWM). Our general goal has been to explore differences and similarities in spatial representations constructed from different sources (navigation, map inspection, spatial texts) and perspectives, and to shed light on whether and how SOD, spatial representation strategies and styles, spatial abilities, and VSWM work together in influencing performance in various spatial tasks.

Studies on this topic originated a long time ago, in 1993, when the first author of this chapter presented a poster together with Cesare Cornoldi at the 34th Annual Meeting of the Psychonomic Society. It is there that we met Barbara Tversky (and a brilliant PhD student: Holly Taylor), and embarked on a long story of research exchanges and friendship that, some years later, came to involve the second author too. The present chapter is a sign of our grateful acknowledgment of how Barbara continues to inspire our work, and how she brought fresh perspectives to our lives.

Acquiring Spatial Knowledge from Different Sources and Perspectives

The ability to acquire spatial knowledge is very important in everyday life, and it has been crucial to the survival of our own and other species. We acquire spatial knowledge from a variety of sensory inputs (e.g. vision, vestibular sense, kinesthesis, motor afference) and experiences (navigation, map reading, listening to directions), which lead to the construction of an internal representation of the environment, which we rely on to perform various spatial tasks. Mental representations have been defined in different terms and illustrated using different metaphors. Probably the most often used is the cognitive map (Tolman, 1948), a map-like representation that can be mentally inspected and that preserves spatial and metric relationships between the relevant elements it contains. Internal representations might be conceived not as a coherent whole (typical of cognitive maps), however – particularly for environments not known in detail – but rather as a concurrence of figures, partial information, and differing perspectives, where fragments of experiences and memories of various formats are collected in a cognitive collage, as Barbara suggested (Tversky, 1993). Of course, the format and properties of mental representations affect the performance of spatial tasks, such as retracing a route, estimating distances and directions, or drawing a map (Hegarty, Montello, Richardson, Ishikawa & Lovelace, 2006; Wolbers & Hegarty, 2010).

If an environment can be experienced from different perspectives (route or survey perspectives, according to a personal or map view, respectively; Taylor & Tversky, 1992; Tversky, 1991), and in different ways (by moving around in it, inspecting it from above, looking at a map, or listening to a verbal description), then it is important to establish whether learning experience and perspective can influence the resulting internal representation and, as a consequence, the performance of spatial tasks (e.g. Thorndyke & Hayes-Roth, 1982). In addition to these external factors, we also need to consider the role of internal variables, including SOD, spatial self-efficacy and anxiety, strategy use, spatial ability, and VSWM. It is important to explore how and to what extent all these variables, alone and/or in combination, affect the construction of mental representations and the consequent performance of spatial tasks.

In the present chapter we examine the role of some of the above-listed external and internal factors in determining individual differences in the performance of spatial tasks, such as way-finding, map learning, and spatial text processing. Our goal is to shed light on how interactions among these variables affect task performance. We first describe a number of instruments widely used to assess SOD, spatial strategies, spatial self-efficacy and anxiety, and then go on to analyze the relationships between these variables, and we review the main outcomes of several studies based on the use of the instruments described. We also examine the role of the variables considered in conjunction with that of spatial ability and VSWM in determining spatial knowledge.

Subjective Variables Influencing Orientation Behavior: How to Measure Them and Their Interconnections

Several subjective measures have been related to way-finding behavior and geographical orientation. Some ask people for an overall estimation of their orientation ability (as in estimating SOD; Hegarty et al., 2006); others more specifically assess the use of spatial strategies during way-finding (route or orientation strategies; Lawton, 1994), or the preference for adopting specific spatial representations (survey, route or landmark-centered representations; Pazzaglia, Cornoldi & De Beni, 2000). Finally, we consider the anxiety individuals experience during orientation tasks (Lawton, 1994) and their reported self-efficacy in performing them (Mitolo et al., 2015).

Sense of Direction: An Overall Index of Orientation Performance

Sense of direction is generally defined as a person's self-reported estimation of their ability to orient themselves geographically. Is it a valid measure? In other words, does a person's self-reported SOD reflect their actual spatial competence? It seems that it does. Several studies conducted so far have found that self-reported SOD correlates directly with success in way-finding tasks. Some of the first evidence was collected in 1977 by Kozlowsky and Bryant, who asked undergraduate students to score their own SOD on a 7-point scale (from 1 = "poor" to 7 = "good"), and then to perform several spatial tasks. They found that participants who felt they had a good SOD performed better when pointing at unseen landmarks in a familiar environment than those who judged their SOD to be poor. Similar results also emerged from more recent studies (e.g. Hegarty, Richardson, Montello, Lovelace, & Subbiah, 2002; Hegarty et al., 2006; Sholl, 1988; Sholl, Kenny, & Della Porta, 2006), which provided further empirical support for the idea that SOD can predict performance in environmental spatial tasks.

The use of instruments specifically devised to assess SOD has helped to shed more light on the relationships between subjective and objective measures of spatial orientation. One of the most often used self-report scales for assessing SOD was devised by Hegarty et al. (2002). This is the Santa Barbara Sense of Direction (SBSOD) scale, which consists of fifteen statements regarding performance in various orientation tasks, to which participants express their degree of agreement on a 7-point Likert scale. The scale generates a general measure of SOD that predicts performance in environmental tasks, such as estimating distance and direction (Hegarty et al., 2006).

Strategies and Representations: Individual Differences in the Perception, Memorization and Representation of the Environment

Another issue addressed by research concerns the strategies people use to mentally represent an environment and move through it. During navigation, some people prefer to pay attention to the landmarks and remember the sequence of streets and turns taken to arrive at a destination. Others focus more on constructing an overall mental picture that maintains the spatial and metric relations among the main landmarks. Two kinds of representation (and related way-finding strategies) have been described (Lawton, 1996; Tversky, 1991). Route representation (associated with a route strategy) adopts the point of view of a person moving through the environment. It is characterized by a linear organization and an intrinsic frame of reference. Survey representation (and the related orientation strategy) provides an overview of the spatial layout, where the relative locations of the main elements are maintained and an extrinsic frame of reference is used. People's preferences for route or orientation strategies can be ascertained using the Way-Finding Strategy Scale (Lawton, 1994, 1996), which consists of fourteen items, nine on the orientation strategy and five on the route strategy. The orientation and route strategies are differently correlated with the performance of spatial tasks. In fact, positive correlations were found between orientation strategy and performance in the Water Level task (Lawton, 1994) and pointing tasks (Lawton, 1996), whereas the use of a route strategy is inversely related to performance in the Mental Rotations Test (MRT; Vandenberg & Kuse, 1978; Lawton, 1994). The exploration of the two strategies revealed interesting gender differences, such that men were more likely to adopt an orientation strategy than women, who tend to prefer a route strategy. Lawton also devised an eight-item Spatial Anxiety Scale (Lawton, 1994) that is used to rate the level of anxiety generated by typical environmental tasks (e.g. finding the car in a large car park). Gender comparisons on spatial anxiety have shown that women are more susceptible to it than men (Lawton, 1996). Spatial anxiety also seems to interfere with performance on pointing tasks (Lawton, 1996).

Another tool capable of detecting individual differences in SOD, spatial strategies, and other associated variables is the Questionnaire on Spatial Representation (QSR; Pazzaglia et al., 2000; Pazzaglia & De Beni, 2001), an 11-item self-report scale devised to record multidimensional scores of SOD, reference to cardinal points, spatial strategies, and spatial language encoding. For each item, respondents are asked to express their degree of agreement on a Likert scale from 1 to 5. The questionnaire's psychometric properties were originally tested on a sample of 285 undergraduates (Pazzaglia et al., 2000).

More recently, a slightly modified version of the QSR was administered to 294 undergraduates (170 females), along with the SBSOD scale (Hegarty et al., 2002), a spatial anxiety scale (Mitolo et al., 2015, adapted from Lawton, 1994), and a scale on spatial self-efficacy that measures how confident individuals feel about their ability to perform specific environmental tasks (Mitolo et al., 2015). Factor analysis on the QSR revealed four factors (Table 9.1): Factor 1 as a factor on general sense of direction in open and closed environments, associated with preference for a survey representation; Factor 2 on the use of compass directions in orientation tasks; Factor 3 grouped together scores on route and landmark-focused representations, and Factor 4 had positive and negative saturations, respectively, for scores on the preference for spatial and verbal encoding of spatial language.

TABLE 9.1 Factor analysis. Extraction: rotated matrix. Eigenvalue >1, varimax rotation loadings equal and higher than .50 (in bold) are used to interpret the factors

Item	*Factor 1 SOD/survey representation*	*Factor 2 Cardinal directions*	*Factor 3 Route-landmark representation*	*Factor 4 Spatial-verbal encoding*
1 Do you think you have a good sense of direction?	**.70**	.24	.15	.27
2 Do your family or friends say that you have a good sense of direction?	**.69**	.24	.08	.18
3 Think about the way you orient yourself in different environments around you. Would you describe yourself as a person:				
a. who orients him/herself by remembering routes connecting one place to another;	.22	−.03	.36	−.24
b. who orients him/herself by looking for well-known landmarks;	.19	−.16	**.64**	−.16
c. who tries to create a mental map of the environment.	**.50**	.41	.07	.23
4 Think of an unfamiliar city. Write the name: … Now try to classify your representation of the city as:				
a. a survey representation, that is a map-like representation;	**.58**	.28	−.05	−.10
b. a route representation, based on memorizing routes;	−.03	.20	**.71**	.14
c. a landmark-centered representation, based on memorizing single salient landmarks (such as monuments, buildings, crossroads, etc.).	−.02	−<.01	**.85**	.04
5 When you are in a natural, open environment (mountains, seaside, country), do you naturally identify cardinal points, i.e. which way is north, south, east and west?	.26	**.87**	−<.01	.09

Item	Factor 1 *SOD/survey representation*	Factor 2 *Cardinal directions*	Factor 3 *Route-landmark representation*	Factor 4 *Spatial-verbal encoding*
6 When you are in your home town, do you naturally identify cardinal points? In other words, do you easily find which way is north, south, east and west?	.20	**.76**	.01	.03
7 Someone is describing the route to an unfamiliar place to you. Do you prefer:				
a. to make a mental image of the route?	.26	.18	.17	**.76**
b. to remember the words of the description?	−.07	.04	.22	**−.85**
8 In a complex building (department store, museum), do you spontaneously and easily think about the direction in which you are moving in relation to the general layout of the building and the outside environment?	**.65**	.23	.03	.03
9 When you are inside a building, can you easily visualize what there is outside the building in the direction in which you are looking?	**.73**	.13	.05	.05
10 When you are in an open space and you are asked to indicate a compass point (north-south-east-west), do you point at it immediately?	.28	**.77**	<.01	.02
11 You are in a complex building (many floors, stairs, corridors) and you have to indicate where the entrance is. Do you point at it immediately?	**.68**	.02	.10	.01

By comparison with the first factor analysis (Pazzaglia et al., 2000), only the factor based on compass directions (now Factor 2) completely overlaps with the previous ones. The others differ in factor composition: the present Factor 1 showed that SOD and survey representation represented a single factor, whereas they were two distinct factors in the previous factor analysis, and the survey factor also included items assessing spatial encoding (and verbal encoding in the opposite direction). These latter items are now covered by Factor 4. The present Factor 3 now groups scores on route and landmark-focused representations together, whereas in the previous factor analysis they were extracted as two distinct factors.

The QSR's internal consistency was high (Cronbach's alpha = .84). A subgroup of 50 participants (32 females) was tested again a fortnight later, and the correlations between the first and second times the questionnaire was administered were >.78 for all factors. Analyzing the correlations calculated between each QSR factor and the SBSOD scale (item scores were converted so that higher scores indicated a greater ability), the spatial anxiety and self-efficacy questionnaires showed correlations for: Factor 1 (sense of direction and survey representation) and SBSOD score ($r = .57, p < .001$), self-efficacy ($r = .56, p < .001$), and anxiety ($r = -.37, p < .001$); and Factor 2 (use of compass directions in orientation tasks) with SBSOD score ($r = .32, p < .001$), self-efficacy ($r = .38, p < .001$), and anxiety ($r = -.22, p < .01$). The results confirmed that SOD, combined with a preference for survey representation, and the use of compass points for orientation were associated with high self-efficacy in performing spatial tasks and protected against spatial anxiety.

SOD, Spatial Representation Strategies, and Spatial Tasks: What Interactions?

The above-mentioned studies provide insight on the relationship between SOD, strategy use, anxiety and performance in spatial and environmental tasks. Overall, they show that people's estimates of their own SOD are consistent and reliable in predicting their performance in a wide range of tasks. Lawton's research also points to the importance of gender-related differences in spatial representations and way-finding strategies, and how they relate to performance in spatial tasks and feelings of spatial anxiety (for further details, see also Ploran, Rovira, Thompson, & Parasuraman, 2015; Prestopnik & Roskos-Ewoldsen, 2000). Overall, individuals with a strong self-reported SOD prefer to adopt a survey representation of the environment and use a configurational strategy. They are more self-confident about their performance in orientation tasks and less prone to experience spatial anxiety than individuals with a weak self-reported SOD, and they also perform better than the latter in a wide range of orientation tasks.

What has emerged so far is the importance of these internal factors in affecting spatial performance. But other variables need to be taken into account (Wolbers & Hegarty, 2010), some of them still internal (such as spatial ability and VSWM), others pertaining to the task (experimental goals, instructions, learning perspectives, media, etc.). They can all have a role in influencing performance, and we believe that they exert their influence both separately and in mutual interaction. In the following sections we review some of our studies showing how tasks and instructions interact with individual variables in influencing success in navigation, map learning, and spatial text processing.

Navigation

An example of how learning perspective, learning test, and individual differences interact in spatial representations comes from an experiment on navigation in a virtual environment. Pazzaglia and Taylor (2007) asked two groups of undergraduates to learn a route in a virtual environment either by navigation or by means of a map. The two groups consisted of high- and low-survey participants, based on the survey scores they obtained in the QSR. After the learning phase, participants were asked to navigate the route just learned and their navigation errors were recorded. The results showed that participants who had learned the route by navigation generally made fewer errors than those who had learned it from a map. When the navigation errors made by the high- and low-survey individuals were considered separately, however, a different pattern of results emerged for the two groups. The high-survey group made the same number of mistakes regardless of whether they had learned the environment by navigation or from a map, whereas the low-survey group made twice as many mistakes in the latter condition, as well as generally making more mistakes than the high-survey group. It is evident that individuals' self-rated preferences for a survey type of spatial representation really reflected the strategies and the types of representation they preferred to adopt and, as a consequence, their actual performance in navigation tasks. It is equally clear that spatial preferences interacted with learning perspective in affecting navigation.

Similar conclusions, but from a different pattern of results, came from another study that examined real navigation in the city of Venice (Denis, Pazzaglia, Cornoldi & Bertolo, 1999, Study 4). The main goal of the study was to investigate the efficacy of qualitatively different route directions in aiding navigation. High-survey and landmark-centered individuals were selected (based on the QSR) and asked to read good or poor route directions and then navigate the route described from start to finish, with a view to examining the influence of good and poor route directions on their navigation. As expected, using poor route directions rather than good ones gave rise to more errors (2.94 and .82 for the poor and good directions, respectively), but their negative impact on navigation was stronger for the high-survey than for the landmark-centered group (4.44 vs. 2.23 errors, respectively). In short, the above-mentioned studies pointed to the importance not only of taking individual differences in spatial representation into account, but also of studying their effect in relation to the experimental tasks and its demands. The experiment on navigation in a virtual environment (Pazzaglia & Taylor, 2007) showed that maps are good virtual navigation aids for high-survey people, but may have a detrimental effect on low-survey people. The experiment conducted in Venice (Denis et al., 1999) demonstrated that everybody can take advantage of good directions for navigating a route, but high-survey individuals are more negatively affected by poor-quality spatial directions than low-survey individuals, possibly because of their tendency to form spatial mental representations with map-like features and to refer to them while navigating – a task made more difficult when the spatial relations between the landmarks are not clearly stated in the directions they receive.

In recent years, several studies have also explored the relationship between working memory and navigation (e.g. Labate, Pazzaglia, & Hegarty, 2014; Wen, Ishikawa & Sato 2011, 2013), and in one of them (Garden, Cornoldi & Logie 2002) an interaction emerged between working memory ability and spatial representation preferences. The study by Garden et al. (2002) investigated the involvement of VSWM and verbal working memory (VWM) in navigation by means of a dual task paradigm. Participants randomly assigned to one of three groups learned a route through the winding streets of an Italian medieval town by navigating through it. Each group was in a different concurrent task condition during this learning phase: an articulatory suppression (AS) group kept repeating the syllables ba-be-bi-bo-bu (a secondary task believed to load the VWM); a spatial tapping group kept pressing four buttons at the corners of a small table (this secondary task is thought to load VSWM); and the third (control) group had no concurrent task to perform. Individual differences in spatial representation were considered too, dividing participants according to whether they had a high or low preference for survey representations. Here again, the experimental conditions were found to interact with the preferences and influence success in navigation: the navigation performance of the high- and low-survey individuals did not differ in the AS and control groups, but the high-survey individuals made more mistakes than their low-survey counterparts in the spatial tapping condition.

Further studies confirmed the interaction between individual differences, the components of working memory (i.e. VWM and VSWM) and navigation ability, expanding our knowledge in this area. For instance, Wen et al. (2013; see also Wen et al., 2011) showed that all working memory components were involved in route learning by individuals with a good SOD, while VWM was more involved in those with a poor SOD. These findings indicate that self-reported individual preferences influence the relationship between working memory and navigation performance.

Map Learning

Another typical way to acquire spatial knowledge is from maps or object configurations. With this type of input too, spatial preferences and spatial abilities, interact with the experimental task and determine how the maps being learned are mentally represented.

In a study by Pazzaglia and De Beni (2006), participants were divided according to their mental rotation (MR) ability. They completed the QSR and their survey scores were calculated. The two groups (good versus poor MR) differed in their survey scores, individuals with a good MR ability scoring higher in the QSR survey scores. Participants were then asked to memorize visual configurations similar to those used by Levine, Jankovic, and Palij (1982), or to study a map (Experiments 1 and 2, respectively). The mental representation of the spatial configuration learned by the participants was tested with a series of pointing tasks in which the imaginary perspectives they adopted were aligned or misaligned with the view they had learned. The performance of the two groups was better for aligned than for misaligned pointing tasks (a finding abundantly confirmed in the literature; e.g. McNamara, 2013). But both experiments also consistently showed a significant group × alignment interaction, supporting the idea that the two groups were differently affected by the perspective (aligned or misaligned of 90°, 135°, 180°) adopted during the pointing tasks. Individuals with a good MR ability performed the pointing tasks better than those with poor MR skills, particularly when they had to adopt a perspective misaligned with the one adopted during the learning phase. The fact that the two groups differed in their survey scores suggests that MR ability could be involved in the construction of spatial representations less anchored to a viewer's orientation and therefore enable information from different views to be managed more flexibly.

Further studies confirmed that map-learning accuracy was positively related to MR ability, spatial visualization style (Pazzaglia & Moè, 2013), and VSWM (Borella, Meneghetti, Muffato, & De Beni, 2015). This last result supports the idea that SOD associated with a preference for survey-based knowledge (as shown by the above-mentioned new factor analysis) efficiently supports the acquisition of the configuration of an environment.

Spatial Text Processing

Although comprehension of spatial language shares a number of cognitive mechanisms with language comprehension *tout court*, there is consistent evidence in favor of a specific involvement of VSWM in understanding and memorizing spatial texts (see Gyselinck & Meneghetti, 2011; Pazzaglia, Gyselinck, Cornoldi & De Beni, 2012, for reviews). Empirical evidence also supports the conviction that spatial abilities, spatial representation strategies, and VSWM interact in affecting spatial text processing. It was found that spatial tapping performed concurrently with spatial text processing impaired the subsequent recall of the text's content, but only in participants with poor MR abilities, whereas good mental rotators' memory performance was not impaired by the concurrent spatial task (Meneghetti, Gyselinck, Pazzaglia & De Beni, 2009). Another study (Meneghetti, Pazzaglia & De Beni, 2011) involved the use of spatial texts from survey and route perspectives (Taylor & Tversky, 1992), and one of the aims of this study was to test whether individuals with very high QSR scores for the use of compass points were particularly good at processing spatial texts. All participants listened to survey and route descriptions and then judged whether survey and route inferential sentences, as well as paraphrased and non-spatial sentences, were true or false. Then they were asked to draw a map of the environment described in the text. The results showed that individuals with a very strong preference for the use of cardinal directions were more accurate than the others in judging the route and survey inferential sentences. They were also better at map drawing than the others, but only for the survey descriptions.

Since spatial abilities (such as MR) and preferences are related (as discussed in the above-mentioned studies), further research was conducted to explore how spatial abilities and spatial preferences work together in supporting environment knowledge acquired from descriptions (Pazzaglia & Meneghetti, 2012; Meneghetti, Ronconi, Pazzaglia & De Beni, 2014). For instance, Meneghetti, Ronconi, et al. (2014) asked participants to listen to route descriptions and their recall was tested by means of a map-drawing task. Participants were also assessed on their spatial abilities (mental rotation with the MRT and VSWM with the Corsi test; Corsi, 1972) and preferences (using the QSR). Given the importance of strategy use in influencing spatial description accuracy (Meneghetti, De Beni, Gyselinck, & Pazzaglia, 2013; Meneghetti, Labate, Ronconi, Grassano, & Pazzaglia, 2014), participants were asked to report how much they used certain strategies (on a Likert scale from 1 = "very little" to 7 = "very much") based on a survey perspective ("I constructed a mental map of the environment"), a route perspective ("I mentally followed the path"), or a verbal strategy based on repetition. The results of path modeling showed that both MR and a preference for a survey-based strategy positively influence recall performance, which is indirectly mediated by VSWM and the use of a survey strategy. This type of result supports the impression that MR ability and a survey-based style are *a priori* individual skills that influence the VSWM resources in processing spatial text information and, as a consequence, the adoption of survey strategies when processing spatial descriptions.

On the whole, these findings corroborate the assumption that, among the various factors coming into play, an effective intervening variable may be of a spatial nature, capable of sharing resources with other factors that qualify people's spatial profile (such as rotation ability and a survey-based style), and encompassing environmental information processing, and this might be the VSWM (see also Meneghetti et al., 2016).

Conclusions

In this overview of our research on individual differences in spatial learning, we have outlined the results of a number of studies exploring the mutual relationships between SOD, spatial representations, VSWM, mental rotation ability and performance in spatial tasks. Overall, these findings show that self-reported SOD and spatial representation preferences (as assessed with the QSR) are reliable and correlate with performance in various spatial tasks.

Research on spatial text processing and map learning indicates that individuals with higher spatial profiles (as assessed with spatial tasks and the QSR) are better able to manage spatial information, find it easier to adopt counter-aligned views (after studying a map), and are more accurate in answering spatial inferential sentences (after studying spatial descriptions). Their superiority in processing spatial information does not prevent these individuals from having difficulty when they use verbal directions for navigation, particularly when they were asked to read poor directions and then navigate by them. Being ambiguous and lacking in substantial spatial information, the poor directions made it difficult to construct a complete and coherent spatial mental model. These outcomes suggest that, even if high-survey individuals have a good comprehension of spatial texts, they can find it difficult to use this information as a navigation aid. It may be that the mental model they derive from route descriptions interferes with their preferential survey representation.

Our studies on navigation in virtual environments showed that high-survey individuals were better able to navigate with the aid of information obtained from a map. They seemed to be more flexible and efficient when asked to navigate a route using information gained from a survey perspective.

To conclude, this review underscores the importance of taking SOD and spatial representation styles (also in relation to spatial and VSWM abilities) into account because they are reliable indicators that relate to individuals' actual performance in spatial tasks. In addition to expanding the theoretical frame on individual differences and environment knowledge, the research discussed in this review has practical implications, such as the need to bear in mind individual differences in spatial representations when implementing navigation aids, because people with different spatial representation styles are likely to need appropriate devices.

Authors' Note

Support for this chapter was provided by a University of Padua grant (PRAT2014) to the second author.

References

Borella, E., Meneghetti, C., Muffato, V., & De Beni, R. (2015). Map learning and the alignment effect in young and older adults: how do they gain from having a map available while performing pointing tasks? *Psychological Research, 79*, 104–119. Doi: 10.1007/s00426-014-0543-y.

Corsi, P. M. (1972). *Human Memory and the Medial Temporal Region of the Brain.* Unpublished doctoral dissertation. McGill University. Montreal.

Denis, M., Pazzaglia, F., Cornoldi, C., & Bertolo, L. (1999). Spatial discourse and navigation: An analysis of route directions in the city of Venice. *Applied Cognitive Psychology, 13*, 145–174. Doi: 10.1002/(SICI)1099-0720(199904).

Garden, S., Cornoldi, C., & Logie, R. H. (2002). Visuo-spatial working memory in navigation. *Applied Cognitive Psychology, 16*, 35–50. Doi: 10.1002/acp.746.

Gyselinck, V. & Meneghetti, C. (2011). The role of spatial working memory in understanding verbal descriptions: a window onto the interaction between verbal and spatial processing. In A. Vandienrendonck & A. Szmalec (Eds.), *Spatial Working Memory* (pp. 159–180). Hove, UK: Psychology Press.

Hegarty, M., Montello, D. R., Richardson, A. E., Ishikawa, T., & Lovelace, T. (2006). Spatial abilities at different scales: Individual differences in aptitude-test performance and spatial-layout learning. *Intelligence, 34*, 151–176. Doi: 10.1016/j.intell.2005.09.005.

Hegarty, M., Richardson, A. E., Montello, D. R., Lovelace, K., & Subbiah, I. (2002). Development of a self-report measure of environmental spatial ability. *Intelligence, 30*, 425–447. Doi: 10.1016/S0160-2896(02)00116-2.

Kozlowski, L.T. & Bryant, K.J. (1977). Sense of direction, spatial orientation, and cognitive maps. *Journal of Experimental Psychology, 3*, 590–598. Doi: 10.1037/0096-1523.3.4.590.

Labate, E., Pazzaglia, F., & Hegarty, M. (2014). What working memory subcomponents are needed in the acquisition of survey knowledge? Evidence from direction estimation and shortcut tasks. *Journal of Environmental Psychology, 37*, 73–79. Doi: 10.1016/j.jenvp.2013.11.007.

Lawton, C. A. (1994). Gender differences in way-finding strategies: relationship to spatial ability and spatial anxiety. *Sex Roles, 30*, 765–779. Doi: 10.1007/BF01544230.

Lawton, C. A. (1996). Strategies for indoor wayfinding: the role of orientation. *Journal of Environmental Psychology, 16*, 137–145. Doi: 10.1006/jevp.1996.0011.

Levine, M., Jankovic, I. N., & Palij, M. (1982). Principles of spatial problem solving. *Journal of Experimental Psychology: General. 111*, 157–175. Doi: 10.1037/0096-3445.111.2.157.

McNamara, T. P. (2013). Spatial memory: Properties and organization. In D. Waller & L. Nadel (Eds.), *Handbook of Spatial Cognition* (pp. 173–190). Washington, DC: American Psychological Association.

Meneghetti, C., De Beni, R., Gyselinck, V., & Pazzaglia, F. (2013). The joint role of spatial ability and imagery strategy in sustaining the learning of spatial descriptions under spatial interference. *Learning and Individual Difference, 24*, 32–41. Doi: 10.1016/j.lindif.2012.12.021.

Meneghetti, C., Gyselinck, V., Pazzaglia, F., & De Beni, R. (2009). Individual differences in spatial text processing: high spatial ability can compensate for spatial working memory interference. *Learning and Individual Differences, 19*, 577–589. Doi:10.1016/j.lindif.2009.07.007.

Meneghetti, C., Labate, E., Ronconi, L., Grassano, M., & Pazzaglia, F. (2014). The role of visuospatial and verbal abilities, styles and strategies in predicting visuospatial description accuracy. *Learning and Individual Differences, 36*, 117–123. Doi: 10.1016/j.lindif.2014.10.019.

Meneghetti, C., Pazzaglia, F., & De Beni, R. (2011). Spatial mental representations derived from survey and route descriptions: When individuals prefer extrinsic frame of reference. *Learning and Individual Differences, 21*, 150–157. Doi:10.1016/j.lindif.2010.12.003.

Meneghetti, C., Ronconi, L., Pazzaglia, F., & De Beni, R. (2014). Spatial mental representations derived from spatial descriptions: the predicting and mediating roles of spatial preferences, strategies, and abilities. *British Journal of Psychology, 105*, 295–315. Doi: 10.1111/bjop.12038.

Meneghetti, C., Zancada-Menéndez, C., Lopez, L., Sampedro-Piquero, P., Martinelli, M., Ronconi, L., & Rossi, B. (2016). Navigation and individual differences: The role of visuospatial abilities and working memory. *Learning and Individual Differences, 49*, 314–322. Doi: 10.1016/j.lindif.2016.07.002.

Mitolo, M., Gardini, S., Caffarra, P., Ronconi, L., Venneri, A., & Pazzaglia, F. (2015). Relationship between spatial ability, visuospatial working memory and self-assessed spatial orientation ability: a study in older adults, *Cognitive Processing, 16*, 165–176. Doi: 10.1007/s10339-015-0647-3.

Pazzaglia, F., Cornoldi, C., & De Beni, R. (2000). Differenze individuali nella rappresentazione dello spazio: presentazione di un questionario autovalutativo [Individual differences in spatial representation and in orientation ability: Presentation of a self-report questionnaire]. *Giornale Italiano di Psicologia, 3*, 627–650. Doi: 10.1421/310.

Pazzaglia, F. & De Beni, R. (2001). Strategies of processing spatial information in survey and landmark-centred individuals. *European Journal of Cognitive Psychology, 13*, 493–508. Doi:10. 1080/09541440042000124.

Pazzaglia, F. & De Beni, R. (2006). Are people with high and low mental rotation abilities differently susceptible to the alignment effect? *Perception, 35*, 369–383. Doi:10.1068/p5465.

Pazzaglia, F., Gyselinck, V., Cornoldi, C., & De Beni, R. (2012). Individual differences in spatial text processing. In V. Gyselinck & F. Pazzaglia (Eds.), *From Mental Imagery to Spatial Cognition and Language. Essays in honor of Michel Denis* (pp. 127–161). Hove, UK: Psychology Press.

Pazzaglia, F. & Meneghetti, C. (2012). Spatial text processing in relation to spatial abilities and spatial styles. *Journal of Cognitive Psychology, 24*, 972–980. Doi: 10.1080/20445911.2012.725716.

Pazzaglia, F. & Moè, A. (2013). Cognitive styles and mental rotation ability in map learning. *Cognitive Processing, 14*, 391–399. Doi: 10.1007/s10339-013-0572-2.

Pazzaglia, F. & Taylor, H. A. (2007). Perspective, instruction, and cognitive style in spatial representation of a virtual environment. *Spatial Cognition & Computation: An Interdisciplinary Journal*, 7, 349–364. Doi:10.1080/13875860701663223.

Ploran, E. J., Rovira, E., Thompson, J. C., & Parasuraman, R. (2015). Underlying spatial skills to support navigation through large, unconstrained environments. *Applied Cognitive Psychology, 29*, 608–613. Doi: 10.1002/acp.3135.

Prestopnik, J. L. & Roskos-Ewoldsen, B. (2000). The relations among wayfinding strategy use, sense of direction, sex, familiarity, and wayfinding ability. *Journal of Environmental Psychology, 20*, 177–191. Doi:10.1006/jevp.1999.0160.

Sholl, M. J. (1988). The relationship between sense of direction and mental geographic updating. *Intelligence, 12*, 299–314. Doi: 10.1016/0160-2896(88)90028-1.

Sholl, M. J., Kenny, R. J., & Della Porta, K. A. (2006). Allocentric-heading recall and its relation to self-reported sense-of-direction. *Journal of Experimental Psychology: Learning, Memory, and Cognition, 32*, 516–533. Doi: 10.1037/0278-7393.32.3.516.

Taylor, H. A. & Tversky, B. (1992). Spatial mental models derived from survey and route descriptions. *Journal of Memory and Language, 31*, 261–292. Doi: 10.1016/0749-596X(92)90014-O.

Thorndyke, P.W. & Hayes-Roth, B. (1982). Differences in spatial knowledge acquired from maps and navigation. *Cognitive Psychology, 14*, 560–589. Doi: OOlO-0285/8UO40560-30$05.00.

Tolman, E. C. (1948). Cognitive maps in rats and men. *Psychological Review, 55*, 189–208. Doi:10.1037/h0061626.

Tversky, B. (1991). Spatial mental models. In G. H. Bower (Ed.), *The Psychology of Learning and Motivation: Advances in Research and Theory, Vol. 27* (pp. 109–145). San Diego: Academic Press.

Tversky, B. (1993). Cognitive maps, cognitive collages, and spatial mental models. In A. U. Frank and I. Campari (Eds.), *Spatial Information Theory: A Theoretical Basis for GIS* (pp. 14–24). Berlin: Springer-Verlag.

Vandenberg, S. G. & Kuse, A. R. (1978). Mental rotations. A group test of three-dimensional spatial visualization. *Perceptual and Motor Skills, 47*, 599–604. Doi: 10.2466/pms.1978.47.2.599.

Wen, W., Ishikawa, T., & Sato, T. (2011). Working memory in spatial knowledge acquisition: Differences in encoding processes and sense of direction. *Applied Cognitive Psychology, 25*, 654-662. Doi: 10.1002/acp.1737.

Wen, W., Ishikawa, T., & Sato, T. (2013). Individual differences in the encoding processes of egocentric and allocentric survey knowledge. *Cognitive Science*, *37*, 176–192. Doi: 10.1111/cogs.12005.

Wolbers, T. & Hegarty, M. (2010). What determines our navigational abilities? *Trends in Cognitive Sciences*, *14*, 138–146. Doi: 10.1016/j.tics.2010.01.001.

Interaction of Mind and World

10

RETELLING EXPERIENCES AND WRITING ESSAYS

How Storytelling Reflects and Changes Memory

Elizabeth J. Marsh and Kathleen M. Arnold

Linking the Laboratory and Everyday Cognition

Barbara Tversky was the first person I (EJM) ever heard use the phrase "cognition in the wild" (Hutchins, 1995). She was not, I quickly learned, referring to animal cognition, but rather to cognition as used in everyday life – navigating real environments, understanding diagrams in articles and newspapers, designing computer graphics, and recognizing caricatures, among many other uses. As a first-year graduate student, I resonated to the real-world implications of this type of work. I frequently traveled to the East Bay to visit my sister at UC Berkeley, and often found myself thinking of her demonstration that many people incorrectly represent Berkeley as being to the east of Stanford (Tversky, 1981). Figure 10.1 shows an adaptation of a Google map of the area, as contrasted to a sketch drawn by my sister (from memory) for this chapter – the tendency to align the bay along a vertical axis is strong, even in the representation of someone who has lived in California for more than 20 years. This example is just one of many that can be found in Barbara's work showing the importance of situating cognition in context and studying complex behaviors. It is a theme that I (EJM) have carried through my own work, from my graduate collaborations with Barbara on retellings to our (EJM and KMA) more recent work on cognition and education.

A focus on cognition in the wild does not mean that research cannot be done in the laboratory; much can and has been learned there. If done thoughtfully, laboratory tasks can capture or mimic complex behaviors, such as when Barbara required subjects to assemble a real TV cart in the laboratory (Heiser, Phan, Agrawala, Tversky, & Hanrahan, 2004). Laboratory studies can also be paired with studies "in the wild", to ensure that the simplified environment of the laboratory does not make the researcher miss an important component of a behavior (Rubin, 1989). The researcher tethered to the laboratory, for example, would miss the

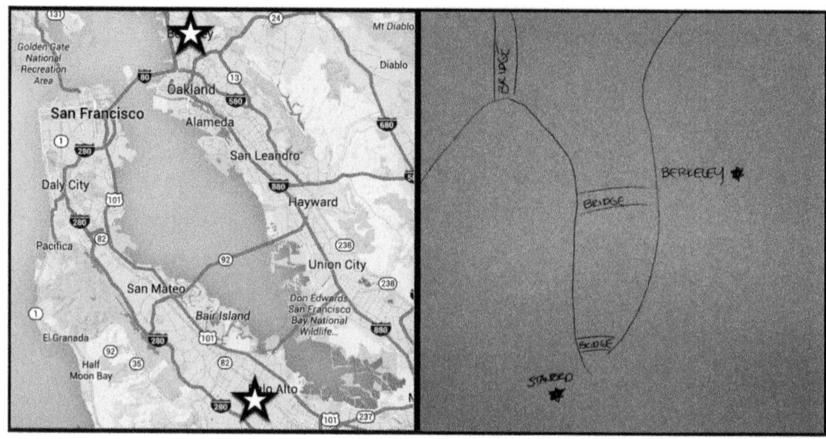

FIGURE 10.1 Left: An accurate map showing Berkeley to the west of Stanford, with the two indicated by stars (map data ©2016 Google). Right: A drawing by a California resident showing the common mistake of locating Berkeley to the east of Stanford

difference between navigation via exploration and navigation via maps (Tversky, 2000). Similarly, while much has been learned about memory based on "cognition in captivity" (verbatim memory for words, by oneself, in a windowless laboratory), this approach must be informed by how memory is used in the world. In real life, few people are worried about their ability to remember random lists of words; they are plagued by names or speeches or remembering other more complex memories. They rely on their smartphones to help them with their memory lapses. Accuracy goals are not the norm, as illustrated in political speeches and the "tall tales" party-goers tell. All of these examples can be studied in the laboratory, just not in the verbal learning tradition. From Barbara, I (EJM) learned the importance of balancing the need for experimental control with relevance to the world.

This chapter also captures a related theme, similarly espoused by Barbara: namely that remembering does not exist solely within the mind. Memory can be translated into an external representation that can be shared with others, and that representation can in turn change what is stored in memory. For purposes of clarity, it should be noted that such external representations of memory are not the same as external memory aids (which are memory supports such as one's smartphone, planner, or Post-it notes). Here, the focus is on external representations as extensions of what is stored in the mind, rather than as crutches for the retrieval of what is stored in the mind. The need for such external representations becomes clear when the many different functions of memory are considered. That is, thinking about how memory is used in everyday situations makes clear that memory can be more than an internal cognitive process in an individual. Barbara wrote eloquently about how "*graphics* externalize internal knowledge" (p. 248, Tversky,

Morrison, & Bétrancourt, 2002) – that is, a sketch, a diagram, and a bar graph are all ways to share one's ideas with the world. More generally, memory plays a social function – which almost by definition includes putting one's memories out there in the world. That is, people talk, email, and Instagram their lives to entertain and to forge connections (Bluck, 2003; Hyman & Faries, 1992; Neisser, 1998). The importance of doing so is highlighted in cases where individuals lose their ability to share memories in conversation, leading to anxiety and social withdrawal (Meltzer, 1983).

This chapter describes work on retellings and essay writing, with a focus on how memory is used and externalized in the real world. These two examples are quite different from each other on the surface but they are related conceptually. Our first example involves the social function of memory, as alluded to previously: people talking about their personal memories in conversation, writing about them in emails, and otherwise recapitulating their lives for others (e.g., Instagram, Facebook albums, etc.). Our second example comes from education, and our argument is that essays written for educational purposes will sometimes be similar to retellings of personal memories. That is, under certain conditions, both can involve selective uses of memory and going beyond what is stored in memory. Good essays should tell good stories, just like interesting anecdotes are stories and not simple recitations of what happened. Our goal in this chapter is to examine how memory is used in these two situations and to understand the downstream consequences of such externalizations.

Memory Reflections: A Note on Accuracy

Much memory research is focused on the accuracy of memories and the ways in which memories become distorted. This focus is important, as errors of memory provide a window into how the normal system functions (Roediger, 1996), and there are many situations (e.g., eyewitness testimony) where accuracy has tremendous ramifications. However, errors (whether of omission or commission) do not always carry the same meaning in the real world as they do in the psychologist's laboratory.

Accuracy in the laboratory often means verbatim recall and remembering the exact words or photos presented (and no more). In this context, it is an error to remember "sleep" after hearing "bed, tired, awake, nap, pillow . . ." (Roediger & McDermott, 1995), as that exact word was not in fact presented. In life, however, the memory researcher's error is often an adaptive inference, such as when one remembers "The ants in the kitchen ate the sweet jelly which was on the table" after reading "The ants ate the sweet jelly which was on the table" and "The ants in the kitchen ate the jelly which was on the table" (Bransford & Franks, 1971). These ideas are reflected in Neisser's (1981) case study of John Dean, the so-called Human Tape Recorder who amazed others with his retellings of White House conversations. Dean was often wrong about particular conversations and details while being accurate about the gist of the events. In other words, "being 'right' is not a simple notion" (Neisser, 1981).

Neisser's notion of accuracy translates well to retellings, in that people often consider their retellings of memories to be accurate so long as they match the gist of past events. Barbara and I (EJM) found evidence for this claim in a diary study in which Stanford undergraduates tracked instances of communicating their memories with others; they filed a reporting form (see Figure 10.2) for each instance of retelling for a one-month period (Marsh & Tversky, 2004). Over 1,000 accounts were collected; undergraduates reported talking about roommate difficulties, romantic encounters, academic work and classes, and extracurricular activities, among many other things. Most interestingly for present purposes, students reported that over a third of their retellings were selective, consistent with Gricean conversational norms not to tell a listener more than is needed to understand (Grice, 1989). For example, a student retelling a story about meeting Chelsea Clinton commented that "I didn't say just how oddly nervous it made me"; a student talking about a disappointing score on a midterm "neglected to say how much time I spent studying for the exam"; a first-year student telling a relative about a dorm scavenger hunt "avoided telling her that we visited a porn shop as part of the scavenger hunt." Conversational norms do not require complete and accurate retellings.

Neisser's notion of accuracy also translates well to education. While a student sometimes needs to remember things exactly as presented, at other times verbatim memory is not required or is just the beginning of the learning process. An educator wants students to make connections across ideas and apply their knowledge to new situations – in other words, to transfer one's knowledge and to create new knowledge. As such, essays rarely involve rote recall of what was read or taught, and in fact often explicitly require the writer to go beyond what is stored in memory, to make inferences and novel connections across ideas. For example, consider what happened in our laboratory experiment when students were asked to write about an astronomy text on detecting extraterrestrial life (Arnold, Umanath, Thio, Reilly, McDaniel, & Marsh, 2017). In one condition, writers were instructed to write a clear and thorough essay that would be understandable to a naive reader. In response, students rarely, if ever, included sections of the passage verbatim in their essays. Instead, they transformed the information to create a new product written in their own words. For example, the studied text included the following sentences:

> Even if favorable conditions and evolution of communicating civilizations were relatively common, one limitation is the length of time a civilization may be communicating. If a civilization is young or only exists for a short period of time, their chances of being present to even hear a message from another star is poor (adapted from Karttunen, Kröger, Oja, Poutanen, & Donner, 2006)

Retelling Recording Form

Date and time of retelling:

Date and time of original event:

General Topic: ____ Social ____ Academic ____ Job ____ Other

Description of original event:

Emotional valence of event: ____ positive ____ neutral ____ negative

Intensity of emotion: ____ very intense ____ somewhat intense ____ not at all

Give an adjective describing the emotional quality of the event:

Audience:		Purpose of Retelling:	
parent:	____	convey facts:	____
teacher:	____	entertain:	____
coach:	____	pride:	____
friend:	____	sympathy:	____
significant other:	____	avoid conflict:	____
acquaintance:	____	other:________________	
sibling:	____		
other ________________			

About how many times have you re-told this story?

Did you give a complete and accurate retelling? Yes____ No____

Did you exaggerate events? If yes, describe:

Did you minimize events? If yes, describe:

Were you selective? If yes, describe:

Did you add anything to the retelling? If yes, describe:

FIGURE 10.2 Form used by participants in Marsh & Tversky (2004) to record incidents of retelling

Students writing essays included the gist of this information, but went beyond the gist to make inferences and connect it to prior knowledge and other passage information:

> *Student A*: This is also, of course, assuming that the hypothetical form of life even has the ability to detect these signals. Had an extraterrestrial form of life sent a signal to our world during the time of the Roman Empire, we would never have even known it was happening.

> *Student B*: Radio waves require a type of receiver to translate the waves into sounds or a message. Without the receiver, the waves would be unintelligible. This means that the reviving [*sic*] alien race needs to have a similar intelligence as the intelligence on Earth. Too primitive a race, the aliens would not be able to receive the message. To [*sic*] intelligent a race, they may not have receivers available to pick up leaked radio waves because their technology has gotten so advanced in accurately sending radio waves as we have.

In contrast, writers in another condition were simply asked to recall as much of the original text as possible (as in standard laboratory recall tasks), and they tended to write things such as the following:

> *Student C*: Most civilizations might be too young or live for such a short period of time that our radio messages might not reach them.

> *Student D*: A young or short-lived civilization would not be able to receive our messages.

> *Student E*: One problem may be that the "civilizations" of life are too young or have spanned too short a time for them to have developed the tools to read and understand our signals.

Neither the recall protocols nor the essays meet the criterion of verbatim memory – but neither are they erroneous. Rather, these are not situations where verbatim memory would be valued (and in fact might even be looked down upon, as it would suggest plagiarism in the essay condition). The essays stray further from the original text, but it is likely that most people would agree that the essay examples show a more advanced understanding of the content, given their connections to other information.

For present purposes, the point is that sometimes verbatim memory is valued (reflecting excellent memory) whereas other times it reveals a lack of awareness of social norms or an inability to go beyond what is given. That is, omissions and inferences can show an awareness of one's audience or an ability to reason beyond what was studied. Of course, they can also be wrong or misleading. That is, an omission is not "inaccurate" when a writer is streamlining her argument or a speaker is accounting for her listener's prior knowledge – but when describing damage to one's car the omission "I left out the part about the guy leaving me his number and insurance information" is misleading as it implies a hit-and-run accident. And of course both retellings and essays can contain errors of commission. Most obviously, students make mistakes because they misunderstand or misremember what they learned, although such errors are unlikely to be introduced intentionally (assuming the student is writing for evaluative or explanatory purposes). On the other hand, people deliberately take liberties when talking about their past experiences. In addition to omitting details, undergraduates recorded exaggerating and/or adding details to a sizeable number of their retellings in the diary study alluded to above – less clear is whether the speakers viewed these as errors or not. That is, when speakers admitted to distorting their retellings – by exaggerating, minimizing, etc. – only two-thirds of those retellings were judged to be "inaccurate." The remaining one-third were admittedly distorted but considered "accurate."

There are two cases that most people would view as inaccurate, regardless of social context: borrowed memories (instances of telling someone else's memory as if it were one's own; Brown et al., 2015) and plagiarized essays. Both happen. For example, more than 40% of a group of undergraduates surveyed at Duke University and Southern Methodist University admitted knowingly telling someone else's story as their own. They did so mostly to entertain (it is a better story to talk about your interaction with a celebrity than a friend of a friend's meeting). Beyond cases of unconscious plagiarism (which is easily elicited in the lab; R. Marsh & Bower, 1993), any educator knows that plagiarism is a problem, as do close observers of political speeches. In our own work, we (EJM and KMA) originally had a problem with plagiarism when we tried to run our studies online using Mechanical Turk (MTurk – Amazon's online platform for recruiting participants) – rather than writing actual essays, some people googled and pasted in an essay that related to our prompt! Less is known about the long-term consequences of such behaviors, a topic we turn to later in this chapter.

Memory Externalizations: Reflections of Goals

What kinds of retellings and essays should be considered "good", given that our traditional definition of accuracy does not always apply? Here we draw inspiration from Barbara's work identifying two principles of good graphics. The first is the *principle of congruity*: the "structure and content of the external representation should correspond to the desired structure and content of the internal representation" (p. 249, Tversky, Morrison, & Bétrancourt, 2002). For example, a line graph should be used to depict your data if you want viewers to take away the impression of a trend over time. In contrast, if you want viewers to make direct comparisons between data points, a bar graph should be used (Zacks & Tversky,

1999). These recommendations are based on the ways people naturally talk about line graphs and bar graphs, to take advantage of the representation these naturally afford. The second is the *principle of apprehension*: "structure and content of the external representation should be readily and accurately perceived and comprehended" (pp. 255–256, Tversky, Morrison, & Bétrancourt, 2002). Oftentimes this principle can be simplified to "less is more." For example, a PowerPoint slideshow packed with animations and flashing objects may overwhelm the viewer, obscuring the intended message. The interpretation of a bar graph with two-dimensional bars may be more accurate than if the bars were three-dimensional (Zacks, Levy, Tversky, & Schiano, 1998). This principle also works for a phenomenon in the educational psychology literature known as the "lure of the seductive detail" (Garner, Gillingham, & White, 1989); a student may be distracted by the pictures accompanying a text or by the jokes the instructor tells during lecture.

Translating these principles to essays and retellings simply means that one's retelling and one's essay should convey what one wants one's audience to take away – in Gricean terms, tell what is needed and no more. We already noted that retellings and essays are rarely verbatim reproductions of everything that happened or was learned. Furthermore, the specific goal may affect *how much* is included. Instructions to be accurate, for example, lead to more content in retelling than do instructions to entertain (Dudukovic, Marsh, & Tversky, 2004).

What we have not discussed, however, is which things are included versus excluded and what is changed when a memory is externalized. The answer to this question will depend in part on the teller's goals when using their memories. As part of my (EJM's) first-year project at Stanford, Barbara and I simulated different goals for retelling after undergraduates read a story about two roommates who did annoying and fun things. The story addressed the participant as "you" and described a series of typical college events, such as going to a party; during each event, each roommate did a mix of fun things (e.g., mixed great drinks) and irritating things (e.g., spilled wine on the carpet). Only after reading did students learn the perspective they would take during retelling. Some students wrote a letter to the Housing Authority requesting a change of roommate, whereas others wrote a letter of recommendation to a fraternity/sorority recommending a roommate for admission to that club. As expected, letters to the Housing Authority made more references to problems like unwashed dishes and loud humming, whereas letters to the social club referred to activities such as playing volleyball and rollerblading. In both conditions, the letters included judgments about the roommate, elaborations that were rare in a verbatim recall control condition (to be clear, the original story consisted mostly of a series of actions, without passing judgments on those actions). The retelling elaborations matched the perspective the teller was taking; letters to the Housing Authority contained complaints such as "David is a slob" whereas letters to the social club contained praises such as "Rachel is bubbly." (Tversky & Marsh, 2000). Two examples are shown below:

> *Social Club*: I have only known David for a week, but my experiences with him have been fabulous. He is definitely one of the most sociable persons I have met, an impression that I didn't expect from a history major. I would attribute his fun-loving attitude to the fact that he's from LA. David knows how to mix drinks at parties amazingly well, and his ability to make new friends very quickly was shown when he told me about his experiences in Spain . . .

> *Housing Authority*: Mike, my roommate, hopefully ex-roommate, has managed to create a hatred for himself in only one week. He is the most inconsiderate man that I have ever met. He has no clue about other's rights, privacy, and space. For example: he hogged the bathroom for 1 hour my first morning! Then he proceeded to leave all his dirty dishes out . . .

These responses were very different from what subjects wrote in a neutral "recall all" condition, where people rarely went beyond the original text to make judgments about the characters. One example is included below:

> one of the main character's new roommates / engineering major from the Midwest / went to Spain, keeps in touch with friends there / spills wine on rugs / ate cake / played volleyball . . .

Returning to the principles guiding successful externalizations of memory, by selectively including certain details and not others the letters made clear a target message about a character (conveying the desired internal representation). In contrast, the control responses, in which people were not trying to create a particular externalization, did not take a perspective on the characters and included both positive and negative details.

Speakers and writers may also change *how* information is told, depending upon their goal. Even if retellings and writings do not differ in the number of events referenced, or which events are mentioned, they may still differ in the way the same events are described.

For example, consider a study where participants read a story about a series of events in a bar; the story was told from the perspective of the bartender and referred to events such as "by ten o'clock, I had thrown two kids with fake IDs out of the place." Participants were video-recorded telling the story three times, over a series of days; they were instructed to recall accurately *or* to entertain their audience. Even when the two conditions referenced the same events, they did so quite differently, as illustrated in the examples below:

> *Accurate condition*: Um . . . before ten tonight I had already kicked out two kids who had fake IDs . . .

> *Entertaining Condition:* And I had already . . . thrown these two kids with fake IDs out cause their fake IDs were just so bad, I mean, they must had made them themselves or something.

Judges blind to the study's hypotheses judged whether each of 105 story events were included in the final retellings, and if so rated each for accuracy (as compared to the original story) and exaggeration. As illustrated in the example above, events were rated as more accurately described in the Accurate Control condition and more exaggerated in the Entertaining condition. Furthermore, entertainers used a "language of storytelling", telling their stories with more certainty and fewer disfluencies like "um" and "uh" (Dudukovic et al., 2004). Entertaining stories contained more affect words and were written in present tense.

There is similar variation when students write about science or history; assignments can take many forms (summaries, stories, essays, etc.) and students write differently depending on the nature of their assignment. For example, essays that make an argument or take a point of view deviate more from the source material than do other kinds of writing. Students in one study read materials related to the Irish Potato Famine (e.g., The Act of Union) and were then instructed to act like historians and "develop an argument (or narrative, summary, or explanation) about what produced the significant changes in Ireland's population between 1846 and 1850" (p. 303, Wiley & Voss, 1999). Each sentence was coded for whether it was "transformative," which was defined as combining information from the original source(s) with new information or making novel connections between studied materials. Argumentative essays contained a higher proportion of transformative sentences than did summaries, narratives, or explanations. In addition, argumentative essays also used more connectors (due to, because of, then, etc.) and causal language. This effect was especially pronounced when students gathered information from multiple sources rather than relying on a single source; students who wrote arguments integrated information from the multiple sources better than those in the other conditions.

In our own work, we observed differences between essays explaining how to detect life in outer space and attempts to recall the original passage. Students wrote more words when writing an essay than when recalling the same passage (311 vs. 219 words; Arnold et al., 2017). However, essays were no more likely than free-recall responses to include "content words" from the original passage (defined as nouns, verbs, and adjectives; a rough measure of content, as measured by the word-counting software Linguistic Inquiry and Word Count (LIWC); Pennebaker, Booth, & Francis, 2007). Subjects in both conditions included a similar, and rather minimal, subset (about 20%) of the passage words. Clearly subjects in both conditions were judicious in choosing which passage content to include – but writing an essay required more words to allow for transitions, elaborations, and connections between ideas.

In an in-progress study, essays written to explain rather than to persuade differed in *how* information was described, not what information was included. For example, a student explaining the role of radio signals in detecting extraterrestrial life listed three relevant facts in a relatively unconnected manner:

> A way to combat these limitations is through listening and sending radio signals. Another life form may be able to pick up these signals, called leakage radiation, and communicate back to Earth. Signals are also sent out through cables and optical fibers.

In contrast, writers in the persuasion condition advocated for research funding, taking on the role of a scientist and arguing that detecting intelligent extraterrestrial life is possible, as illustrated below:

> By sending out radio transmissions, we can cause another civilization orbiting a nearby star to pick up small bits of our transmissions, called leakage transmissions, with a large radio telescope. However, this signal is very weak given that . . . recent technology has enabled us to send transmissions with reduced power due our increasingly sensitive radio receivers. This lessens the signals that leak into space and thus decreases our chance of being detected by a nearby civilization. Seeing that this phenomenon is caused by the growing prevalence of cables and optical fibers (which reduce leakage transmission), we must divert research into expanding the use of radio transmissions – possibly even purposely sending signals to potential receivers so that they may detect us faster.

Although both of these writers included the same facts, they structured those facts in different ways to achieve their different goals. Explanation essays were more similar to the original passage, which was not surprising since the textbook passage was itself an explanation of the strategies used to detect alien life. In persuasive essays, these facts were transformed into a new structure; ideas were connected in new ways to create a new argument not present in the source material.

Summary of Memory Reflections

Our examinations of retellings and essays make clear that people use memory flexibly, for different purposes, leading to very different external representations. In short, "accurate and complete recall" is just one of many different ways that an event may be remembered, and in real life it is a less frequent goal than in the lab. These differences raise the question: does it matter? Does taking liberties when talking or making arguments when writing matter beyond the moment when one is writing and speaking? Beyond the possible influence on others (as ideas propagate through people; see Coman & Hirst, 2012), we argue that these differences matter as they have the potential to change what the tellers remember and understand.

Memorial Consequences

Externalizing memory through retellings and essays can in turn change the internal representations of past events and knowledge. For autobiographical memories, these downstream consequences are a byproduct of using memories in social contexts. In education, these downstream consequences are often the goal of creating these external representations in the first place – that is, essays and other writing tasks are assigned to help students develop an understanding of the material. We briefly describe two examples of memorial consequences; additional memory effects will be discussed in the section where we argue for a particular mechanism of change.

Example 1: Differences in retelling lead to differences in later memories of events. In the study about roommates and their activities, memory for the story was biased by the perspective taken during the retelling period. For example, after complaining about a roommate, students remembered more of his/her annoying characteristics and also misattributed another character's annoying actions to him/her. In contrast, a student who promoted a character to a social organization remembered more activities consistent with that perspective than the annoying roommate perspective.

Example 2: Different external representations of science have different consequences for learning. For example, both note-taking and highlighting involve creating external representations; however, these externalizations involve copying or marking content and do not involve the same kind of transformation as the writing tasks we studied. We compared the memorial consequences of essay writing and free recall with these two less-transformative learning activities. Two days after completing their learning activity, students took a test on the science material, answering questions that required inferences and problem-solving such as:

> You have spent your whole career trying to prove that extraterrestrial intelligent life currently exists. Others do not believe, citing lack of communication from extraterrestrials. Describe the three reasons you use to explain why lack of communication is not sufficient evidence to prove that we are currently alone in the universe.

Essay and free recall-writers were able to answer more of these questions correctly; both notes and highlighted texts were more similar to the original text, and yet these external representations yielded less learning (see Figure 10.3).

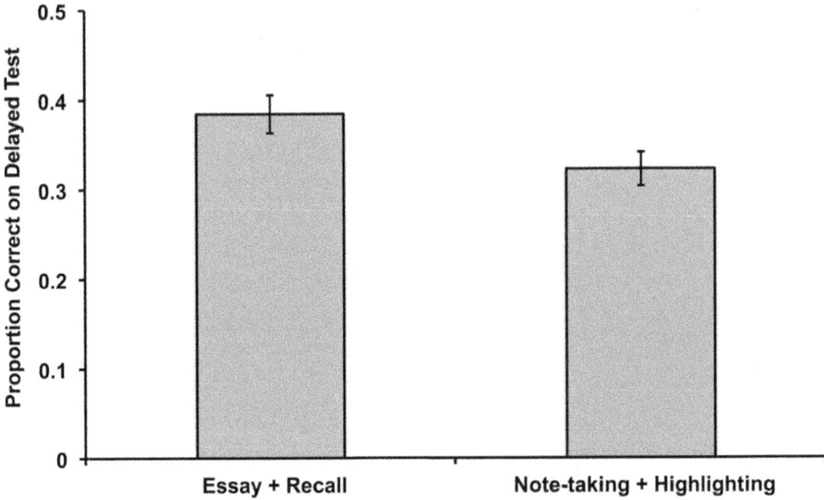

FIGURE 10.3 Proportion correct on a test two days after reading a passage about detecting extraterrestrial life and completing a relatively transformative writing task (writing an essay or recalling the passage) or a non-transformative task (note-taking or highlighting the passage). Error bars indicate standard errors of the mean. From Arnold et al. (2017)

Mechanisms of Change

Why do externalizations of memory have downstream consequences, changing the way events are later remembered or what is learned? One possibility is that externalizations may interfere with retrieval of the original memories, given that externalizations are rarely copies of what is stored in memory. More intriguingly, externalizations can involve creating a new structure for what is remembered, which can in turn guide later retrieval, for better or worse.

For example, externalizing a memory may involve the activation and application of a schema, and this structure in turn can guide later memory. Schemas are organized knowledge structures based on past experience; they can help to fill in the gaps and to make predictions. For example, most people have a schema about robberies; the perpetrator is often male and may be masked, weapons are often involved, threats may be made, things will be taken. While schemas are often activated at encoding, our point is that they can also be activated later, when one is thinking about an event or talking about it with others. For example, one may reinterpret seemingly innocuous actions after learning that one just walked through a holdup or forget details that do not fit with the schema (one reason why the Cognitive Interview includes recalling events backwards, to thwart reliance on a schema and thus potentially allow the retrieval of information that does not fit the schema; Fisher, Milne, & Bull, 2011).

Returning to the Roommate study described earlier, our Stanford undergraduates clearly knew what to put in their letters to the Housing Authority and to fraternities/sororities; they had *schemas* for this information. They used these schemas to select which information to include in their letters, resulting in a similar bias in downstream memory. Such a result is also consistent with a selective retrieval effect: participants retrieved a subset of original events, limited to those consistent with their goals, and it is not surprising that retrieving and externalizing such events might be at the expense of remembering events from the other perspective (as has been observed in numerous text processing studies; e.g., Pichert & Anderson, 1977). However, retelling condition also affected how participants later attributed actions – claiming that Dave cracked his gum, for example, when really Mike had done so. Critically, these misattributions were not included in the retellings, and thus suggest that the schema activated at retelling also guided later memory.

Different retellings and writings change memory, even if they do not involve differential rehearsal of events, so long as the structure of the externalization differs from that of the original memory. We do know, for example, that witnesses who accept a suggestion and then talk about it will later on be more likely to repeat that misinformation (e.g., Lane, Mather, Villa, & Morita, 2001). However, a retelling can change memory and lead to errors, even if no errors are rehearsed. In a study done at Stanford, I (EJM) and Barbara examined how people talked about a violent film clip and the consequences of these retellings for later memory (Marsh, Tversky, & Hutson, 2005). People who talked about their emotional reactions to the film later continued to include more thoughts and feelings on memory tests, even when instructed to recall as accurately as possible. More importantly for present purposes, people who talked about their emotional reactions tended to make more major errors when recalling (e.g., misattributing responsibility for a crime to the wrong perpetrator) than did people who talked about the facts. An emotional retelling may be at the expense of remembering perceptual information (e.g., Suengas & Johnson, 1988)[1].

We can make a similar argument for essays, revisiting the comparison between recalling and writing an essay, two forms of writing that involved similar rehearsal of the original text (and hence similar benefits for learning). A deeper examination of these responses revealed that the structure of the response, especially of the recall response, was highly predictive of later performance. When recalling, students varied in their response to the prompt to write down everything they could remember about the passage. Some subjects interpreted these instructions as requesting lists of facts:

- In 1960 there was an important SETI experiment.
- Most civilizations might be too young or live for such a short period of time that our radio messages might not reach them.
- Two important biological indicators of life are methane and ozone.

Others wrote in paragraph form, but used unconnected sentences with very little organization or transitions between ideas:

> Frank Drake did the first serious search for extra-terrestrial life scanning at 23 cm wavelengths at the stars CET and Eris. Ozone is produced from oxygen. Ozone and methane are two key indicators of life on a planet. Plants reflect IR radiation as well as green visible light. Microbial life is probably common, but intelligent life is probably very rare due to evolutionary obstacles . . .

However, other free-recall responses strongly resembled many of the essay responses in structure:

> There are several ways that we could trace and detect intelligent civilizations. Such detection involves both biological and astronomical approaches in explaining the indicators of life. With this knowledge, we have attempted to communicate with foreign civilizations through spectroscopic signals, emissions, and radio waves . . .

Our hypothesis was that structure mattered, rather than instruction. To get an objective measure of how "essay-like" a response was, we turned to crowdsourcing. Over 300 "workers" were recruited from Amazon's Mechanical Turk; each rated 10–20 essays and/or free-recall responses. They judged each response on a 5-point Likert scale, rating the writing from 1 "very list-like" (defined as unconnected sentences or phrases that read like a list of facts) to 5 "very cohesive" (defined as connected and well-organized sentences that read like an essay). The results of this crowdsourcing can be seen in Figure 10.4. As expected, essays were rated as

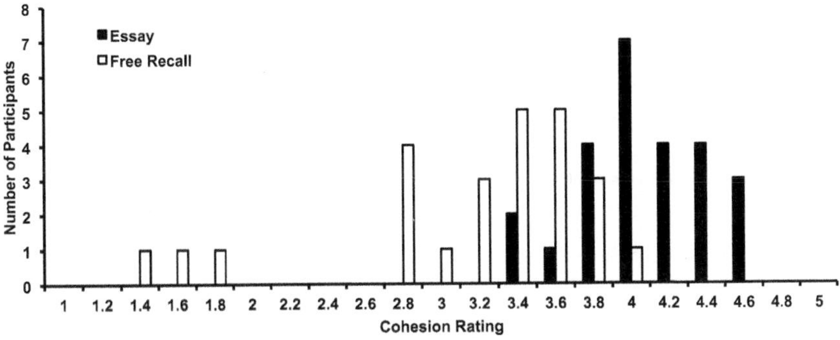

FIGURE 10.4 Histogram showing the average cohesion rating for each participant's essay or free recall responses. Cohesion ratings were made by MTurk workers, using a Likert scale from 1 ("very list-like") to 5 ("very cohesive"). From Arnold et al. (2017)

more "essay-like" than recall responses, but, more importantly, the large variation in how subjects chose to structure recall responses is clearly visible. Using this measure, we found that the more "essay-like" the recall response was rated, the better the subject did on the delayed problem-solving test. In other words, students learned more from their external representations when they engaged in more transformation, structuring the information into an essay.

The effect of structure on memorial consequences can also be seen when comparing different kinds of essays. As a reminder, persuasive essays were generally more transformative than explanatory essays, probably because the text was itself an explanation. The interesting preliminary finding is that writing a persuasive essay especially benefited low-ability students. People differ in their ability to build mental models, or structures, as they read, a skill vitally important for comprehension. We measured this individual difference using a scale called the Multi-Media Comprehension Battery (MMCB; Gernsbacher & Varner, 1988), and found that, in general, the better subjects were at structure building, the better they did on the later science test. The exception was that some low structure-builders who wrote persuasive essays did just as well on the later test as high structure-builders. This pattern was not found in the explanatory essays condition; there, high structure-builders always did better than low structure-builders. This exception suggests that the transformation that is involved in writing a persuasive essay helped low structure-builders to learn this information in a way that the more verbatim use of details in writing an explanatory essay did not. Of course this effect needs to be replicated, but it allows the hypothesis that creating an argument may be an effective way to help low structure-builders create an effective mental model.

Summary of Mechanisms of Change

Paralleling the text literature, an organization created when using memory for social or other purposes can affect what is later remembered. This organization can take the form of a schema, a way of telling ("language of storytelling"), or a better mental model of a scientific process. The ability to update and use memory flexibly is an adaptive one, allowing people to remember things in a way that is consistent with their goals.

Conclusions

It is exciting when memory is used to create something new, beyond reliving the past. Externalizing one's memory is one way of doing so; a diagram differs from the image in one's mind, a retelling selectively elaborates on one's past experiences, and an essay shapes memory to make an argument. These new creations in turn will affect (or at least interfere with) the stored internal representations. In many cases going beyond specific experiences is adaptive – one wants to extract general principles of science, understand the essence of an artist's style (Kornell & Bjork, 2008), and more generally extract the essence of concepts.

One exciting direction was raised by Barbara in the question period following the talk that this chapter is based upon. She asked whether a visual externalization might be more powerful than a verbal one, pointing to one of her student's work showing exactly that (Bobeck & Tversky, 2014). For example, drawing a picture of a bicycle pump was better for learning than writing an explanation of how the pump works. We believe it is likely that the nature of to-be-learned material may interact with whether a verbal or visual externalization is better; for example, some things are hard to put into words and thus a visual externalization may be better. We look forward to a lively discussion of this hypothesis with Barbara in the future.

Note

1 A digression to reminisce about a positive memory from graduate school: I (EJM) remember rushing to Barbara's office upon discovering this paper, and she was putting on her coat to leave – she saw my excitement, took off her coat, and sat down to discuss the paper with me even though it was quite late.

References

Arnold, K. M., Umanath, S., Thio, K., Reilly, W., McDaniel, M. A., & Marsh, E. J. (2017). Understanding the cognitive processes involved in writing to learn. *Journal of Experimental Psychology: Applied*. Advance online publication. DOI: 10.1037/xap0000119

Bluck, S. (2003). Autobiographical memory: Exploring its functions in everyday life, *Memory*, *11*, 113–123, DOI: 10.1080/741938206.

Bobeck, E. & Tversky, B. (2014). Creating visual explanations improves learning. *Proceedings of the 36th annual conference of the Cognitive Science Society*, 206–211.

Bransford, J. D. & Franks, J. J. (1971). The abstraction of linguistic ideas. *Cognitive Psychology*, *2*, 331–350.

Brown, A. S., Caderao, K. C., Fields, L. M., & Marsh, E. J. (2015). Borrowing personal memories. *Applied Cognitive Psychology*, *29*, 471–477.

Coman, A. & Hirst, W. (2012). Cognition through a social network: The propagation of induced forgetting and practice effects. *Journal of Experimental Psychology: General*, *141*, 321–336.

Dudukovic, N. M., Marsh, E. J., & Tversky, B. (2004). Telling a story or telling it straight: The effects of entertaining versus accurate retellings on memory. *Applied Cognitive Psychology*, *18*, 125–143. DOI: 10.1002/acp.953.

Fisher, R. P., Milne, R., & Bull, R. (2011). Interviewing cooperative witnesses. *Current Directions in Psychological Science*, *20*, 16–19.

Garner, R., Gillingham, M. G., & White, C. S. (1989). Effects of "seductive details" on macroprocessing and microprocessing in adults and children. *Cognition and Instruction*, *6*, 41–57.

Gernsbacher, M. A. & Varner, K. R. (1988). *The multi-media comprehension battery.* Eugene, OR: Institute of Cognitive and Decision Sciences.

Grice, H. P. (1989). Logic and conversation. In H. P. Grice (Ed.), *Studies in the ways of words* (pp. 41–58). Cambridge: Harvard University Press.

Heiser, J., Phan, D., Agrawala, M., Tversky, B., & Hanrahan, P. (2004). Identification and Validation of Cognitive Design Principles for Automated Generation of Assembly Instructions. *Proceedings of Advanced Visual Interfaces '04*, 311–319.

Hutchins, E. (1995). *Cognition in the wild*. Cambridge, MA: MIT Press.

Hyman, I. E. & Faries, J. M. (1992). The functions of autobiographical memory. In M. A. Conway, D. C. Rubin, H. Spinnler, & W. A. Wagenaar (Eds.), *Theoretical perspectives on autobiographical memory* (pp. 207–221). Netherlands: Kluwer Academic Press.

Karttunen, H., Kröger, P., Oja, H., Poutanen, M., & Donner, K. J. (2006). *Fundamental astronomy*. Berlin: Springer.

Kornell, N. & Bjork, R. A. (2008). Learning concepts and categories: Is spacing the "Enemy of Induction"? *Psychological Science, 19*, 585–592.

Lane, S. M., Mather, M., Villa, D., & Morita, S. K. (2001). How events are reviewed matters: Effects of varied focus on eyewitness suggestibility. *Memory & Cognition, 29*, 940–947.

Marsh, E. J. & Tversky, B. (2004). Spinning the stories of our lives. *Applied Cognitive Psychology, 18*, 491–503.

Marsh, E. J., Tversky, B., & Hutson, M. (2005). How eyewitnesses talk about events: Implications for memory. *Applied Cognitive Psychology, 19*, 531–544.

Marsh, R. L. & Bower, G. H. (1993). Eliciting cryptomnesia: Unconscious plagiarism in a puzzle task. *Journal of Experimental Psychology: Learning, Memory and Cognition, 19*, 673–688.

Meltzer, M. I. (1983). Poor memory: A case report. *Journal of Clinical Psychology, 39*, 3–10.

Neisser, U. (1981). John Dean's memory: A case study. *Cognition, 9*, 1–22.

Neisser, U. (1998). Stories, selves, and schemata: A review of ecological findings. In M. A. Conway, S. E. Gathercole, & C. Cornoldi (Eds.), *Theories of memory volume II* (pp. 171–186). East Sussex, UK: Psychology Press Ltd.

Pennebaker, J. W., Booth, R. J., & Francis, M. E. (2007). *LIWC2007: Linguistic inquiry and word count*. Austin, TX: LIWC.

Pichert, J. W. & Anderson, R. C. (1977). Taking different perspectives on a story. *Journal of Educational Psychology, 69*, 309–315.

Roediger, H. L. (1996). Memory illusions. *Journal of Memory and Language, 35*, 76–100.

Roediger, H. L. & McDermott, K. B. (1995). Creating false memories: Remembering words not presented in lists. *Journal of Experimental Psychology: Learning, Memory, and Cognition, 21*, 803–814.

Rubin, D. C. (1989). Issues of regularity and control: Confessions of a regularity freak. In L. W. Poon, D. C. Rubin, & B. A. Wilson (Eds.), *Everyday cognition in adulthood and late life* (pp. 84–103). New York, NY: Cambridge University Press.

Suengas, A. G. & Johnson, M. K. (1988). Qualitative effects of rehearsal on memories for perceived and imagined complex events. *Journal of Experimental Psychology: General, 117*, 377–389.

Tversky, B. (1981). Distortions in memory for maps. *Cognitive Psychology, 13*, 407–433.

Tversky, B. (2000). Some ways that maps and graphs communicate. In C. Freksa, W. Brauer, C. Habel, and K. F. Wender. (Eds.), *Spatial cognition II: Integrating abstract theories, empirical studies, formal methods, and practical applications* (pp. 72–79). New York, NY: Springer.

Tversky, B. & Marsh, E. J. (2000). Biased retellings of events yield biased memories. *Cognitive Psychology, 40*, 1–38.

Tversky, B., Morrison, J. B., & Bétrancourt, M. (2002). Animation: Can it facilitate? *International Journal of Human Computer Systems, 57*, 247–262.

Wiley, J. & Voss, J. F. (1999). Constructing arguments from multiple sources: Tasks that promote understanding and not just memory for text. *Journal of Educational Psychology, 91*, 301–311.

Zacks, J. & Tversky, B. (1999). Bars and lines: A study of graphic communication. *Memory & Cognition, 27,* 1073–1079.

Zacks, J., Levy, E., Tversky, B., & Schiano, D. J. (1998). Reading bar graphs: Effects of extraneous depth cues and graphical context. *Journal of Experimental Psychology: Applied, 4,* 119–138.

11

SPATIAL PROBLEM SOLVING AND COGNITION

Christian Freksa, Thomas Barkowsky, Frank Dylla, Zoe Falomir, Ana-Maria Olteţeanu, and Jasper van de Ven

Spatial Problems and Physical Space

A spatial problem is (1) a question about a given spatial configuration (of arbitrary physical entities) that needs to be answered (e.g. is there wine in the glass?) or (2) the challenge to construct a spatial configuration with certain properties from a given spatial configuration (e.g. add two matchsticks to the given configuration to obtain four squares) (Bertel, 2010). By spatial configurations we mean arrangements of entities in 1-, 2-, or 3-dimensional physical space, where physical space is commonsensically observable Euclidean space and motion, rather than relativistic space-time. Physical space is contrasted here to abstract space of arbitrary dimensionality. Physical space affords certain actions, like (1) rotation (circular motion of objects around a given location); (2) motion from one location to another; (3) deformation of objects; (4) separation of objects into parts; (5) aggregation of objects; and (6) combinations, i.e. rotation around a changing location.

A special feature of *commonsense physical space* (CPS) is that operations such as motion are severely constrained and comply with rigid rules we cannot change, whereas in abstract spaces we are free to make up arbitrary rules about which operations are possible and which are not. For example, in *abstract representations of space* (AbsRS) we could allow a 'jump' operation that moves an entity directly from one location to a remote location (as in some board games). In CPS this is not possible: objects always first move to neighboring locations and then to a neighbor of that location, etc., before they can reach a remote location[1]. This has implications on the trajectories (including the time course) of motion.

As a second example, in abstract space we could come up with an operation that allows an entity to be in two places at the same time. In CPS this is not possible because of the nature of physical space and matter. This has implications on unique identity, presence in a space, containment within it and access to it. In abstract space, the types of operations possible are defined by the agent conceiving the abstract space, while in CPS they depend on the nature of physical space itself. The types of actions that can be performed in CPS define the characteristic structure of physical space (Freksa, 1997) that is exploited by Euclidean geometry and vice versa (Euclid, 300 BC/1956).

In this chapter, we discuss (1) how cognitive agents such as humans, other animals, or robots can use concrete CPS and AbsRS for solving spatial problems and (2) what are the relative merits of both approaches. We describe how the approaches can be combined. We look at the roles of spatial configurations and of cognitive agents in the process of spatial problem solving from a cognitive architecture perspective. In particular, we discuss (a) the role of the structures of space and time; (b) the role of conceptualizations and representations of these structures; and (c) the role of knowledge about these structures.

The chapter is organized as follows. In this section, we describe how and why geographic maps help us solve spatial problems in the real world; then point out cognitive difficulties of communicating about space and spatial representations; and offer a wayfinding example that illustrates how various levels of abstraction can be involved in spatial problem solving and reasoning. A fresh look at spatial problem solving is taken in the second section, where we describe components of problem solving; put the components together; and discuss the difference between *solving* spatial problems and *understanding* problem solving processes. On the basis of this discussion, the third section proposes mild abstraction as a third way between direct spatial and indirect formal problem solving, discusses how much abstraction is useful; illustrates how mild abstraction is performed in geographic maps; moves the discussion of mild abstraction from geographic space to other spatial domains; and discusses strategic aspects of applying this approach to spatial problem solving. The final section concludes with a discussion of three levels of cognitive processing in spatial problem solving and implications for cognitive approaches to spatial problem solving.

Physical Representation of Space: Geographic Maps

Maps distort the space in which we want to navigate. Most notably, maps shrink the space to such an extent that it is not possible to walk or drive in map space. Or stated differently: although maps represent space physically by means of a concrete spatial medium[2], they abstract from certain aspects of the spaces they represent. Specifically, they systematically substitute distances by smaller distances in such a way that certain other aspects of space (e.g. connectivity, orientation, angles, relative distances, or relative areas) are preserved.

Thus, spatial relations in environmental space are projected into similar spatial relations in map space. Due to the specific analogical way of representing spatial relations by identical or projections of spatial relations (Sloman, 1971; Robinson et al., 1995) we perceive these spatial relations in the map as if we would perceive them in the environment under more favorable perception conditions (more suitable perspective, scale adapted to our field of view, no obstructions) (MacEachren, 1995). As far as spatial relations are concerned, it is as if we would look at the spatial environment with a de-magnifying lens or from a large distance above the ground. If we have the map at our current location, we can do this without the effort of moving about the environment.

The map offers a bird's-eye view of an ample set of spatial relations that we could rarely observe all at once in the environment, without the help of a high point, like the peak of a mountain or a hot air balloon. Allowing us to perceive many more spatial relations at once, rather than keep in mind some objects while we move around and discover others, and then establish the relation, the map thus acts as an extended memory with visual access, and supports a form of external cognition (Scaife & Rogers, 1996; Tversky & Lee, 1999; Card et al., 1999). The operations we can perform on the map are basically the same as the ones we can perform in the environment (e.g. triangulation, measuring distances, path following); however, we must be aware of distortions if we project from a sphere to the flat surface of a map (Monmonier, 1996). As geographic maps *preserve essential spatial relations* implicitly *as spatial relations* and do not abstract them away, we consider map representations as *mild abstractions* of the spatial environment they represent.

Barbara Tversky early on pointed out that *cognitive* maps are spatially distorted with respect to the represented space (Tversky, 1981, 1992, 1993; Mark et al., 1999); this insight inspired the spatial cognition community including the present authors to investigate potential advantages of spatial distortions. For example, why is it easier to navigate with distorted subway maps than with veridical maps even though it should be more difficult to match those maps to the environment (Berendt et al., 1998)? Once we recognize that (physical or cognitive) spatial distortions actually may simplify spatial problem solving, we open up a whole new domain for studying spatial problem solving.

On the Difficulty of Communicating About Space and Spatial Representations

A cognitive issue that causes problems when discussing spatial representations and spatial cognition is the following: in human language we often do not distinguish between entities in the real world and their physical or mental representation. For example, we point with a finger to a location on a map and explain to another person, *now we are here*; we intend to express that we are located at the place in the environment that is represented by the corresponding location on the map that we are pointing at.

An interesting aspect that contributes to the confusion between the environment and its representation is that, really, we do not care so much about where we are *on the map*; we are in fact interested to know where we are in the environment. The answer to the latter, however, would be trivial and not useful: we are *right here* where we are standing; this answer even is highly context-adaptive, i.e. it is valid wherever we are!

Interestingly, it is frequently easier to find out in a completely different space (map space) where we are, than in the environmental space itself. The reason is that, on the map, our perception provides us with an overview of a multitude of known locations (pardon: representatives of known locations) (Tversky, 2000); in this way, we are able to relate the representation of our location to the representations of the locations of other entities, and thus perceive relations (in front, right, left, north, south, etc.) between these representations. These representations allow us to derive relations between the corresponding locations in the environment. It is through these relations that we are able to orient ourselves and understand our environment, in the same way in which a listener requires a few bars of music to pass before they can tell in which tonality they are 'located' – finding their 'place' through a web of musical relations.

Therefore, for orientation purposes, there is no necessity to distinguish between the environment and its map representation: the map serves as an aid to perceive the environment and may equally well be considered a part of our perception apparatus (a de-magnifying lens) as it can be viewed as a space that is conceptually outside the geographic environment.

When we discuss cognitive processes as scientists, we have a different situation than when we try to locate ourselves: as scientists, we need to carefully distinguish the spatial environment from its representation. But in practice, the problem domain and the representation domain are conflated even in scientific contexts as if they were identical. For example, in much of the artificial intelligence (AI) work, spatial problems are defined on the formal representation level, where – unlike in our map example – no relevant spatial relations are intrinsically given (Russell & Norvig, 1995). On the formal level, however, we are dealing with *descriptions of* spatial relations rather than with spatial relations. Formally trained people read these descriptions as if they were the spatial relations themselves, just as trained map-readers read maps as if they were the environments themselves.

Descriptions of spatial relations make some properties explicit which are implicitly present in physical spatial structures; they convert these properties into *knowledge about* the properties. For example, a distance between two cities is implicitly given through the distance between the cities' locations on the map; knowledge about this distance could be expressed explicitly for example by 'distance ($city_A$, $city_B$) = 40 km' or by specifying the cities' coordinates and computing the distance through an explicitly specified algorithm.

Symbol systems in AI (and formally trained people) use these descriptions to *reason about* spatial relations. This allows solving spatial problems indirectly, by arguing about what effects spatial relations and properties of spatial structures would have if we were to solve a real spatial problem. Some AI researchers seem to suggest that cognitive agents including humans and other animals must solve spatial problems by reasoning about them (Davis, 2013); but do toddlers or dogs reason about spatial relations when they open a door? How can cognitive agents solve spatial problems if they are lacking the explicit symbolic knowledge needed for reasoning? Explanations are rarely given.

A Wayfinding Example: Finding a Shortest Path Between Two Locations

To appreciate some of the issues involved in spatial problem solving and reasoning, let us consider approaches to determine a shortest path between two locations in a route network. We will first sketch how this problem could be solved directly in the spatial environment; we will then discuss different ways of solving this problem with the support of various kinds of representations.

Finding a Shortest Path in the Spatial Environment

To determine a shortest path in a route network, we must (1) be able to compare lengths of paths and determine which of two paths is shorter; and (2) take into account all possible paths between the start and the end points of the respective route network, to be sure we identified a shortest path.

Unless we can directly relate and perceive the extent of two paths, it is difficult to compare their lengths, as we lack sensors to compare path lengths; therefore we have to resort to some indirect way of comparing lengths: for example, we can identify the start point of a route with one end of a rope that we stretch out along the route; we can mark the rope at the end of the path (provided it is long enough); we then can move the marked rope section to another path and determine whether its length is less than, equal to, or greater than the marked segment of the rope. In doing so, we assume that the length of ropes is preserved when they are moved and we make use of the transitivity property of length: if the length of the rope section is the same as the first path, then comparing the second path to the rope yields the same result as comparing the second path to the first path would yield if we could do it. Note that we do not have to measure lengths quantitatively in order to compare them.

There are other methods for indirectly comparing lengths in spatial environments; popular ones include: counting the number of steps of constant length and comparing the step counts; moving along the paths at constant speed and comparing the traversal times (this can be done qualitatively by comparing contents of sand clocks or quantitatively by measuring times that then can be compared).

An additional challenge will be to make sure that we take into account all possible paths; this requires an ability to identify paths and to record whether they have been compared to another path, and if so, to which.

In summary, if we solve the shortest path problem directly in the spatial environment, we will require tools for comparing lengths and for keeping track of the problem-solving progress. These tools can be part of the spatial environment. A perceiving agent is required to assess differences (in lengths and path identity).

Solving the shortest path problem directly in the spatial environment is cumbersome. Largely this is due to the size of the environment and our lack of sensors that can cope with this size; therefore we scale down the size. As we are interested in the role the representation medium or the structure of the representation plays for the problem-solving process, we will first consider various media that we can use to solve navigation problems: a map or visual graph; an abstract graph; and a list.

Finding a Shortest Path in a Map

Let us suppose you are using a map like that in Figure 11.1 and you want to find a shortest path from the intersection of Normandie Ave. and W 35th Pl (symbol ⊗ on the map) to University of Southern California (symbol ⊙ on the map). In order to find a shortest path, one could naïvely apply the same methods as in the 'spatial environment', i.e. comparing all possible routes. One advantage of a map representation is the provision of overview knowledge. The straight connection between start position and destination provides a direct means to compare the currently considered path to a shortest possible connection, the linear distance. If there are several candidates whose length cannot be discriminated visually, one may have to compare them by some indirect means, e.g. by using a string in the same way as the rope in the 'spatial environment' example.

Task-irrelevant information, like buildings or parks, does not have to be represented. In the abstraction of the spatial environment that leads to the map, no task-relevant information is lost, except perhaps altitude information or some other spatial distortion, depending on the specific map projection employed. The resulting schematic map (Figure 11.2) is spatially equivalent to the map as long as spatial relations are preserved, i.e. the graph provides the same task-relevant spatial information.

We can go one step further to facilitate the task of finding a shortest path: we can construct the schematic map as a 'string map' from flexible non-elastic strings, that connect the nodes of the spatial graph and preserve the lengths of the edges. A shortest path then can be found by a simple physical action: we pull apart the nodes that correspond to the starting position and the target position until we obtain a straight connection between them; the strings on the taut connection represent a shortest path (Dreyfus & Haugeland, 1974; Freksa et al., 2016).

Finding a Shortest Path in an Abstract Graph Structure

The next representation we consider is an abstract graph. Spatial information is provided by means of vertices representing road junctions and edges representing road connections. Abstract graphs do not convey distance information of paths implicitly as maps do; therefore, we label edges explicitly with numerical

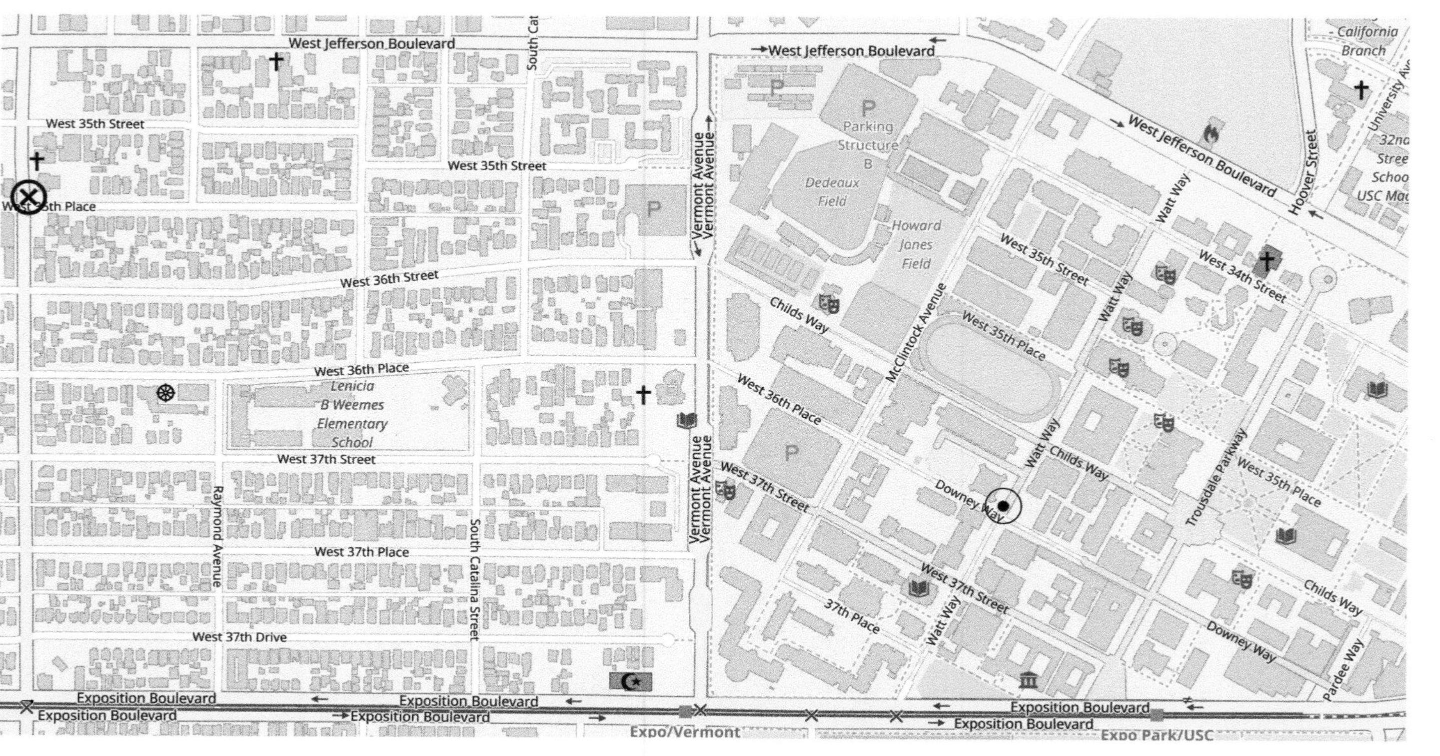

FIGURE 11.1 Section of a city map for solving a wayfinding problem with visual and haptic support [© OpenStreetMap contributors www.openstreetmap.org/copyright]

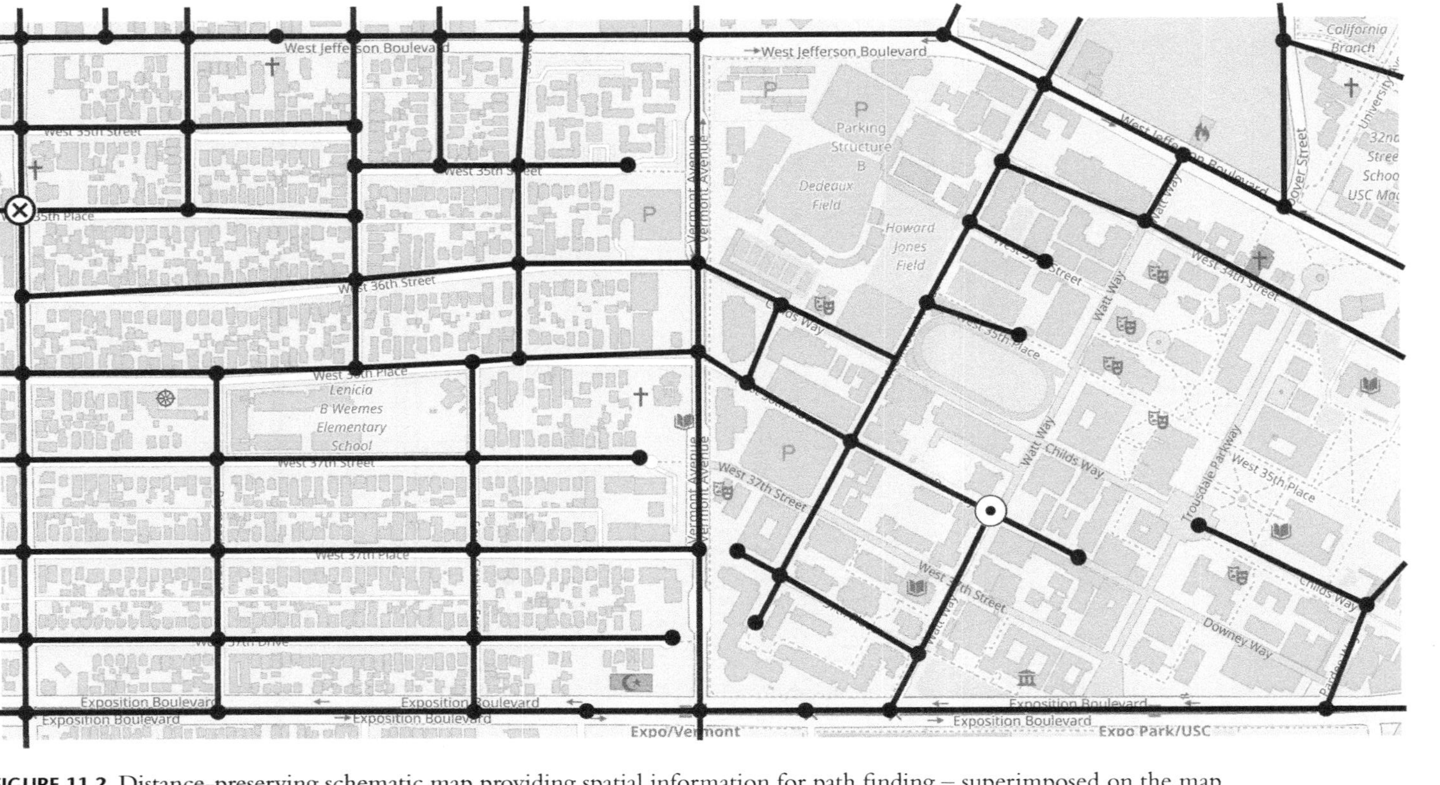

FIGURE 11.2 Distance-preserving schematic map providing spatial information for path finding – superimposed on the map

values that reflect the distance between junctions along the corresponding path. With the abstraction from a map, the connection between the spatial environment and the representation is lost. Although this connection is not relevant for solving the abstract shortest path problem, it will be required to apply the abstract solution to the real world. This can be achieved by explicitly annotating abstract graphs with coordinates or names of locations.

Our abstract graphs focus on road junctions and connections between them. Apart from that, space is not represented. Abstract graphs can be coded in various ways. A popular representation scheme for graphs is an adjacency matrix. In our case, the matrix will contain one column and one row for each vertex in the graph (Figure 11.3). The elements of the matrix indicate whether the pairs of vertices are adjacent or not in the graph. As we want to identify shortest paths, we will enter the length of the corresponding path segment in the matrix and leave the entries for non-adjacent vertex pairs empty. This will enable suitable computer algorithms to determine accumulated path lengths of chains of path segments. Note that – unlike in the map where each location in the environment is represented by a unique location – each vertex is represented twice in the adjacency matrix: once as a starting node (row) and once as an ending node (column) of a connection.

Figure 11.3 also uses a (2D) spatial medium for the representation; but the space of the medium no longer carries spatial information about the environment. The *spatiality of the medium*, however, still facilitates our perception of the connection

	...	McCAve_DowAWay	⊙ WatWay_DowWay	DEnd_DowWay	WatWay_W37Pl	...	NomAve_WJBlvd	NomAve_W35St	RayAve_W35St	⊗ NomAve_W35Pl	RayAve_W35Pl	NomAve_W36St	SBuAve_W35Pl	NomAve_W36Pl	SBuAve_W36St	...
...	...	...	...	...	...	...	...	...	...	...	...	...	...	...	...	...
McCAve_DowAWay	...	0	32													
⊙ WatWay_DowWay	...	32	0	12	27											
DEnd_DowWay	...		12	0												
WatWay_W37Pl	...		27		0											
...	...	...	...	...	...	...	...	...	...	...	...	...	...	...	...	
NomAve_WJBlvd	...						0	15								
NomAve_W35St	...						15	0	33	16						
RayAve_W35St	...							33	0		15					
⊗ NomAve_W35Pl	...							16		0	32	15				
RayAve_W35Pl	...								15	32	0		32			
NomAve_W36St	...									15		0		16	65	
SBuAve_W35Pl	...										32		0			
NomAve_W36Pl	...											16		0		
SBuAve_W36St	...											65			0	
...	...	...	...	...	...	...	...	...	...	...	...	...	...	...	...	...

FIGURE 11.3 Adjacency matrix representing a segment of the visual graph shown in Figure 11.2

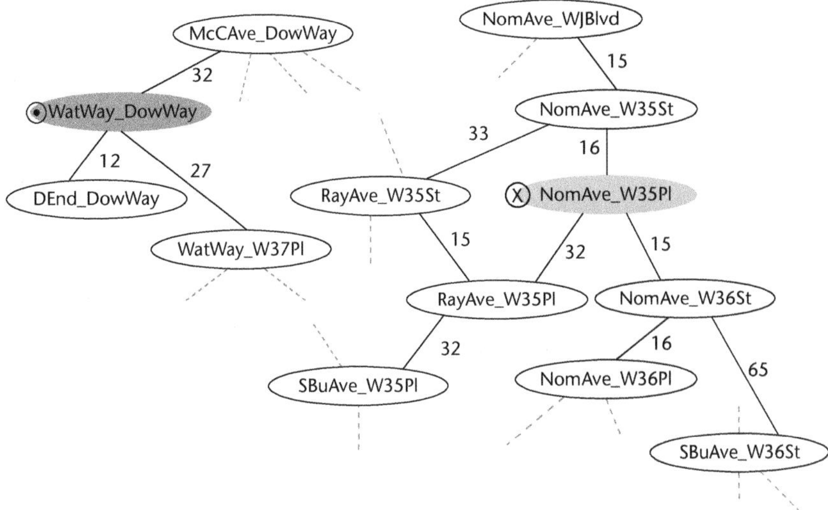

FIGURE 11.4 Visualization of the abstract graph represented in Figure 11.3. Vertices depict road junctions and edges depict road connections; the labels indicate lengths of route segments

relations between the vertices, as it provides an easy overview of these relations to our visual system at a glance. Computer algorithms usually do not make use of the *spatiality of representations*; they 'look up' one connection after another and construct abstract chains of the route segments and accumulate their length values to determine a shortest path.

Figure 11.4 visualizes the abstract graph represented in Figure 11.3 in a more human-friendly fashion. As the spatial medium no longer carries spatial information, this visualization is informationally equivalent to Figure 11.3.

The graph visualization in Figure 11.5 depicts the same road network as Figure 11.1. This depiction is just one possible visualization, which does not necessarily reflect spatial relations in the spatial environment. An arbitrary number of different visualizations can be generated from an abstract graph. This implies that the spatial methods to determine a shortest path, described above, are not applicable to this kind of representation. For comparing lengths, we can no longer compare routes visually; instead, we must interpret and compare numerical values. The overall path length is determined by the accumulation of the lengths of the individual segments. As a consequence, we must compare all possible paths, e.g. by means of an algorithm like the Dijkstra algorithm (Dijkstra, 1959).

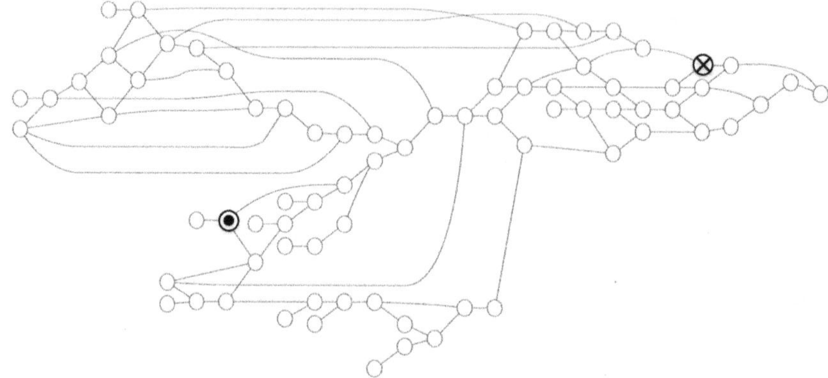

FIGURE 11.5 One possible visualization of the complete abstract graph representation of the road map shown in Figure 11.1 without vertex names and distance labels

Finding a Shortest Path in a List of Path Segments

Adjacency matrices (Figure 11.3) for route connections typically comprise a large fraction of empty entries, as vertices typically are directly connected only to some of the other vertices. As a consequence, we can compress the relevant information without losing task-relevant information by focusing on the edges between the vertices and explicitly representing only those relations between vertices that comprise a direct connection. To this end, the information about the edges can be represented by a list of triples that each contain two labels representing the vertices and an associated path length: (<start-of-path-segment>, <end-of-path-segment>,<length-of-path-segment>).

For example, we may have a list that contains the following triples (cf. Figure 11.3):

- (WatWay_DowWay, McCave_DowWay, 32)
- (DEnd_DowWay, WatWay_DowWay, 12)
- (NomAve_W35Pl, RayAve_W35Pl, 32)
- (RayAve_W35Pl, SBuAve_W35Pl, 32).

The list requires only as many entries as there are direct paths between vertices. Each vertex appears as many times in the list as it functions as a starting or end point of a connection. The order of the triples in the list is insignificant (i.e. the list is interpreted as a set; no information is conveyed by the sequence of its elements).

In this representation, the graph has been chopped into pieces; spatial integrity is lost. However, all the information required to reconstruct the graph correctly has been maintained; thus, the graph can be reconstructed computationally by linking triples that comprise identical vertex names. Consequently, shortest path-finding algorithms like the Dijkstra algorithm can be applied.

Summary

Table 11.1 summarizes the progressive transformation from spatially implicit information in environments and maps to symbolically explicit information about spatial paths in abstract graphs and lists of edges. The mild abstraction of spatial information in the environment into veridical or schematized maps maintains task-relevant essential spatial features and adds perceptual, haptic, and mental affordances for human use, by adapting to the visual and haptic field of humans and permitting the use of global path-finding heuristics.

The transformation from maps to abstract graphs switches from a space-based representation with implicitly maintained spatial relations to a feature-based representation with symbolically explicit representation of spatial features. In our examples, the abstract graph is represented by a junction-based adjacency matrix that makes limited use of structural landmark association by means of rows and columns to represent information implicitly. Most other task-relevant spatial features are made symbolically explicit.

The transformation from abstract graphs to a list of edges that represent direct path connections serves as compaction of the task-relevant information and no longer makes use of spatial/positional information (except within the triples that denote the edges). In the transformed representations, some information is implicitly assumed that permits to reconstruct spatial integrity to some extent. For example, we assume that identical location identifiers refer to a unique location (and in some systems we assume that distinct location identifiers refer to distinct locations); this permits us to reconstruct correctly connected graph structures from rather sparse information about edges.

The spatial integrity that collocates all features of a spatial location at that location in a spatial environment is progressively dissolved in the transitions to map, graph, and list respectively, such that all spatially implicit information in the environment that is represented will be made symbolically explicit at the final stage.

A Fresh Look at Spatial Problem Solving

Many spatial problems are solved every day *without representing* them as spatial problems in the mind or the computer. For example, my keys open locks mechanically without a representation of the lock's mechanism needing to exist in my mind; doors open by my leaning against them or 'magically' through sensor-controlled mechanisms that respond to my approaching the door. In these cases, physical affordances (Gibson, 1979) established in the interaction between the environment and the agent enable solutions to spatial problems without reasoning needing to be involved.

While this type of problem solving may be intellectually unsatisfactory for computer scientists, as cognitive scientists we must acknowledge that such an action and perception-based approach developmentally precedes reflective thinking and most likely is a prerequisite for building up mental representations of spatial problems and for spatial problem solving (Johnson, 2009; Needham, 2009; Keen, 2003). Initially,

TABLE 11.1 Progressive transformation from spatially implicit information in spatial environments and maps (left) to symbolically explicit information about paths in abstract graphs and lists (right)

	Environment	*Map*	*Abstract graph*	*List of edges*
Spatial abstraction	(none)	**Mild abstraction:**	**Transformation:**	**Compaction:**
		Space-based => space-based	Space-based => junction-based	Junction-based => path segment-based
		• Relative locations preserved • Scale: absolute distances => relative distances	• Locations of junctions: implicitly unique => conceptually separated into beginning & end of multiple path segments	• Location of junctions: start & end of multiple path segments => beginning & end of individual path segments
		• Dimensions: 3D => 2D • 2D connectivity preserved • 2D orientations preserved	• Distances: implicit => explicit • Path segment connectivity: implicit through matrix structure and labels	• Distances: explicit • Path segment connectivity: implicit through label uniqueness
		Spatial integrity is largely maintained	Spatial integrity is partially dissolved	Spatial integrity is fully dissolved
Spatial features	(all present)	• Absolute 2D location explicit (map section) • Relative 2D locations implicit (spatial medium) • Spatial scale (explicit/implicit) • Connectivity relations (spatially implicit) • 2D orientations (spatially implicit)	• Locations of junctions (explicit by label) • Direct distances between junctions (explicit by label) • Junction identity (partly spatially implicit in matrix; partly symbolically implicit through label) • Direct connections between junctions explicit	• Locations of junctions (explicit by label) • Direct distances between junctions (explicit by label) • Junction identity (symbolically implicit through label) • Direct connections between junctions explicit
		• Connectivity between path segments implicit • Implicit representation of missing connections	• Connectivity between path segments implicit • Explicit representation of missing direct connections	• Connectivity between path segments implicit • Implicit representation of missing direct connections
Spatial affordances	• Physical motion through environment until goal is reached • Random path selection	• Overview perspective • Perceptual path length comparison • Orientation-based heuristic path selection • Haptic or mental simulation of path traversal	• Partial junction identity due to matrix structure	(none)

cognitive agents can relate cause and effect of actions; later, they can describe and possibly understand the underlying process. At that point, cognitive agents have a representation that may enable them to find problem solutions mentally or computationally by reasoning. Once they have generated a solution by reasoning, they can apply it to the actual spatial situation in the environment.

We can distinguish two types of processes involved in spatial problem solving: problem-solving processes that operate in a given medium such as the physical space, a geographic map, a logic formalism, or some other representation of space; and problem transformation processes that transform problems between different media or kinds of representations. AI problem solving has been largely concerned with the first type of process (e.g. Fikes & Nilsson, 1971); but there also are approaches on the formal level that re-represent a given problem in a different formalism in order to determine a problem solution more easily (Yan et al., 2003). The role of different representations has been discussed by Bobrow (1975), Palmer (1978), Marr (1982), Sloman (1985), and Freksa (2015); the importance of paying attention to the transformation between media or forms of organizing knowledge to achieve such transformations were demonstrated by Freksa (1988) and Olteţeanu (2016).

Different media (physical space, map space, diagrams, logic representation, etc.) afford different operations and thus favor different kinds of problem solving. Therefore, solving the same problem in different media or representations results in different process structures and possibly in a different scalability of the problem-solving process (Larkin & Simon, 1987).

Components of Spatial Problem Solving

Spatial problems can be given in physical space or in an abstract form; similarly, the problem solution can be given as a spatial configuration or in the form of an abstract description. Accordingly, we can distinguish different kinds of spatial problem-solving processes, depending on whether they are performed entirely within the spatial domain, entirely within the abstract domain, or by some sort of a combination.

For the present discussion, we will focus on problems that are given in physical space and for which the solution sought is a spatial configuration. For this situation, we can identify four basic spatial problem-solving components that may be involved in these processes:

1. Solving a physically-spatial problem by operating on the problem configuration *within* the spatial medium.
2. Solving a spatial problem by processing the description of the problem.
3. Transforming a physically-spatial problem into a differently structured (e.g. abstract) representation medium.
4. Transforming the description of a problem solution from the representation medium to a spatial configuration.

These components and their interrelationships are depicted in Figure 11.6.

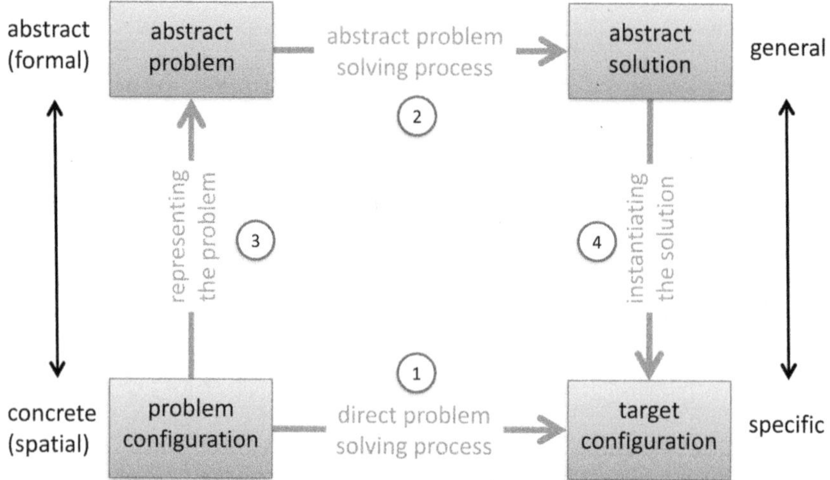

FIGURE 11.6 From spatial problem to spatial solution: A spatial problem configuration (bottom left) can be operated on directly in space to obtain a spatial target configuration (bottom right); alternatively, it can be transformed by abstraction into a mental or formal representation (top left), mentally or computationally processed into a solution (top right), which then can be re-transformed into a spatial configuration

Putting the Components Together

Cognitive agents may get away with limiting their approach to process component 1 applied directly to the spatial medium: operating on the spatial problem configuration through a physical action, in order to obtain a spatial solution configuration that manifests the desired effect (e.g. opening a door by leaning on it). This can be achieved by trial and error that accidentally solves the problem (due to spatial affordances) or by an intentional action that has known effects, but has no explanation of how the effects are produced in terms of process.

Cognitive agents can solve spatial problems in a variety of ways: they can (A) take an action that solves the problem (i) accidentally or (ii) by means of known effects; in either case spatial affordances enable the problem solution process. Or they can (B) transform the spatial problem into a formal problem for which (i) a solution can be searched for on the formal level or for which (ii) a solution is already known. Or they can (C) transform the spatial problem into a non-formal representation such as a map or a diagram that (i) may facilitate visual search for a solution or for which (ii) a solution is already known (see Mild Abstraction section).

The fact that cognitive agents have such a variety of options for spatial problem solving at their disposal suggests that being capable of pursuing several of these options requires some sort of meta-knowledge (or intuition) regarding which direction to pursue in order to solve a given problem. This meta-knowledge involves knowledge about the objectives to be achieved and knowledge or beliefs about strategies that may be successful. In Solving Problems vs. Understanding Problem Solving, we will address the issue of objectives; in From Geographic Space to Other Spatial Domains we will address the issue of strategies.

Solving Problems vs. Understanding Problem Solving

Spatial problem solving may serve different objectives: we may solve a problem in order to obtain a desired spatial configuration (e.g. an open door to pass through) or we may investigate problem solving in order to *understand* spatial transformation processes and principles intellectually as scientists. Although these two objectives are related, they require different kinds of models: spatial reconfiguration requires physical action, and actions need to be controlled by some sort of a mind; a mind that controls actions requires different knowledge than a mind that understands spatial transformations and their implications. Understanding spatial transformations does not necessarily require physical action; it requires notions of causality, topological transformation, geometric equivalence, and logical inference.

Much of the research on spatial problem solving since Euclid has focused on the intellectual challenge of *understanding spatial structures and principles* underlying spatial operations, as well as their implications regarding spatial problem solving: it concerned general spatial problems that we wanted to solve as scientists and whose solutions indirectly also could solve a common agent's problem of how to transform specific spatial configurations into desired target configurations. Consequently, this research has been concerned with formal descriptions of space and its properties: a representation that has proven particularly useful for intellectual treatment and analysis.

Understanding the principles of physical space certainly is most useful for characterizing the abstract space of potential approaches to (concrete) spatial problem solving. But is an understanding of formal spatial principles and structures sufficient to replicate or synthesize the kind of *commonsense spatial problem solving* exercised by animals and common people (including toddlers) who lack the explicit knowledge to reason about spatial principles and structures?

We believe that the difference between solving problems and understanding their solution is underappreciated. This is partly due to the mental identification of spatial situations and their representation that was described in the first section, Spatial Problems and Physical Space. Although *embodiment* and *situatedness* have become elaborately described and generally accepted notions, we find little work that employs this approach to spatial problem solving. We are convinced that it is worthwhile investigating naïve spatial problem solving by studying spatial affordances generated in the interaction between cognitive agents and spatial configurations. Our aim is to understand and synthesize naïve cognitive agents who depend on pre-intellectual shortcuts in spatial problem solving; these agents make direct use of spatial structures without knowing any principles that could guide their actions. Thus, our approach can be viewed as an action and perception-based approach that complements existing symbol-based approaches.

Mild Abstraction: A Third Way Between Direct and Formal Problem Solving

As we have seen, solving spatial problems directly in a spatial medium and solving problems abstractly both may have remarkable advantages, depending on the specific problem-solving requirements. We have seen that cognitive agents applying their perception and action capabilities to maps and visual graphs can make use of implicit spatial structures to solve spatial problems – why should we not equip computational problem-solving systems with the same type of capabilities? This will enable them to make direct use of multiple levels of features that are integrated into spatial structures. This also will provide shortcuts to purely computational spatial problem solving as it avoids spatial disintegration and re-integration steps involved in symbolic information processing.

The key idea is to implicitly maintain those aspects of the problem domain that can directly support the spatial problem-solving process, and to formalize only those aspects that do not support a solution in the spatial domain, but can be used for explicit reasoning in the formal domain (Freksa, 1991; Freksa et al., 2000). A main advantage will be that, by manipulating spatial structures, we will simultaneously manipulate coarse and fine levels of space, as well as all aspects that are integrated in the spatial representation. Spatial integration thus also offers a solution to the frame problem (McCarthy & Hayes, 1969).

How Much Abstraction Is Useful?

A great advantage of using spatial structures for spatial problem solving is that crucial properties of space, such as topological and geometric laws including dimensionality and inherent relations between dimensions, are maintained intrinsically and therefore can be directly exploited without any need to reason about them (Palmer, 1978; Dirlich et al., 1983; Freksa, 2015; Furbach et al., 2016). Generalization to a wider range of sizes, orientations, and geometries may be desirable; but generalization beyond the general constraints of space would not be useful when we want to use our representation exclusively to solve truly spatial problems. On the contrary: if we relax constraints generally applicable to spatial domains, we have to invest additional computational effort on the representation level in order to guarantee results that conform to the realm of space (Freksa, 1997).

On the other hand, generalization to less constrained representations may be quite useful for other kinds of problems, e.g. if we want to reason about abstract mathematical spaces or conceptual spaces (Gärdenfors, 2000), where we explicitly intend to escape the confinements of physical space.

But also for purely spatial problems there are aspects where we can take advantage of abstraction. In the path-finding example we already discussed the advantages of linearly scaling an entire scenario. This is a spatially benign abstraction from absolute size, as the geometric and topological properties of the domain are globally preserved; however, if specific geometric properties such as sizes, distances, and angles change locally, global spatial relations will also be affected. Thus, we may want to have abstractions that only generalize over similar spatial configurations, that is, we may abandon full geometric correctness in favor of a qualitative abstraction that maintains more general spatial characteristics, such as ordering relations and topological relations (Barkowsky et al., 2000).

In addition, we may want to use representations that omit aspects not related to the spatial problem and/or we may want to apply spatially invariant transformations that preserve crucial spatial properties, such as relative distance or relative orientation, and in addition enable new operations. For example, if a geographic problem essentially is a 2-dimensional problem, we can project the 3D spatial environment to a 2D map; by scaling the map from environmental space to the scale of vista space or figural space (Montello, 1993), we permit perceptual and haptic operations on the map that we could not perform on the corresponding entities in geographic space (see the Finding a Shortest Path in a Map section).

Mild Abstraction in Geographic Maps

In A Wayfinding Example: Finding a Shortest Path Between Two Locations, we illustrated for the shortest path problem how we can adapt the representation of a given problem to the problem-solving tools available. We argued that for embodied and situated perceiving and acting agents, such as humans, a map representation as a mild abstraction of the spatial environment has advantages over the environment itself, as well as over formal representations in which spatially implicit knowledge is made explicit. In this section, we will sketch how mild abstraction supports the use of different map types by human users, for solving different types of tasks.

Again, we will maintain the intrinsic properties of spatial structures, where spatial affordances can provide useful shortcuts, while we will abstract from those aspects that benefit from generalization. We will discuss the following familiar types of geographic maps:

- Aerial photograph (abstraction 3D → 2D)
- Topographic map (high-resolution 2D; vertical dimension symbolically represented)
- City map (density of settlements → type of urbanization)
- Road map (many spatial features symbolically abstracted (e.g. width of road → road type)
- Symbolic sketch map (only topological arrangement spatially represented).

Figure 11.7 depicts a section of the city of Heidelberg by each of these map types.

In geographic maps, the idea is to maintain as much spatial structure as may be helpful for solving the problem and to add as much symbolic information as may be helpful for dealing with non-spatial aspects of a problem. Spatial information and symbolic information compete for the space of the spatial representation medium. The assessment of the helpfulness can be done on the basis of meta-knowledge through answers to questions such as the following ones:

1. Is the problem given spatially or symbolically?
2. Do we require a spatial or a symbolic solution?
3. Can we treat the problem as an instance of a class of problems for which we know or can find a general approach?
4. Do we know solutions to similar problems?
5. Is the problem at hand peculiar and requiring a highly specific approach?
6. Do we need a specific practical (one-shot) solution quickly or can we afford to invest time to search for a general solution that may have multiple uses (one-time or long-term optimization)?
7. Is the problem ill-structured or well-structured?

The example of a map may illustrate that, for typical navigation tasks, a reduction from a 3D spatial environment to a 2D projection may be OK, but a reduction to 1D would give up important advantages of spatial integrity. In particular, we lose spatial orientation information when we reduce from 2D to 1D; together with path connectivity, spatial orientation provides important information for selecting suitable path candidates in wayfinding problems. Formally, we can easily construct an information-equivalent representation of all aspects of 3D space by means of 1D relations. In effect, this would correspond to a disintegration of the overall spatial structure; to reconstruct this structure, extensive computation is required.

Thus, in order to decide on a suitable representation for a spatial problem, we should take into account (1) which relations and structures of space we need to *rely on* and (2) which we need to *reason about*. We then can design representations that preserve structures we *rely on implicitly* (like certain distance and orientation relations in a map) and structures that we want to *reason about explicitly*.

From Geographic Space to Other Spatial Domains

After illustrating the notion of *mild abstraction* using familiar map representations and familiar wayfinding problems, we will now sketch how we can make use of the concepts described when we want to solve novel spatial problems for which we have to find suitable representations in order to find a solution to the problem. In the following discussion, we will refer to the Putting the Components Together

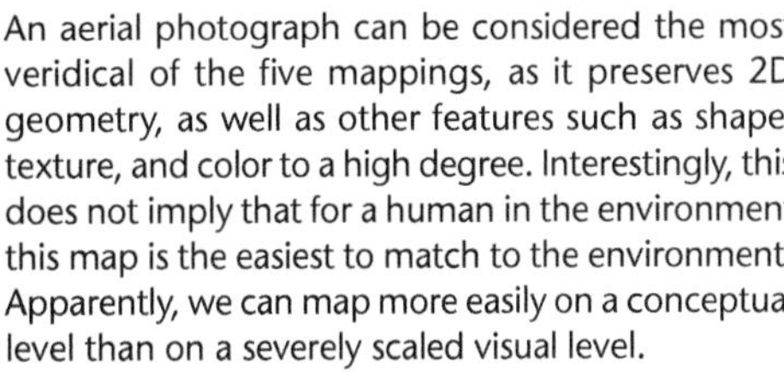

An aerial photograph can be considered the most veridical of the five mappings, as it preserves 2D geometry, as well as other features such as shape, texture, and color to a high degree. Interestingly, this does not imply that for a human in the environment this map is the easiest to match to the environment. Apparently, we can map more easily on a conceptual level than on a severely scaled visual level.

Bilder © 2017 DigitalGlobe, GeoBasis-DE/BKG, GeoContent, Kartendaten © 2017 GeoBasis-DE/BKG (©2009), Google

Topographic maps make height information that is lost in the 3D => 2D projection symbolically explicit. Height information is useful for finding hiking routes and scenic views, for example.

http://www.glade-web.de/GLADE_Geocaching/maps/HD-S.jpg

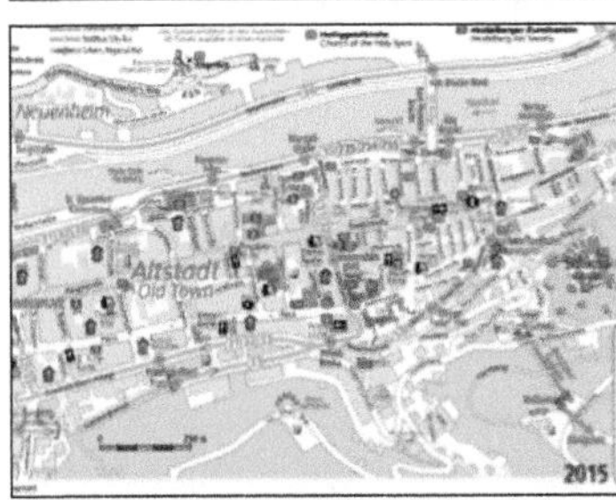

Typical city maps make street names and landmarks symbolically explicit by including their names into the map. In addition, churches or other landmarks are symbolically represented. This produces an interface that permits easy matching of entities in the environment with entities in the map.

http://static.wixstatic.com/media/4bb853_a01f31b221474c5583db122cb3112f1b.jpg_srz_3992_2811_85_22_0.50_1.20_0.00_jpg_srz

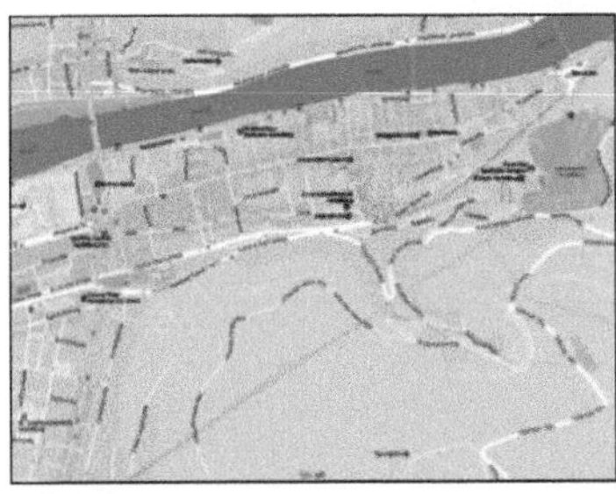

Typical road maps transform aspects of spatial veridicality into aspects of conceptual identity: the width (and color) of road symbols represents the road type rather than the width of the corresponding road.

Kartendaten © 2017 GeoBasis-DE/BKG (©2009), Google

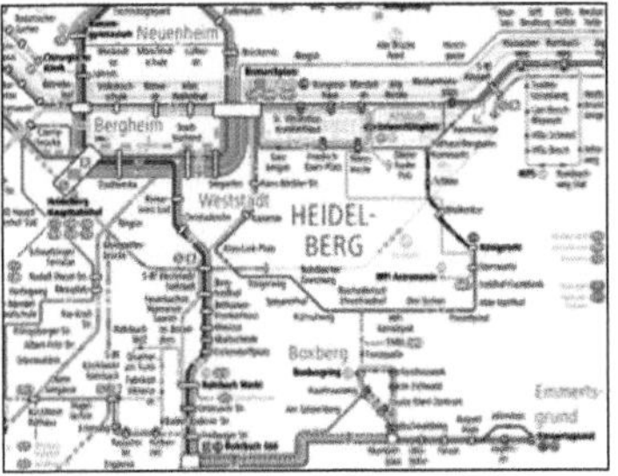

Schematic maps of various types emphasize specific aspects of the environment by selectively symbolizing them to support the solution of specific problems. Maps of transportation systems, such as subway maps, focus on supporting the transition from one transport line to another. They abstract from other aspects, the representation of which would clutter up the map.

http://s3.exploredoc.com/store/data/009847193_1-5f8f9af4f6aa7986ab5221ba1db4b220.png

FIGURE 11.7 Different levels of mild abstraction for different uses of maps

section, which introduced various components that can be configured for solving spatial problems. As we now have a variety of spatial problem solving approaches at our disposal, meta-knowledge will be helpful to select from the alternatives. We will use spatial puzzles in this section as examples for spatial problems for which successful approaches are not obvious. Spatial puzzles typically are given in the form of a spatial configuration; the goal of the puzzle is to obtain a specific new configuration.

If the objective is to obtain a certain spatial configuration, approach A (ii) (take an action that solves the problem by means of a known effect) is the method of choice. If the necessary knowledge about specific effects of actions is not available, approach A (i) (trial and error) may work if spatial affordances are known and if the number of actions in space is limited; then the odds may be good enough to find a solution, or the agent can keep track of the steps that have already been attempted.

The approaches A only require the process component 1 (transforming a *spatial* problem into a *spatial* solution). As the problem-solving process takes place directly in the spatial medium, transformations into a formal or mental representation of the problem and back are not required. A drawback is that the solution only will fit the given specific problem, as it is not generalized; however, the solution may serve as a source of knowledge for future problems that appear related (for example by means of case-based reasoning (Aamodt & Plaza, 1994)).

If knowledge about the problem is not available, cognitive agents have a choice between approaches A (i) and B (transform spatial problem into a formal problem) – a situation we frequently may be confronted with when we attempt to solve spatial puzzles, such as the snake cube puzzle or Rubik's Cube (Figure 11.8).

Can we solve the problem quickly by trial and error (possibly combined with limited knowledge about effects of local actions) or should we solve the problem via graphical or formal representation and analysis? In addition to process component 2 (transforming a *formal* problem into a *formal* solution), formal analysis requires the process component 3 that transforms the spatial problem into a formal representation of the problem (approach B). This transformation may be hard to find unless we recognize a pattern for which we already have an approach.

FIGURE 11.8 Snake cube puzzle and Rubik's Cube: How can we decide how we are going to approach the problem?

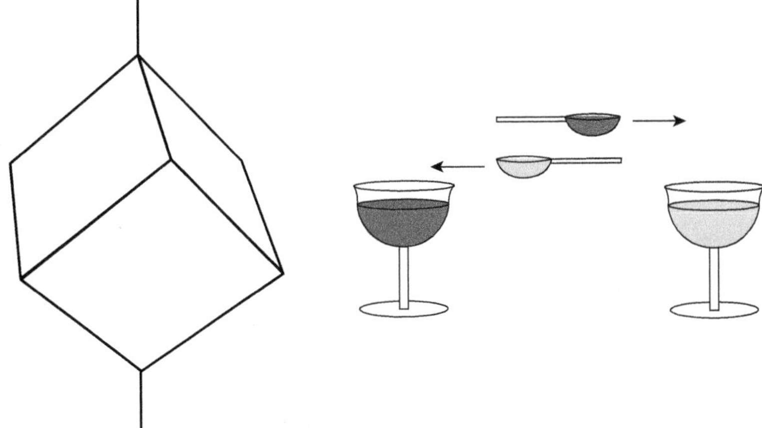

FIGURE 11.9 Left: Geoff Hinton's cube. Right: The wine/water mixing problem

In case of graphical or formal analysis we again can distinguish between two cases: B (i) where we know an approach that will solve the corresponding formal problem and B (ii) where we hope to find a solution on the formal level once we have a suitable description of the problem. While B (i) usually makes it easy to find a good problem representation, as the representation is suggested by the known solution to the formal problem, B (ii) can pose severe challenges even for simple-structured problems, as usually there are many ways to represent a given spatial problem and these ways differ in their suitability or ease of solving a given problem. Examples are Geoff Hinton's cube[3] and the wine/water mixing problem[4] (Figure 11.9). Both problems are good examples to demonstrate that the difficult part of solving novel problems is finding a suitable representation (Polya, 1945); once a good representation for the specific problem has been identified, the solution to the problem may become almost trivial[5].

If the problem solution requires actually carrying out a spatial task as in the spatial puzzles, the process component 4 (transforming formal solution into spatial solution) is also needed; this is usually straightforward if the transformation 3 was performed correctly, as the form of the solution is constrained by the structure of the spatial problem domain. For example, once our formal representation has computed an angle for Hinton's cube, there will be only one axis in the physical cube situation to which this angle may refer, due to the correspondence established in the formalization of the problem.

Discussion on Strategic Aspects

The sketched approach to spatial problem solving is particularly economical if we have to solve many spatial problems in the same spatial environment, as the environment needs to be modeled only once for all the problems we have to solve, provided that we represent all the information relevant to these problems and provided that we can represent the environment in such a way that all the problems can be easily solved in that representation. In other words, the spatial problem-solving component 3 (transforming a physically-spatial problem into differently structured representation media) that we did not need for solving the problem directly in the spatial environment may turn out to be a worthwhile investment if (1) we can find a form of representation that can be used for a variety of problems; (2) we need to solve many problems using the same data sets; and (3) we find effective and efficient procedures to solve the problems. Otherwise the search for a suitable problem solving representation may become disproportionally expensive.

In today's world of computer power and computerization we are able to use information in so many new ways that we may be easily led to believe that there will be no limits to solving problems with computers. But we very well know that the computational complexity of some problem classes is so unfavorable that even simple-structured problems may quickly exceed any computer's capabilities.

If we compare the wayfinding procedure in string maps (Finding a Shortest Path in a Map section) with wayfinding algorithms we use in computers, we observe that, unlike in computer algorithms, we do not have to consider laws of mathematics to identify a shortest path; consequently, no effort is required to apply such laws to make sure we will compute correct results.

Why do we have to invest in computation in the formalized problem that is not required for solving the original spatial problem? The answer is straightforward: in the spatial environment, all spatial properties relevant to solving spatial problems are *intrinsically* given (Palmer, 1978); that is, they cannot be violated or otherwise overcome. In contrast, in our general computer formalisms we are free to describe many more domains than spatial environments and spatial problems; specifically, we can describe impossible worlds, conflicting situations, and much more. Consequently, we must apply a 'computational straitjacket' to make sure the computer conforms to the laws of physical space when solving spatial problems.

Conclusion

A theory of spatial problem solving cannot start and end on the knowledge representation level. It must include the spatial medium, its perception, its representation, the processes operating on the representation, and the spatial actions that result from these processes.

In this chapter we have discussed alternative ways in which cognitive systems can solve spatial problems: (1) by perception and action directly in a spatial medium whose structure reflects the spatial structure of the problem domain; (2) by reasoning in a formal medium in which knowledge about space is explicitly described; or (3) in a combination thereof. As there are several alternatives in which a given problem can be approached, we require an entity that constructs the approach to be taken or that decides on an available selection. This entity will be able to take better decisions the better it understands the problem to be solved.

In classical AI programming, the task of deciding on suitable representations for problem solving usually is carried out by the program designer. His or her creativity constitutes much of the intelligence that is later attributed to the program. If we want to model the creativity of designers of versatile spatial problem solving agents, we should equip spatial problem-solving programs with the knowledge about spatial problem solving that has been described in this chapter.

Figure 11.10 depicts three levels of processing that are involved in spatial problem solving:

1. The object level is manifested by the substrate that hosts spatial configurations. The substrate effectively integrates (i.e. collocates) the attributes of spatial entities. For example, location, size, orientation, and also molecular structure, color, density, weight, etc. are all integrated at the same place. Spatial configurations of arbitrary entities are the objects of spatial problems and their solutions. Spatial perception, such as vision, haptics, and audition, as well as spatial actions, such as rotation or motion, operate on the object level. In the end, spatial problems must be solved on the object level. So, the object level is the level on which direct solutions in the spatial medium are performed.
2. The knowledge level *describes* the object level. It makes knowledge about relevant properties of the substrate and the spatial configurations explicit, typically in the form of statements about facts and relations. Different aspects of the object level (e.g. location, size, orientation) are described individually in a linear fashion, i.e. in some formalism or as text. This means that the spatial structure of the object level is disintegrated into the various aspects that are made explicit. Explicit knowledge is the basis for argumentation and reasoning. Thus, we may have inference rules and calculi on the knowledge

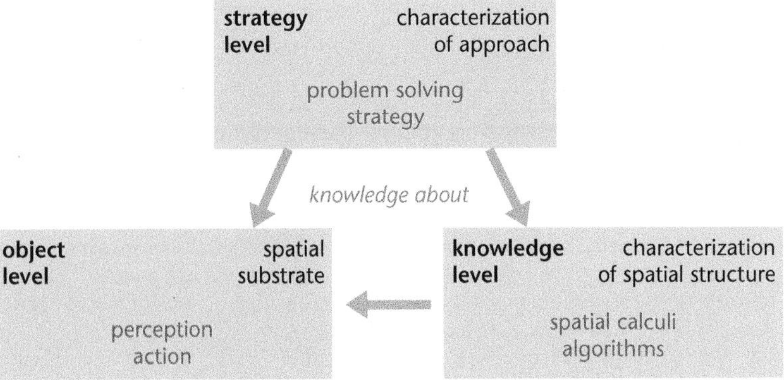

FIGURE 11.10 Levels of cognitive processing in spatial problem solving

level that enable us to derive new facts and relations about the object level. So, the knowledge level is the level on which indirect solutions in abstract media are computed.

3. The strategy level contains meta-knowledge about actions and affordances on the object level, about rules and processes on the knowledge level, as well as about their effects. The strategy level controls perception, action, problem and knowledge transformation, as well as reasoning for solving the spatial problem at hand. Thus, it decides about the distribution of tasks between the object level and the knowledge level. By maintaining certain spatial structures and 'aspectualizing' others (Bertel et al., 2004), the strategy level can make use of the advantages of mild abstraction.

We suggest that physical spatial structures play a special role in cognitive processing, as they are capable of integrating multiple aspects of a domain at the same place and of manipulating them simultaneously. We demonstrate how spatial structures can be exploited in spatial problem solving and how they can be combined with more abstract knowledge processing approaches.

At this time, we do not have computer architectures that replicate integrated spatial structures as described in this chapter. We therefore propose to investigate the *strong spatial cognition* paradigm in physical space by means of embodied and situated cognitive agents, such as people and robots, to better understand how to make use of integrated spatial structures in cognitive processing.

Acknowledgments

We acknowledge generous support by the German Research Foundation (DFG SFB/TR 8 projects R1 and R3; DFG project SOCIAL—FR 806/15) and by the Central Research Development Fund of the University of Bremen (project CogQDA). We thank Holger Schultheis, Ahmed Loai Ali, and the editors of this volume for critical and constructive comments.

Notes

1 This holds for arbitrary granularities of neighborhoods.
2 We will use 'representation' and 'medium' synonymously in this chapter. While 'representation' emphasizes structural aspects, 'medium' emphasizes physical and spatial aspects.
3 Geoff Hinton's cube: Imagine a cube suspended (by a string) at one of its corners, such that the most distant corner points down vertically. Imagine a vertical axis through these corners. Now turn the cube around this axis in one direction. By how many degrees do you have to turn the cube until for the first time all corners of the cube will coincide with the corners and all edges will coincide with the edges of the cube before rotation? (Hinton, 1979; Freksa et al., 1985).
4 Wine/water mixing problem: You have two drinking glasses. One contains wine, the other contains water of equal volume. One spoonful of wine is taken from the wine glass and added to the water in the second glass. Then an equal amount of the water-wine

combination is transferred from the water glass into the wine glass. Which mixture is purer: the one in the water glass, or the one in the wine glass? (Freksa, 1988).

5 Solution to Hinton's cube problem: We can abstract from the vertical dimension and consider a projection of the cube to the horizontal plane. The three edges connecting to the suspending string will divide the 360° space surrounding the axis into three equal sectors of 120°; a turn of 120° will move the cube into complete alignment with its original position. Solution to the wine/water mixing problem: After the transactions, each glass contains the same volume of fluid as before; the volume of wine missing in the wine glass has been replaced by water and vice versa; both volumes are identical. The purity of both fluids therefore is the same.

References

Aamodt, A. & Plaza, E. (1994). Case-based reasoning: Foundational issues, methodological variations, and system approaches, *Artificial Intelligence Communications*, 7 (1), 39–52.

Barkowsky, T., Latecki, L. J., & Richter, K.-F. (2000). Schematizing maps: Simplification of geographic shape by discrete curve evolution. In C. Freksa, W. Brauer, C. Habel, & K. F. Wender (Eds.), *Spatial Cognition II – Integrating Abstract Theories, Empirical Studies, Formal Models, and Practical Applications* (41–53). Berlin: Springer.

Berendt, B., Barkowsky, T., Freksa, C., & Kelter, S. (1998). Spatial representation with aspect maps. In C. Freksa, C. Habel, & K. F. Wender (Eds.), *Spatial Cognition – an Interdisciplinary Approach to Representing and Processing Spatial Knowledge* (313–336). Berlin: Springer.

Bertel, S. (2010). *Spatial Structures and Visual Attention in Diagrammatic Reasoning*. Lengerich: Pabst Science Publishers.

Bertel, S., Freksa, C., & Vrachliotis, G. (2004). Aspectualize and conquer. In J. S. Gero, B. Tversky, & T. Knight (Eds.), *Visual and Spatial Reasoning in Design III* (255–279). Sydney: Key Centre of Design Computing and Cognition, University of Sydney.

Bobrow, D. G. (1975). Dimensions of representation. In D. G. Bobrow, & A. Collins (Eds.), *Representation and Understanding* (1–34). New York: Academic Press.

Card, S. K., Mackinlay, J. D., & Shneiderman, B. (1999). *Readings in Information Visualization: Using Vision to Think*. San Francisco: Morgan Kaufmann.

Davis, E. (2013). Qualitative spatial reasoning in interpreting text and narrative. *Spatial Cognition and Computation, 13* (4), 264–294.

Dijkstra, E. W. (1959). A note on two problems in connexion with graphs. *Numerische Mathematik, 1*, 269–271.

Dirlich, G., Freksa, C., & Furbach, U. (1983). A central problem in representing human knowledge in artificial systems: The transformation of intrinsic into extrinsic representations. *Proc. 5th Cognitive Science Conference*. Rochester: Cognitive Science Society.

Dreyfus, H. & Haugeland, J. (1974). The computer as a mistaken model of the mind. In S. C. Brown (Ed.), *Philosophy of Psychology* (247–258). London: Palgrave Macmillan.

Euclid (1956). *The Thirteen Books of Euclid's Elements*. (T. L. Heath, Trans.). New York, NY: Dover. (Original work published 300 BC.)

Fikes, R. E. & Nilsson, N. J. (1971). STRIPS: A new approach to the application of theorem proving to problem solving. *Artificial Intelligence, 2*, 189–208.

Freksa, C. (1988). Intrinsische vs. extrinsische Repräsentation zum Aufgabenlösen oder die Verwandlung von Wasser in Wein. In G. Heyer, J. Krems, & G. Görz (Eds.), *Wissensarten und ihre Darstellung* (155–165). Berlin: Springer.

Freksa, C. (1991). Qualitative spatial reasoning. In D. M. Mark, & A. U. Frank (Eds.), *Cognitive and Linguistic Aspects of Geographic Space* (361–372). Dordrecht: Kluwer.

Freksa, C. (1997). Spatial and temporal structures in cognitive processes. In C. Freksa, M. Jantzen, & R. Valk (Eds.), *Foundations of Computer Science. Potential – Theory – Cognition* (379–387). Berlin: Springer.

Freksa, C. (1999). Spatial aspects of task-specific wayfinding maps: A representation-theoretic perspective. In J. S. Gero, & B. Tversky (Eds.), *Visual and Spatial Reasoning in Design* (15–32). Sydney: Key Centre of Design Computing and Cognition, University of Sydney.

Freksa, C. (2015). Strong spatial cognition. In S. I. Fabrikant, M. Raubal, M. Bertolotto, C. Davies, & S. Bell (Eds.), *Spatial Information Theory* (65–86). Heidelberg: Springer.

Freksa, C., Furbach, U., & Dirlich, G. (1985). Cognition and representation. In J. Laubsch (Ed.), *GWAI-84. 8th German Workshop on Artificial Intelligence* (119–144). Berlin: Springer.

Freksa, C., Moratz, R., & Barkowsky, T. (2000). Robot navigation with schematic maps. In E. Pagello, F. Groen, T. Arai, R. Dillmann, & A. Stentz (Eds.), *Intelligent Autonomous Systems, 6*, 809–816. Amsterdam: IOS Press.

Freksa, C., Olteţeanu, A. M., Ali, A. L., Barkowsky, T., van de Ven, J., Dylla, F., & Falomir, Z. (2016). Towards spatial reasoning with strings and pins. *Advances in Cognitive Systems 4* Poster Collection #22, 1–15.

Furbach, U., Furbach, F., & Freksa, C. (2016). Relating strong spatial cognition to symbolic problem solving – An example. *Proc. 2nd Workshop on Bridging the Gap Between Human and Automated Reasoning*, IJCAI, New York, 9 July 2016, arXiv:1606.04397 [cs.AI].

Gärdenfors, P. (2000). *Conceptual Spaces*. Cambridge, MA: MIT Press.

Gibson, J. J. (1979). *The Ecological Approach to Visual Perception*. New Jersey: Lawrence Erlbaum Assoc.

Hinton, G. (1979). Some demonstrations of the effects of structural descriptions in mental imagery. *Cognitive Science, 3*, 231–250.

Johnson, S. P. (2009). Developmental origins of object perception. In A. Woodward, & A. Needham (Eds.), *Learning and the Infant Mind* (47–65). New York: Oxford University Press.

Keen, R. (2003). Representation of objects and events: Why do infants look so smart and toddlers look so dumb? *Current directions in Psychological Science, 12*, 79–83.

Larkin, J. H. & Simon, H. A. (1987). Why a diagram is (sometimes) worth ten thousand words. *Cognitive Science, 11*, 65–100.

MacEachren, A. M. (1995). *How Maps Work: Representation, Visualization, and Design*. New York, NY: Guilford Press.

Mark, D. M., Freksa, C., Hirtle, S. C., Lloyd, R., & Tversky, B. (1999). Cognitive models of geographic space. *Int. J. of Geographical Information Science, 13*, 8, 747–774.

Marr, D. (1982). *Vision*. Cambridge, MA: MIT Press.

McCarthy, J. & Hayes, P. J. (1969). Some philosophical problems from the standpoint of artificial intelligence. *Machine Intelligence, 4*, 463–502.

Monmonier, M. S. (1996). *How to Lie with Maps*, 2nd ed. Chicago IL: University of Chicago Press.

Montello, D. (1993). Scale and multiple psychologies of space. In A. U. Frank, & I. Campari (Eds.), *Spatial Information Theory: A Theoretical Basis for GIS* (312–321). Berlin: Springer.

Needham, A. (2009). Learning in infants' object perception, object-directed action, and tool use. In A. Woodward, & A. Needham (Eds.), *Learning and the Infant mind* (208–226). New York: Oxford University Press.

Olteţeanu, A. M. (2016). *A Cognitive Systems Framework for Creative Problem Solving*. Doctoral dissertation. Bremen: University of Bremen.

Palmer, S. E. (1978). Fundamental aspects of cognitive representation. In E. Rosch, & B. B. Lloyd (Eds.), *Cognition and Categorization*, 259–303. Hillsdale: Lawrence Erlbaum.

Polya, G. (1945). *How to Solve it*. Princeton: Princeton University Press.

Robinson, A. H., Morrison, J. L., Muehrcke, P. C., Kimerling, A. J., & Guptill, S. C. (1995). *Elements of Cartography*, 6th edition. New York: Wiley.

Russell, S. & Norvig, P. (1995). *Artificial Intelligence – A Modern Approach*. Upper Saddle River: Prentice Hall.

Scaife, M. & Rogers, Y. (1996). External cognition: How do graphical representations work? *International Journal of Human-Computer Studies*, *45*, 185–213.

Sloman, A. (1971). Interactions between philosophy and artificial intelligence: The role of intuition and non-logical reasoning in intelligence, *Artificial Intelligence*, *2*, 209–225.

Sloman, A. (1985). Why we need many knowledge representation formalisms. In M. A. Bramer (Ed.), *Research and Development in Expert Systems*, 163–183. Cambridge: Cambridge University Press.

Tversky, B. (1981). Distortions in memory for maps. *Cognitive Psychology*, 13, 407–433.

Tversky, B. (1992). Distortions in cognitive maps. *Geoforum*, 23, 131–138.

Tversky, B. (1993). Cognitive maps, cognitive collages, and spatial mental models. In A. U. Frank & I. Campari (Eds.), *Spatial Information Theory: A Theoretical Basis for GIS*, 14–24, Berlin: Springer.

Tversky, B. (2000). Some ways that maps and diagrams communicate. In C. Freksa, W. Brauer, C. Habel, & K. F. Wender (Eds.), *Spatial Cognition II – Integrating Abstract Theories, Empirical Studies, Formal Models, and Practical Applications*, 72–79, Berlin: Springer.

Tversky, B. & Lee, P. (1999). Pictorial and verbal tools for conveying routes. In C. Freksa, & D. Mark (Eds.), *Spatial Information Theory*, 51–64, Berlin: Springer.

Yan, J., Forbus, K., & Gentner, D. (2003). A theory of rerepresentation in analogical matching. *Proc. Twenty-fifth Annual Meeting of the Cognitive Science Society*, New York: Psychology Press.

12

EVENTS IN MIND, MEDIA, AND MEMORY

Jeffrey M. Zacks

Event Models: A Distinct Format of Cognitive Representation?

Have you ever caught yourself in the middle of watching a movie needing to remind yourself that the characters on the screen are fictions sustained by mere dancing light? Have you ever had the experience of getting lost in a book? Has a friend ever told you the story of a scary experience that gave you goose bumps—despite the fact that the story happened to someone else and is long over? Not everyone will say "yes" to these questions, but for many of us there seems to be something powerful in common between mediated experiences of events—movies, reading, and listening—and live experiences of events. In this chapter I am going to propose an explanation of the parallels in our experience of life and various media and to explore the consequences of this proposal for human cognition and action.

Here is the core of my suggestion: In normal perception and action, we depend strongly on a particular kind of working memory representation, which captures the functionally relevant components of the event that we are experiencing now. I will refer to this as an *event model*. Humans (and other animals) evolved event models over a long period of time, well before the emergence of language or of pictorial depictions. Our ability to comprehend depictions of events in pictures or movies, and to understand stories about events, is built on top of our systems for representing events from perception. Most of the time, it is not critical to keep track of whether a represented event originated from perception, from a depiction, or from someone telling us a story. In this way our perception of mediated events parasitizes (in a benign way) our evolved mechanisms for representing unmediated events.

Why Do We Have Event Models?

When I was a PhD student working with Barbara Tversky in the mid-1990s, I dropped into her office with a question: "Why does our experience feel like it consists of discrete events, when the physical signals that impinge on our sensory systems are continuous and fluid?" This turned out to be one of those questions that can ambush you as a student: At first it appeared well-formed, tractable and modest in scope, but then emerged layers within layers of ambiguity, intractability and sprawl. Barbara was patient and wise, and with her guidance I got started trying to wrestle this problem into experiments. I have continued to work on this question in one form or another for 20 years, sometimes in collaboration with Barbara and often with the benefit of her insight. Over the last few years, working with a number of collaborators, this has led to a theory of how event models are represented and updated (Kurby & Zacks, 2008; Radvansky & Zacks, 2014; Zacks, Speer, Swallow, Braver, & Reynolds, 2007). The theory starts from a functional analysis, which proposes that we evolved event models because maintaining a stable representation of the situation around us improves our perceptual abilities. The sensory signals that we must use to guide our actions are patchy, incomplete, and noisy. Consider vision. The eyes can register only a small part of the visual world in detail at any given moment. We make saccades to sample information from throughout the visual field, and the information obtained from multiple glances must be reconciled. We also blink our eyes, lose track of objects when they are occluded, and suffer lapses of attention in which we fail to adequately process information from some glances. An event model is a representation that stitches together these fragmentary glimpses with similarly fractured information from other sensory systems and other sources into a coherent form. Such a representation improves our ability to predict how the events around us will unfold, and this is of singular advantage for guiding action. For example, to catch a thrown or falling object, one must predict its path of motion. For humans, predicting others' behavior is particularly challenging and particularly important. When meeting a stranger, the ability to predict whether their actions would be friendly or hostile no doubt determined the survival of many a prehistoric person.

How Are Event Models Updated?

Updating an event model amounts to chunking experience into spatiotemporal units. This is a fundamental operation that provides for cognitive economy—efficiency that is necessary given the complexity of our environments. Moreover, carving the world into parts tells us important things about its functional structure (Tversky, 1989; Tversky & Hemenway, 1984). How do we parse activity into events? The theory we have developed is called *event segmentation theory* (EST; Zacks et al., 2007). It proposes that the main challenge in developing an effective event model is to control its updating. Update too frequently, and the model can add nothing to the currently-available perceptual information. Update too infrequently, and the model will fail to register the real changes in states of affairs in the world, and thus will lead to erroneous predictions. According to EST, the control system for event model updating is based on monitoring the quality of perceptual prediction. When predictions are good and prediction error is low, the model is likely to be appropriate to the situation. When prediction error spikes, this indicates that something has changed in the situation and it would be adaptive to re-initialize the event model. This control architecture is motivated by a hypothesis about the nature of experience: We hypothesize that everyday activity contains predictable sequences of action punctuated by junctures where predictability is lower. To test this, Jeremy Reynolds, Todd Braver, and I built a neural network model that made predictions about the movements of a human actor whose body posture had been recorded while he performed a number of actions (Reynolds, Zacks, & Braver, 2007). After training on a large corpus of actions containing repetitions of each type, the model showed the predicted spikes in prediction error at action boundaries. Further, adding an additional component to the network improved its ability to predict the actions. (A funny thing about this proposed architecture is that though it explains segmentation, it turns out that the model does not have segmentation as a goal. It does not get rewarded or punished based on segmentation. Instead, segmentation arises as a side-effect of predicting more effectively.)

For naturalistic activity, EST predicts that spikes in prediction error, and thus event model updating, will tend to happen when features of the situation in the world change. This is the case because activity tends to become less predictable when things change. To test this hypothesis, we conducted a series of experiments in which we measured features of activity in movies and stories and looked at the relationship between feature changes, event segmentation, and neural processing. The activities we have studied include simple animations, movies of everyday activities, commercial films, and stories. We first asked how low-level movement features related to event segmentation. Our point of departure was an experiment conducted by Newtson, Engquist, and Bois (1977), in which they found that event boundaries tended to correspond with large changes in the position of human actors. In one set of experiments, we presented simple animations of geometric objects and asked participants to segment them into meaningful events by pushing a button while they watched. For fine segmentation, we asked observers to identify the smallest units that were natural and meaningful to them. For coarse segmentation, we asked them to identify the largest units that were natural and meaningful. For both grains of segmentation, changes in movement features such as objects' acceleration significantly predicted segmentation (Zacks, 2004). We also tracked the movement of an actor's head and hands while he performed a set of everyday activities, allowing us to calculate similar features from live action. The relationship between movement and segmentation was again strong, for both fine and coarse segmentation (Zacks, Kumar, Abrams, & Mehta, 2009). Similar results were obtained by Hard, Recchia, and Tversky (2011).

We then asked whether more conceptual features of activity are associated with event boundaries (Zacks, Speer, & Reynolds, 2009). To do so, we adapted a coding of situational features from the *event indexing model* developed by Zwaan and colleagues (Zwaan, 1999; Zwaan, Langston, & Graesser, 1995). The event indexing model proposes that representations of a narrative are organized around situational dimensions that are relevant to a reader; these often include the dimensions of space, time, characters, objects, causes, and goals. When one of these dimensions changes, the reader updates the current situation model. We coded a feature film and a set of narrative texts for changes in these dimensions. EST proposes that this updating occurs because situational changes produce prediction errors. Consistent with this hypothesis, readers tended to segment events at points in time when more features were changing. This was true for both written narratives and for movies. (See also Magliano, Miller, & Zwaan, 2001.) For the texts, we also were able to obtain ratings of predictability during reading. As hypothesized by EST, readers rated activity as less predictable when more features were changing, and this tended to correspond with the points they identified as event boundaries.

Another implication of EST's prediction-error-driven updating mechanism is that event boundaries should correspond with focal increases in neural activity. For both movies and narratives, we have investigated the neural mechanisms of segmentation by measuring brain activity with functional MRI (fMRI) while participants simply experience the events and then asking the same participants to segment the activity. We then can time-lock their brain activity to the event boundaries, assaying where in the brain there were transient changes at event boundaries. We have consistently found that a consistent collection of brain areas increases in activity when people experience event boundaries while watching movies (Zacks et al., 2001; Zacks, Speer, Swallow, & Maley, 2010) and reading stories (Speer, Reynolds, & Zacks, 2007; Whitney et al., 2009); similar responses have been observed while listening to music (Sridharan, Levitin, Chafe, Berger, & Menon, 2007).

If these increases reflect event model updating, then they should be associated with the same feature changes that are associated with event boundaries. This has been found to be the case for movement features (Zacks, Swallow, Vettel, & McAvoy, 2006) and for more abstract situational features such as changes in characters, locations, goals, and causes (Speer et al., 2007). For the situational features, activity associated with changes in features has been shown to mediate the relationship between feature changes and the brain responses observed at event boundaries. That is, about half of the brain's response to event boundaries can be explained by the brain's response to situational feature changes (Speer, Reynolds, Swallow, & Zacks, 2009; Zacks et al., 2010). This provides relatively strong evidence for the proposal that feature changes lead to the updating of event models.

What Is the Representational Format of Event Models?

An important question about any cognitive representation is "What format is it in?" There are at least two important dimensions on which representations vary. First, representations can be *isomorphic* to the things they represent, or stand in an *arbitrary* relation (Shepard & Chipman, 1970). For example, an aerial photograph of a city is isomorphic to the space it depicts—there is a smooth one-to-one mapping between locations in the picture and locations in the city. In contrast, a set of written directions for taking the subway from one location to another has an arbitrary relation to the locations; the words in the directions do not correspond in any simple way to locations within the space. Second, representations can be *holistic* or *componential*. Componential representations can be broken down into parts and the parts can be manipulated separately while preserving the functioning of the representation, whereas holistic representations cannot. Language, in addition to being arbitrary, is componential. The words in the sentence "The designed world is a diagram" can be recombined to represent other ideas, such as "The diagram is a designed world." In contrast, a photograph is holistic in addition to being isomorphic. A photograph of a building cannot generally be cut up and rearranged to experiment with alternative floor plans.

In the brain, neural representations early in the sensory and perceptual system tend to be holistic, isomorphic maps of dimensions in the world. For example, the visual system contains multiple retinotopic maps, which map locations in visual space to locations in the cortex (Tootell, Silverman, Switkes, & De Valois, 1982). The motor cortex also contains holistic isomorphic maps of the body (Penfield & Rasmussen, 1950), which map locations on the body to locations in the cortex. Retinotopic visual maps and somatotopic body maps use space to represent space, but that is not necessary for isomorphism. In the auditory system, the primary auditory cortex uses space to represent pitch (Humphries, Liebenthal, & Binder, 2010). In contrast, some representations of higher cognitive features including language and concepts (Fodor, 1975; Mahon & Caramazza, 2008) are thought to be arbitrary and componential. One possibility, which has accrued recent evidence, is that circuits in the prefrontal cortex can implement arbitrary "pointers" to other neural representations, forming a neurobiological basis for arbitrary, componential representations (Kriete, Noelle, Cohen, & O'Reilly, 2013). (For a view that questions the hypothesis that human symbolic processing is arbitrary, see, e.g., Barsalou, 1999.)

My working hypothesis is that event models have a distinctive representational format that is important for the special role they play in cognition; namely, they are both isomorphic and componential. This combination is unusual. Most representations in psychology and neuroscience seem to be either isomorphic and holistic or arbitrary and componential. The aerial photograph I mentioned previously is isomorphic and holistic, as are paintings, maps, and sketches in the world and topographic maps in the brain. There are also plenty of representations that are arbitrary and componential; consider linguistic descriptions, computer programs, data tables, and tally marks. A good example of a representation that is both isomorphic and componential is a doll house. In a doll house, the individual pieces are isomorphic to the real objects they represent, but the function of the system as a whole can be manipulated by moving the pieces around. Other examples include construction toys such as Lego or Tinker Toys and computer-assisted design models. In the preceding chapter (p. 172), Freksa and colleagues describe how event "mild abstraction" of an isomorphic-holistic representation can add a componential component, enabling new forms of reasoning. My view is that this amounts to creating an event model.

I think there is a good possibility that event models represent situations in the world by representing features of objects, surfaces, and other elements of situations isomorphically, but using arbitrary representations to code the role of these objects and surfaces within a larger spatiotemporal framework. (This view owes much to Barsalou's characterization of perceptual symbol systems; see Barsalou, 1999, 2008.) I think that this combination of isomorphism and componentiality is a powerful one for cognition because it allows for both verisimilitude and generativity. Why do toys like doll houses and Lego or Tinker Toys provide such enduring entertainment? Because they allow a child to capture an endless variety of situations with fidelity. Just so with event models.

In terms of the neurophysiology of event models, a number of hypotheses are tenable at this point, and the following are not necessarily mutually exclusive. First, my colleagues and I have previously noted that patients with prefrontal lesions have selective deficits in processing complex events (Humphreys, Forde, & Riddoch, 2001; Sirigu et al., 1995, 1996) and that sustained activity in parts of the prefrontal cortex is associated with reasoning about events (Barbey, Krueger, & Grafman, 2009; Crozier et al., 1999), and therefore suggested that prefrontal regions may be particularly important for maintaining event models (Zacks et al., 2007). This accords with theories that suggest the prefrontal cortex is specialized for representing temporal sequences (Fuster, 1997) or semantic representations of event classes (Grafman, Partiot, & Hollnagel, 1995; Wood & Grafman, 2003). It also fits with the possibility that the prefrontal cortex may have the capacity to implement symbolic indirection—the ability to store in one representation the address of another representation, a key feature of computer programming languages (Kriete et al., 2013). Second, Barsalou (1999) has observed that tertiary "convergence zones" are well positioned to integrate information from multiple sensory modalities, and to implement componential representations. Convergence zones are hypothesized to be distributed throughout the cortex rather than localized to one area (Damasio, 1989). Third, studies comparing the retrieval of event information from long-term memory to the imagination of future or counterfactual events implicate regions of the parietal cortex, particularly the angular gyrus, as being important for constructing a bound representation of a remembered or imagined event (Rugg & Vilberg, 2013). (One reason to think that the parietal lobes are not the whole story for maintaining event representations is that patients with lesions to this area are not notably impaired in reasoning about events or in sequencing their actions.) An important feature of *all* of these hypotheses is that they propose representations that abstract features of a situation away from the details of any single sensory modality; rather, in all cases the proposed representations are multimodal or supramodal. This comports well with event models as integrated representations of situations in the world rather than isolated features of those situations.

Whatever the neural specializations are that we evolved to support event models, I think the existence of those specializations explains some important features of how we respond to mediated events. I turn next to several examples that illustrate the striking commonality between how we respond to live events and to mediated ones.

Common Responses to Movies and Stories

The first thing that strikes me about the psychology of mediated events is that mediated events can be experienced as so real. For many of us, when we hear ghost stories we shudder, when we read science fiction we see strange worlds in our mind's eye, and when we watch a movie we flinch from looming trains. Gabriel Radvansky and I (2014) have argued that this is so because whether we experience an activity live, watch it on a screen, read about it, or hear about it, our understanding of the events in that activity depends on building event models that represent them, and the underlying format of the representation is the same independent of those input modalities. One train of evidence for this comes from our studies of event segmentation. In these studies, participants are often asked to identify the boundaries between events in an ongoing activity. Most adults have no problem doing so, whether that activity is presented as movie, a written narrative, or a spoken narrative (Newtson, 1976; Zacks, Speer, et al., 2009). As I noted previously, these easily-identified boundaries are associated with phasic increases in brain activity (Zacks et al., 2001, 2010).

A second train of evidence comes from the studies of situational changes, described previously. In those studies, participants viewed a feature movie or read stories presented one word at a time on a screen, while brain activity was recorded with fMRI. Brain responses to situational changes had similar topography whether they occurred in movies or stories (Speer et al., 2009, 2007; Zacks et al., 2010). This is illustrated for two classes of feature change in Figure 12.1. Here, I have concentrated on two feature changes associated with well-characterized neurophysiological responses. First, we hypothesized that spatial changes would be associated with activity in the *parahippocampal place area*, a region of the medial temporal lobes that is selectively activated when people look at pictures of places (Epstein & Kanwisher, 1998). Second, we hypothesized that object changes would be selectively associated with activity in parietal and posterior frontal regions known to be involved in making grasping movements (Castiello, 2005). More specifically, we hypothesized that the evoked responses would be limited to the left cortical hemisphere; this is so because the motor system is organized contralaterally, and our participants (and the movie's main actor) were right handed. As can be seen in the figure, the evoked responses for both spatial changes and object changes corresponded impressively well across the movie and narrative datasets, despite the fact that the materials were completely different and different participants were included in the two experiments. Of course, the whole brain's response is not identical. For example, object changes in movies evoked great activity in the superior parietal lobes than did stories. (This activity could reflect effects of visual attention or eye movement control that would not be expected for reading single successive words.) But in the relevant parts of the system, the correspondence is predictable and strong. In short, event segmentation seems to work in highly similar ways, whether the events in question are experienced by watching them in front of your eyes or through language.

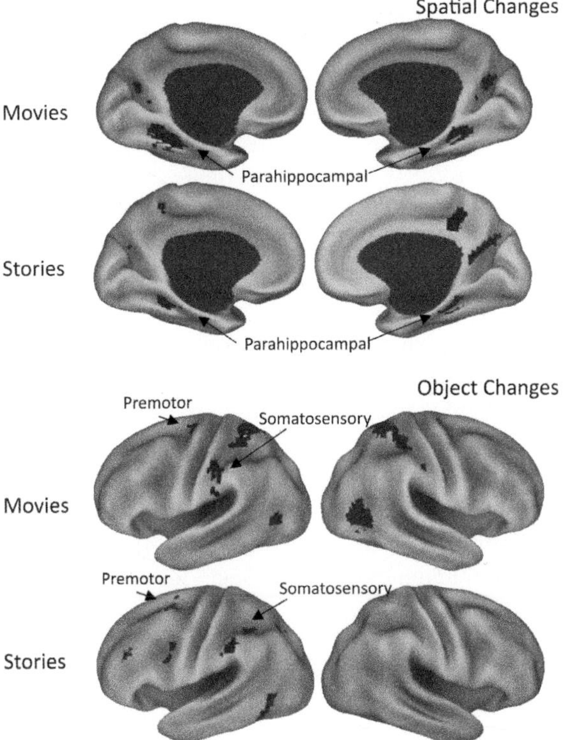

FIGURE 12.1 Brain activity evoked at changes in movies and stories. The top images show medial views of the cortical hemispheres; the bottom panels show lateral views. Data are from Speer et al., 2009, and Zacks et al. 2010, and are thresholded at z = 4.50 and corrected for multiple comparisons

Another striking thing about events experienced from life, movies, and language is that we can sometimes have a hard time telling them apart in memory. Neurological patients have been reported to develop elaborate confabulations in which they take on outlandish plots as their own life stories (Kalisky & Uzzell, 1996). In the laboratory, people can show high rates of confusing events they performed with events they only imagined (Johnson, 2006), and with repeated repetition people become increasingly likely to believe they performed an action (Goff & Roediger, 1998). Retelling an event alters subsequent memory, a sign that in the act of telling we create representations that become confused with the original memory (Tversky & Marsh, 2000). We also can have trouble discriminating events we read about from events we saw in movies. For example, Butler and colleagues presented students with a historical article, and then with an excerpt from a commercial film that depicted the same events but with known inaccuracies (Butler, Zaromb, Lyle, & Roediger, 2009). When tested on the history, the students were quite prone to intruding the misinformation from the movies. Giving a general warning that there might be errors in the movies did not help people to avoid intruding them. It took a specific warning describing which information was inaccurate to reduce its negative impact.

The proposal that event models underlie comprehension and memory for everyday activity helps to explain how viewers can sometimes miss changes in a visual scene that would seem to be large and salient, a phenomenon known as *change blindness* (Levin & Simons, 2000; Simons & Ambinder, 2005). Dramatic examples of change blindness can be seen in continuity errors in movies. A typical commercial film is composed of a large number of *clips* joined by *edits*, of which the simplest is a *cut*—when two clips are joined with no visual transition. Cuts are by far the most common type of edit in commercial cinema. Across cuts in commercial films, objects and object features often change unintentionally because two clips that are adjacent in a film may have been shot at different times during a session or even on different days, and props and costumes may not have been perfectly matched across takes. These are called *continuity errors*, and they are notable because, on the one hand, viewers rarely spot them spontaneously, but on the other hand once they are pointed out they can be quite striking. For example, Figure 12.2 shows images from two consecutive shots in *Terminator 3: Rise of the Machines*. As the actors board the plane, the tail number reads "N3035C." But a moment later, the flying plane reads "N3973F" ("*Terminator 3: Rise of the Machines* movie mistake picture 1," n.d.). In the laboratory, Levin and Simons (1997) showed viewers short films in which they used editing to introduce changes in objects, clothing, and actors. In the Levin and Simons movies, elements of the situation were switched at cuts and viewers were astonishingly bad at detecting these changes. One film showed a man working at a desk when a phone rang. The man got up and walked to the phone to answer it. During a cut as he was walking, the actor was switched for a different actor wearing different clothing. Two thirds of the participants failed to detect the switch.

FIGURE 12.2 Continuity error in *Terminator 3: Rise of the Machines*. Two characters hop into a small plane and fly off. When the camera cuts to the plane in flight it has a different tail number

Not only do viewers miss when objects change across cuts, they also often miss the cuts themselves—a phenomenon that has been dubbed *edit blindness* (Smith & Henderson, 2008). For example, Smith and Henderson (2008) showed viewers excerpts from commercial movies and asked them to push a button while watching whenever they saw an edit. Overall, participants missed 15.8% of the cuts. Edit blindness was greatest (32.4%) for cuts that took place in the middle of an action. It was lowest (9.4%) for edits at breaks between scenes.

I suggest that change blindness and edit blindness happen because of two things that our event model construction system does to construct an integrated, coherent event model. First, it abstracts away sensory features that vary as a function of momentary changes in viewpoint or attention. For example, objects' relative location, orientation, and lighting vary as we move our eyes and move relative to a scene so they are abstracted away. Event models should represent information about objects' categories, and sometimes their identity, but not necessarily information about their appearance that may be noisy or changeable. This means that if those features change, we may not be able to register such changes, leading to change blindness. Second, the event model construction system is built to bridge discontinuities in sensory input that arise during natural vision. One important source of visual discontinuity is eye movements, particularly saccades. Saccades are the most frequent type of eye movement, typically occurring several times a second and taking a bit less than 100 ms (Rayner & Castelhano, 2007). We make saccades in order to bring a region of the visual world into the high-resolution central part of the visual field, the fovea. During a saccade, visual information cannot be obtained due to the high velocity of the eyeball in its socket. A second source of visual discontinuity is blinking, which typically occurs every few seconds and lasts about

200–300 ms (Stern, Walrath, & Goldstein, 1984). Finally, occlusion is an important source of visual discontinuity. As we move around, objects in the scene are hidden by other objects. Similar considerations apply to other sensory modalities. To construct a coherent, stable event model in the face of these discontinuities, higher level perceptual processing systems identify correspondences between successive glances (or touches or sounds) and fuse them into a common representation. If a false correspondence is made, change blindness can result. Edit blindness can result because the bridging mechanism masks the discontinuity of the edit, just as it does with saccades and blinks. In short, we are insensitive to continuity errors and to edits because they fit themselves into the gaps between what our event models track. My hunch is that over the course of the development of cinema, filmmakers worked out which violations were jarring and which "worked" by intuition and trial and error, thereby doing a form of implicit perceptual psychology.

Episodic Memory, Autobiographical Memory, and Event Memory

An event model is a representation of a situation in the here-and-now (though it may be a here-and-now that one is reading about, imagining, or remembering). However, the act of forming an event model leaves strong traces that help determine how that event is represented later. Gabriel Radvansky and I have proposed a model of how this happens, called the *event horizon model* (Radvansky, 2012; Radvansky & Zacks, 2014). The model asserts five principles of event memory (see Table 12.1).

The first two principles are inherited from EST; the remaining three describe how the encoding of events is reflected in subsequent memory. The segmentation and working memory models lead to new predictions about how events are organized in long-term memory. One prediction is that information that is bound together in a common working model will become associated in long-term

TABLE 12.1 Five principles of the Event Horizon Model (Radvansky & Zacks, 2014)

1. **Segmentation:** Continuous ongoing activity is segmented into discrete events, and an event model is constructed for each event.
2. **Working models:** The event model corresponding to the event you are currently experiencing at any particular timescale has special status. It is actively maintained by recurrent neural activity, rather than being solely stored in patterns of synaptic weights.
3. **The causal network:** Long-term memory links event models by their causal relations.
4. **Noncompetitive attribute retrieval:** When elements of events are represented in multiple event models, access to those elements is facilitated.
5. **Competitive event retrieval:** When several event models are similar, accessing any specific event model is more difficult.

memory. Ezzyat and Davachi (2011) studied this using narrative texts. They presented people with stories that manipulated the locations of event boundaries using temporal predicates. For example, one story contained the sentence "He turned on some music to help him focus on his work," followed by one of two sentences: "A while later, he discovered some useful information and made a few notes," or "A moment later, he discovered some useful information and made a few notes." The version that used "while" created an event boundary, whereas the version that used "moment" was less likely to do so. After studying these narratives, participants completed a cued recall test in which they were given the first sentence and asked to recall the second. They were better able to do this in the "moment" condition than in the "while" condition, indicating that in the "moment" condition they were more likely to bind the two sentences together in long-term memory. Furthermore, this was associated with greater activity during encoding in brain areas associated with perceiving event boundaries.

If segmentation during encoding determines the subsequent structure of representation in long-term memory, then people who segment more adaptively should show better long-term memory. In a series of studies, we have found this to be the case. Assessing how well someone segments an activity requires a bit of finessing, because there is no objectively correct answer as to where the event boundaries are in a stimulus. However, it is straightforward to assess how consistent is one person's segmentation with the typical segmentation provided by others. This measure, *segmentation agreement,* is basically a correlation between an individual's segmentation and the likelihood of segmentation across a normative group. Segmentation agreement is a highly reliable predictor of subsequent memory across the adult lifespan (Sargent et al., 2013). It is sensitive to the effects of Alzheimer's disease and of genetic risk for Alzheimer's disease, and accounts for part of the effect of disease and genetic risk on long-term memory (Bailey et al., 2013, 2015).

If effective segmentation is important for long-term memory, then interventions that improve segmentation should improve memory. One way to test this is by editing films to encourage effective segmentation. For example, in one study Boltz (1992) presented viewers with an episode of a detective drama in which varying numbers of commercials had been inserted either at event boundaries or at the middles of events. Adding commercials at event boundaries improved memory, whereas adding commercials at event middles hurt memory. Similar results have been found for shorter films using subtler manipulations such as inserting pauses or edits (Gold, Zacks, & Flores, under review; Schwan, Garsoffky, & Hesse, 2000). This result offers a promise of interventions to benefit people with memory impairment. It may be possible to design systems that estimate the event boundaries in a film or story and present it to viewers or readers with modifications that facilitate adaptive segmentation, thereby improving memory encoding. Another possibility is to focus not on the stimulus but on the viewer. In a series of recent studies, we have asked whether simply attending to segmentation improves memory (Flores, Bailey, Eisenberg, & Zacks, in press). We manipulated attention to segmentation by instructing participants to segment events during encoding or merely watch them and try to remember as much as possible. Segmentation consistently improved memory, and the effect was durable at delays of up to a month.

The fact that event structure during encoding affects subsequent memory is probably important for film comprehension. As we watch a feature film, we are continuously encoding new events at the same time we are retrieving information from previous events—just as we do in real life. In films, however, events can be presented in any temporal order, and naturally occurring cues to segmentation can be subverted. For example, in Alain Resnais' *Last Year at Marienbad* (Resnais, 1962) or Christopher Nolan's *Memento* (Nolan, 2000), events are reordered in ways that subvert the retrieval of associated past events, and this surely affects the encoding of new events as they unfold. It may well be that our improved understanding of event segmentation will afford filmmakers new tools to manipulate viewers' experience.

Recently, there has been much interest in the overlap between processes involved in remembering past events, simulating future events, and imagining fictional events (Buckner & Carroll, 2007; Schacter et al., 2012). One important observation from these studies is that remembering, simulating, and imagining all are associated with a common set of brain regions, including the medial temporal lobes, midline areas in the prefrontal cortex, and midline and lateral areas in the inferior parietal cortex and adjacent regions. These areas comprise a functionally connected network: If one measures brain activity with fMRI during quiet wakefulness, the cortical areas all fluctuate along with the medial temporal lobe area. It has been proposed that this commonality reflects the ability to construct simulations of what might happen or of what the situation might look like from another point of view (Buckner & Carroll, 2007), and that this evolved in order to support long-term planning (Boyer, 2008).

I would suggest that what is in common across remembering, predicting, and imagining is *the construction of an event model*. The view from the science of memory contributes an important insight: As we construct event models, we make use of information retrieved from representations of previous events. However, I would suggest that this view, steeped as it is in the psychology of deliberate recollection, misconstrues one important aspect of event model construction: Often, retrieval of information from previous events is automatic and associative rather than deliberate (Berntsen, 2010). Moreover, at the same time we are retrieving representations of specific previous events, we are also retrieving knowledge about generic events. This sort of knowledge is usually described as an *event schema* or *script*, and it captures how particular classes of events typically unfold (Abelson, 1981; Rumelhart, 1980). Further, we are of course retrieving information about objects, people, and all the other things that make up events. I see no reason to privilege the role of representations of previous specific events in the construction of event models; rather, that sort of retrieval is likely to be smoothly integrated with retrieval of event schemas, object knowledge, person knowledge, and fact knowledge.

This view fits well with the account of long-term memory recently proposed by Rubin and Umanath (2015). They define an event memory as "the mental construction of a scene, real or imagined, for the past or the future" (p. 1). Rather than viewing episodic memory as a natural kind implemented by a particular neural system, they argue that the construction of a scene is the natural kind, and that episodic memory as described by Tulving (1983) corresponds to a subset of event memory—memories that are of relatively specific instances and are accompanied by a sense of reliving. On this view, what the hippocampus and surrounding structures contribute to memory is the binding of disparate features at encoding and during scene construction at retrieval. However, on this view the format of information storage for event memories is not fundamentally different from the format for other sorts of memories, including knowledge about events, objects and people.

Why Do We Have This System?

Thus, the primary function of event memory is not to make deliberately controlled inferences from episodic representations, but to construct a representation of what is happening now that is effective for guiding action control online (Glenberg, 1997). Along with this, I would suggest that the greater value of event memory may not be to engage in deliberate planning for the long-term future (Boyer, 2008), but to anticipate developments in the unfolding situation.

Since Helmholtz, physiologists and psychologists have noted that prediction plays an important role in perception (Boring, 1950, p. 308), but recent research in psychology and neuroscience has brought prediction to front and center (e.g., Aron et al., 2004; Bar, 2009; Loewenstein, Rick, & Cohen, 2008; Rao & Ballard, 1999; Wolpert & Flanagan, 2001). The evolutionary significance of prediction is easy to see: Prairie dogs avoid predation from falcons by detecting shadows that predict an attack is imminent and proactively taking evasive action and calling out. From the predator's point of view, dolphins anticipate the trajectories of prey fish and of their hunting partners, thereby improving success. In even simpler cases such as throwing a rock or jumping over an obstacle, anticipating the consequences of potential actions allows animals to select actions adaptively.

The philosopher Andy Clark (2013) has gone so far as to argue that "brains . . . are essentially prediction machines" (p. 181). He cites examples ranging from predictive coding of patterns of illumination in the retina to predictions of the consequences of deliberate actions. Are these all the same thing? I think it is unlikely that all—or even most—of the predictive processing mechanisms in the human brain can be subsumed under one general mechanism (and Clark's analysis treats low-level perception and motor control almost exclusively). However, I propose that there is an important class of predictive processing that may correspond to a natural kind implemented by a mechanism that can be conceptually isolated from other aspects of neural processing. This kind of processing encompasses predictions about how objects and entities on a human spatial scale (millimeters to meters) will behave on a human temporal scale (tenths of seconds to tens of minutes). This is the sort of prediction that allows one to anticipate that an approaching postal carrier will hand you your mail, to judge whether a boulder rolling downhill will intercept your current path or pass you by, or to judge whether a strange dog will behave aggressively. Event models are well positioned to facilitate this sort of prediction. Because they maintain a representation of the current state of affairs, they include the things that can participate in causal interactions—objects, animate agents, and relevant features of the scene. Because they are componential, they afford runnable simulations that result in representations of future states of affairs. Because they combine inputs from memory with inputs from perception, they allow us to use relevant previous instances and general knowledge to drive predictions. I will refer to predictions about the immediate scene on the spatial scale of millimeters to meters and the temporal scale of tenths of seconds to tens of minutes as *event predictions*.

Event predictions are at the center of event segmentation theory (EST; Zacks et al., 2007). Specifically, as I described previously, EST proposes that errors in event prediction tend to increase at event boundaries—in fact, it is this increase that leads to event model updating and the subjective experience of an event boundary. To test this hypothesis, we designed a task in which participants viewed movies of everyday activities and were asked from time to time to predict what would happen next in the movie (Zacks, Kurby, Eisenberg, & Haroutunian, 2011). In most of the experiments, they made their predictions by viewing two pictures and selecting the one that showed what would happen. The correct choice showed what would happen 5 seconds later, and the incorrect choice was selected from a movie of the same actor performing a similar activity. The movies had previously been segmented by a large number of viewers, and we used those previous data to define event boundaries based on the consensus of those previous viewers. We then designed the prediction trials such that half of the time 5 seconds later was a new event, and half of the time 5 seconds later was still part of the same event. EST entails that predictions should be less accurate when they cross event boundaries, and that is exactly what we observed. EST also makes specific predictions about the neurophysiological aspects of the prediction updating mechanism. These predictions are based on two observations about the neurophysiology of prediction errors in human and nonhuman animals. The first is that experiences that produce surprise, conflict, or error are associated with activation of the anterior cingulate cortex, in the medial frontal lobes. It has been proposed that this region is involved in monitoring levels of prediction error or conflict between representations (Bush, Luu, & Posner, 2000; Carter et al., 1998; Cohen, Botvinick, & Carter, 2000). The second observation is that spikes in prediction error are associated with discrete firing of dopamine neurons in the midbrain (Düzel et al., 2009; Schultz, 2007). These dopamine cells project broadly throughout the prefrontal cortex, both directly and through relays in the striatum. Thus, they are well positioned to serve as a reset signal for event boundaries. We hypothesized that attempting to predict across an event boundary would activate the midbrain dopamine system and its striatal targets, and that is what we found. Using brief movies of an actor tying knots, Schiffer, Krause, and Schubotz (2014) found that seeing another person perform an action in an unexpected manner led to activity in the anterior cingulate cortex. Importantly, the design allowed the authors to dissociate prediction error from performance error. Participants were trained to expect that the actor would finish some knots correctly but make errors on other knots. Cingulate activity was associated with unexpected completions whether they were unexpectedly correct or incorrect.

More recently, we have been investigating event predictions by tracking where people look as they are viewing an activity (Eisenberg & Zacks, in preparation). When people engage in activity or observe others' activities, they look predictively, gazing at objects that are about to be picked up before the object is actually contacted (Eshuis, Coventry, & Vulchanova, 2009; Gredebäck & Falck-Ytter, 2015). We hypothesized that this predictive looking would be slower and less accurate for objects contacted near event boundaries than for objects contacted in the middle of an event. To test this, we showed viewers movies of everyday activities while the viewers' eye gaze was tracked. Each movie had previously been segmented by other observers to identify fine and coarse event boundaries. We coded the movies to identify when objects were picked up by the actor, and where those objects were when they were contacted. Objects were divided into three classes: those that were picked up in the middle of an event, those that were picked up within 3 seconds of a fine event boundary, and those that were picked up within 3 seconds of a coarse event boundary. We then tabulated the frequency of looking to the to-be-contacted object in the 3 seconds leading up to the object contact. As hypothesized, we found that viewers looked earlier and more frequently at to-be-contacted objects during event middles than during fine or coarse boundaries.

These results provide some initial hints about how event predictions work—in particular, how event models are regulated by prediction error monitoring. Many more questions remain to be answered. How do individuals differ in their event prediction ability? Is this related to other aspects of cognition such as memory and decision-making? How does event prediction develop? How is it affected by neurological disease and injury? My hunch is that this component of "the predictive brain" will turn out to be a coherent entity, and that investigating event prediction will tell us much about basic issues in cognition.

Why We Tell Stories

Event models are probably not at all unique to humans. Rather, I believe that the capacity to construct an event model and to use it to drive predictions about the immediate future is one that is shared broadly across mammalian taxa and could even exist in similar form in birds and other species (Clayton & Dickinson, 1998).

However, there is one aspect of event cognition that is clearly unique to humans: we share stories of events (see also Marsh and Arnold, this volume). Originally, this took the form of stories around the campfire and instructions about how to forage for plants and to hunt game. Now, we read newspapers and magazines, pulp and literary fiction, graphic novels, and histories. We listen to podcasts, news radio, and books on tape. We watch plays and operas, movies and television. Human culture is awash in stories. (See Tversky, 2004.)

All of this storytelling, evolutionarily new as it is, piggybacks on our older evolved mechanisms for storytelling (Donald, 1991). Thus, it depends on two key adaptations. First is the event model system, which is evolutionarily old and shared across species. The second is language, which is evolutionarily very young and is basically unique to humans. Other species certainly have impressive communications abilities, and there is room for disagreement as to where to draw the bounds around the term "language," but only humans have the sort of language that can allow a speaker or writer to give detailed directions for a listener or reader to construct a rich event model.

Recently, scientific attention has focused on one particular function of one particular kind of storytelling: social reasoning in literary fiction. As Mar and Oatley (2008) put it, "The function of fiction is the abstraction and simulation of social experience." They argue that literary fiction in particular provides a testbed for readers to train their ability to form representations of social situations and to test predictions about what may happen in varying social situations. This makes intuitive sense: As we comprehend a story, we construct a sequence of event models. For each model, during the period in which it is current we use it to drive predictions about what will happen next in the story—in particular, how the people in the story will behave. We can test our predictions against what actually happens, and use the same prediction-error-driven mechanism that leads to event model updating to provide a training signal to teach us about how human behavior works. There is a powerful computational learning mechanism, reinforcement learning, that can support just this sort of training (Holroyd & Coles, 2002; Maia, 2009). Reinforcement learning works by adjusting associations based on differences between one's expectation of reward or punishment and the rewards or punishments one receives. Each adjust serves to reduce the error between one's predictions and what actually happens. After training, reward learning can produce impressive prediction performance. The unique advantage of driving reinforcement learning from stories is that the rewards—and more importantly, the punishments—are virtual. If you make a wrong prediction in a heated social situation in the real world, there could be strong negative consequences. By providing a safe training environment, stories give us the opportunity to hone our social event prediction skills offline, without the risks of practicing in real situations.

The data in support of this thesis are intriguing. First, in the 1960s and 1970s, researchers used stories to attempt to reduce white children's prejudice against black children and to increase empathy, by editing the English readers they were using to include black characters. This worked—and worked better than having black and white children work together on a shared task. Second, correlational studies have shown that adults who read more literary fiction are better at tasks that require empathy (Mar, Oatley, Hirsh, dela Paz, & Peterson, 2006). Most striking, a single episode of reading literary fiction (defined as recent literary prize nominees) improved people's ability to read others' states of mind, and did so better than reading nonfiction or popular fiction (defined as recent bestsellers; Kidd & Castano, 2013).

On this account, the reason we tell stories is to practice social reasoning. I would like to close by taking this proposal and broadening it dramatically[1]. I think that the reason we are so attracted to stories is that they give us the chance to practice event model construction in a safe, virtual environment. As Mar and Oatley (2008) note, erroneous social predictions can be dangerous in real life, and so practicing them offline is valuable. However, this point applies not just to social predictions but also to all aspects of event prediction. What might happen if the ship's radio goes out? If the roof takes on too much snow? If the creek floods? Further, the value of training predictions applies to rewards as well as to threats. What might happen if one orders the octopus at an expensive restaurant? Confesses one's feelings to an admired someone? Takes the trip of a lifetime? Fictional stories—be they literary or not, and be they spoken, written, or filmed—give us the chance to build event models of situations that might be difficult or expensive or dangerous in real life. They provide a safe space to train our event models, to hone our predictive brains, to ready us for the world.

I think this is an eminently Tverskyan suggestion. For me, one of the most salient characteristics of Barbara's theoretical work—be it on memory, spatial thinking, or event cognition—is its attention to common mechanisms that can unite online behavior with offline cognition. This feature—and so many others—I have tried to emulate in the work described here.

Author Note

The research described in this chapter was supported by the National Institutes of Health (R01MH070674, R01AG031150, P50AG0568), the National Science Foundation (BCS-023665) and the Defense Advanced Research Projects Agency (D13AP00009).

Note

1 I thank Suparna Rajaram for this suggestion.

References

Abelson, R. P. (1981). Psychological status of the script concept. *American Psychologist, 36*, 715–729.

Aron, A. R., Shohamy, D., Clark, J., Myers, C., Gluck, M. A., & Poldrack, R. A. (2004). Human midbrain sensitivity to cognitive feedback and uncertainty during classification learning. *Journal of Neurophysiology, 92*(2), 1144–1152.

Bailey, H. R., Sargent, J. Q., Flores, S., Nowotny, P., Goate, A., & Zacks, J. M. (2015). APOE ε4 genotype predicts memory for everyday activities. *Aging, Neuropsychology, and Cognition, 22*(6), 639–666.

Bailey, H. R., Zacks, J. M., Hambrick, D. Z., Zacks, R. T., Head, D., Kurby, C. A., & Sargent, J. Q. (2013). Medial temporal lobe volume predicts elders' everyday memory. *Psychological Science, 24*(7), 1113–1122. Doi: 10.1177/0956797612466676

Bar, M. (2009). The proactive brain: memory for predictions. *Philosophical Transactions of the Royal Society B – Biological Science, 364*(1521), 1235–1243. Doi: 10.1098/rstb.2008.0310

Barbey, A., Krueger, F., & Grafman, J. (2009). Structured event complexes in the medial prefrontal cortex support counterfactual representations for future planning. *Philosophical Transactions of the Royal Society B – Biological Science, 364*(1521), 1291–1300. Doi: 10.1098/rstb.2008.0315

Barsalou, L.W. (1999). Perceptual symbol systems. *Behavioral and Brain Sciences, 22*(4), 577–660.

Barsalou, L.W. (2008). Grounded cognition. *Annual Review of Psychology, 59*, 617–645.

Berntsen, D. (2010). The unbidden past: Involuntary autobiographical memories as a basic mode of remembering. *Current Directions in Psychological Science, 19*(3), 138–142.

Boltz, M. (1992). Temporal accent structure and the remembering of filmed narratives. *Journal of Experimental Psychology: Human Perception & Performance, 18*(1), 90–105.

Boring, E. G. (1950). *A history of experimental psychology*. New York: Appleton-Century-Crofts, Inc.

Boyer, P. (2008). Evolutionary economics of mental time travel? *Trends in Cognitive Sciences, 12*(6), 219–224.

Buckner, R. & Carroll, D. (2007). Self-projection and the brain. *Trends in Cognitive Sciences, 11*(2), 49–57.

Bush, G., Luu, P., & Posner, M. I. (2000). Cognitive and emotional influences in anterior cingulated cortex. *Trends in Cognitive Sciences, 4*(6), 215–222.

Butler, A. C., Zaromb, F. M., Lyle, K. B., & Roediger, I. (2009). Using popular films to enhance classroom learning: the good, the bad, and the interesting. *Psychological Science, 20*(9), 1161–1168.

Carter, C., Braver, T., Barch, D., Botvinick, M., Noll, D., & Cohen, J. (1998). Anterior cingulate cortex, error detection, and the online monitoring of performance. *Science, 280*(5364), 747–749.

Castiello, U. (2005). The neuroscience of grasping. *Nature Reviews Neuroscience, 6*(9), 726–736.

Clark, A. (2013). Whatever next? Predictive brains, situated agents, and the future of cognitive science. *Behavioral and Brain Sciences, 36*(3), 181–204.

Clayton, N. S. & Dickinson, A. (1998). Episodic-like memory during cache recovery by scrub jays. *Nature, 395*(6699), 272–274. Doi: 10.1038/26216

Cohen, J. D., Botvinick, M., & Carter, C. S. (2000). Anterior cingulate and prefrontal cortex: who's in control? *Nature Neuroscience, 3*(5), 421–423.

Crozier, S., Sirigu, A., Lehéricy, S., Moortele, P.-F., van de, Pillon, B., Grafman, J., ... LeBihan, D. (1999). Distinct prefrontal activations in processing sequence at the sentence and script level: An fMRI study. *Neuropsychologia, 37*, 1469–1476.

Damasio, A. R. (1989). The brain binds entities and events by multiregional activation from convergence zones. *Neural Computation, 1*(1), 123–132.

Donald, M. (1991). *Origins of the modern mind: three stages in the evolution of culture and cognition.* Cambridge, MA: Harvard University Press.

Düzel, E., Bunzeck, N., Guitart-Masip, M., Wittmann, B., Schott, B. H., & Tobler, P. N. (2009). Functional imaging of the human dopaminergic midbrain. *Trends in Neurosciences, 32*(6), 321–328. Doi: 10.1016/j.tins.2009.02.005

Eisenberg, M. L., & Zacks, J. M. (in preparation). *Predictive looking is impaired at event boundaries.*

Epstein, R. & Kanwisher, N. (1998). A cortical representation of the local visual environment. *Nature, 392*(6676), 598–601.

Eshuis, R., Coventry, K. R., & Vulchanova, M. (2009). Predictive eye movements are driven by goals, not by the mirror neuron system. *Psychological Science, 20*(4), 438–440. Doi: 10.1111/j.1467-9280.2009.02317.x

Ezzyat, Y. & Davachi, L. (2011). What constitutes an episode in episodic memory? *Psychological Science, 22*(2), 243–252.

Flores, S., Bailey, H. R., Eisenberg, M. L., & Zacks, J. M. (in press). Event segmentation improves event memory up to one month later. *Journal of Experimental Psychology: Learning, Memory & Cognition.*

Fodor, J. A. (1975). *The language of thought.* Cambridge, MA: Harvard Univ Press.

Fuster, J. M. (1997). *The prefrontal cortex: anatomy, physiology, and neuropsychology of the frontal lobe.* Philadelphia: Lippincott-Raven.

Glenberg, A. M. (1997). What memory is for: Creating meaning in the service of action. *Behavioral and Brain Sciences, 20*(1), 41–50.

Goff, L. M. & Roediger, H. L. I. (1998). Imagination inflation for action events: Repeated imaginings lead to illusory recollections. *Memory & Cognition, 26*(1), 20–33.

Gold, D. A., Zacks, J. M., & Flores, S. (under review). Effects of cues to event segmentation on subsequent memory.

Grafman, J., Partiot, A., & Hollnagel, C. (1995). Fables of the prefrontal cortex. *Behavioral and Brain Sciences, 18*(2), 349–358.

Gredebäck, G. & Falck-Ytter, T. (2015). Eye movements during action observation. *Perspectives on Psychological Science, 10*(5), 591–598.

Hard, B. M., Recchia, G., & Tversky, B. (2011). The shape of action. *Journal of Experimental Psychology: General, 140*(4), 586–604.

Holroyd, C. B. & Coles, M. G. (2002). The neural basis of human error processing: reinforcement learning, dopamine, and the error-related negativity. *Psychological Review, 109*(4), 679–709.

Humphreys, G.W., Forde, E. M. E., & Riddoch, M. J. (2001). The planning and execution of everyday actions. In B. Rapp (Ed.), *The handbook of cognitive neuropsychology: what deficits reveal about the human mind* (pp. 565–589). Philadelphia: Psychology Press.

Humphries, C., Liebenthal, E., & Binder, J. R. (2010). Tonotopic organization of human auditory cortex. *NeuroImage, 50*(3), 1202–1211.

Johnson, M. K. (2006). Memory and reality. *American Psychologist, 61*(8), 760–771.

Kalisky, Z. & Uzzell, B. P. (1996). Florid confabulation following brain injury. In B. P. Uzzell & H. H. Stonnington (Eds.), *Recovery after traumatic brain injury* (pp. 149–161). Mahwah: L. Erlbaum Associates.

Kidd, D. C. & Castano, E. (2013). Reading literary fiction improves theory of mind. *Science, 342*(6156), 377–380.

Kriete, T., Noelle, D. C., Cohen, J. D., & O'Reilly, R. C. (2013). Indirection and symbol-like processing in the prefrontal cortex and basal ganglia. *Proceedings of the National Academy of Sciences, 110*(41), 16390–16395.

Kurby, C. A. & Zacks, J. M. (2008). Segmentation in the perception and memory of events. *Trends in Cognitive Sciences, 12*(2), 72–79.

Levin, D. T. & Simons, D. J. (1997). Failure to detect changes to attended objects in motion pictures. *Psychonomic Bulletin & Review, 4*(4), 501–506.

Levin, D. T. & Simons, D. J. (2000). Perceiving stability in a changing world: Combining shots and integrating views in motion pictures and the real world. *Media Psychology, 2*(4), 357–380.

Loewenstein, G., Rick, S., & Cohen, J. D. (2008). Neuroeconomics. *Annual Review of Psychology, 59*(1), 647–672.

Magliano, J. P., Miller, J., & Zwaan, R. A. (2001). Indexing space and time in film understanding. *Applied Cognitive Psychology, 15*(5), 533–545.

Mahon, B. Z. & Caramazza, A. (2008). A critical look at the embodied cognition hypothesis and a new proposal for grounding conceptual content. *Journal of Physiology-Paris, 102*(1–3), 59–70.

Maia, T. V. (2009). Reinforcement learning, conditioning, and the brain: Successes and challenges. *Cognitive, Affective, & Behavioral Neuroscience, 9*(4), 343–364. Doi: 10.3758/CABN.9.4.343

Mar, R. A. & Oatley, K. (2008). The function of fiction is the abstraction and simulation of social experience. *Perspectives on Psychological Science, 3*(3), 173–192.

Mar, R. A., Oatley, K., Hirsh, J., dela Paz, J., & Peterson, J. B. (2006). Bookworms versus nerds: Exposure to fiction versus non-fiction, divergent associations with social ability, and the simulation of fictional social worlds. *Journal of Research in Personality, 40*(5), 694–712.

Marsh, E. J., & Arnold, K. M. (2018). Retelling experiences and writing essays. In *Representations in Mind and World: Essays Inspired by Barbara Tversky* (pp. 137–155). New York: Routledge.

Newtson, D. (1976). Foundations of attribution: The perception of ongoing behavior. In J. H. Harvey, W. J. Ickes, & R. F. Kidd (Eds.), *New directions in attribution research* (pp. 223–248). Hillsdale, New Jersey: Lawrence Erlbaum Associates.

Newtson, D., Engquist, G., & Bois, J. (1977). The objective basis of behavior units. *Journal of Personality and Social Psychology, 35*(12), 847–862.

Nolan, C. (2000). *Memento.* [Film]

Penfield, W. & Rasmussen, T. (1950). *The cerebral cortex of man.* New York: Macmillan.

Radvansky, G. A. (2012). Across the event horizon. *Current Directions in Psychological Science, 21*(4), 269–272.

Radvansky, G. A. & Zacks, J. M. (2014). *Event Cognition.* New York: Oxford University Press.

Rao, R. P. & Ballard, D. H. (1999). Predictive coding in the visual cortex: a functional interpretation of some extra-classical receptive-field effects. *Nature Neuroscience, 2*(1), 79–87.

Rayner, K. & Castelhano, M. (2007). Eye movements. *Scholarpedia, 2*(10), 3649. Doi: 10.4249/scholarpedia.3649

Resnais, A. (1962). *Last Year at Marienbad.* [Film]

Reynolds, J. R., Zacks, J. M., & Braver, T. S. (2007). A computational model of event segmentation from perceptual prediction. *Cognitive Science, 31*, 613–643.

Rubin, D. C. & Umanath, S. (2015). Event memory: A theory of memory for laboratory, autobiographical, and fictional events. *Psychological Review, 122*(1), 1–23.

Rugg, M. D. & Vilberg, K. L. (2013). Brain networks underlying episodic memory retrieval. *Current Opinion in Neurobiology, 23*(2), 255–260.

Rumelhart, D. E. (1980). Schemata: The building blocks of cognition. In R. J. Spiro, B. C. Bruce, & W. F. Brewer (Eds.), *Theoretical issues in reading comprehension: Perspectives from cognitive psychology, linguistics, artificial intelligence, and education* (pp. 33–58). Hillsdale, N.J.: L. Erlbaum Associates.

Sargent, J. Q., Zacks, J. M., Hambrick, D. Z., Zacks, R. T., Kurby, C. A., Bailey, H. R. . . . & Beck, T. M. (2013). Event segmentation ability uniquely predicts event memory. *Cognition, 129*(2), 241–255.

Schacter, D. L., Addis, D. R., Hassabis, D., Martin, V. C., Spreng, R. N., & Szpunar, K. K. (2012). The future of memory: Remembering, imagining, and the brain. *Neuron, 76*(4), 677–694.

Schiffer, A.-M., Krause, K. H., & Schubotz, R. I. (2014). Surprisingly correct: Unexpectedness of observed actions activates the medial prefrontal cortex. *Human Brain Mapping, 35*(4), 1615–1629.

Schultz, W. (2007). Multiple dopamine functions at different time courses. *Annual Review of Neuroscience, 30*(1), 259–288.

Schwan, S., Garsoffky, B., & Hesse, F. W. (2000). Do film cuts facilitate the perceptual and cognitive organization of activity sequences? *Memory & Cognition, 28*(2), 214–223.

Shepard, R. N. & Chipman, S. (1970). Second-order isomorphism of internal representations: Shapes of states. *Cognitive Psychology, 1*(1), 1–17.

Simons, D. & Ambinder, M. (2005). Change Blindness: Theory and consequences. *Current Directions in Psychological Science, 14*(1), 44–48.

Sirigu, A., Zalla, T., Pillon, B., Grafman, J., Agid, Y., & Dubois, B. (1995). Selective impairments in managerial knowledge following pre-frontal cortex damage. *Cortex, 31*(2), 301–316.

Sirigu, A., Zalla, T., Pillon, B., Grafman, J., Agid, Y., & Dubois, B. (1996). Encoding of sequence and boundaries of scripts following prefrontal lesions. *Cortex, 32*(2), 297–310.

Smith, T. J. & Henderson, J. M. (2008). Edit blindness: The relationship between attention and global change in dynamic scenes. *Journal of Eye Movement Research, 2*(2), 1–17.

Speer, N. K., Reynolds, J. R., Swallow, K. M., & Zacks, J. M. (2009). Reading stories activates neural representations of perceptual and motor experiences. *Psychological Science, 20*, 989–999.

Speer, N. K., Reynolds, J. R., & Zacks, J. M. (2007). Human brain activity time-locked to narrative event boundaries. *Psychological Science, 18*(5), 449–455.

Sridharan, D., Levitin, D., Chafe, C., Berger, J., & Menon, V. (2007). Neural dynamics of event segmentation in music: converging evidence for dissociable ventral and dorsal networks. *Neuron, 55*(3), 521–532.

Stern, J. A., Walrath, L. C., & Goldstein, R. (1984). The endogenous eyeblink. *Psychophysiology, 21*(1), 22–33.

Terminator 3: Rise of the Machines movie mistake picture 1. (n.d.). Retrieved March 28, 2016, from www.moviemistakes.com/picture28864

Tootell, R., Silverman, M., Switkes, E., & De Valois, R. (1982). Deoxyglucose analysis of retinotopic organization in primate striate cortex. *Science, 218*(4575), 902–904.

Tulving, E. (1983). *Elements of episodic memory*. New York: Oxford University Press.

Tversky, B. (1989). Parts, partonomies, and taxonomies. *Developmental Psychology, 25*(6), 983–995.

Tversky, B. (2004). Narratives of space, time, and life. *Mind & Language, 19*(4), 380–392.

Tversky, B. & Hemenway, K. (1984). Objects, parts, and categories. *Journal of Experimental Psychology: General, 113*(2), 169–193.

Tversky, B. & Marsh, E. J. (2000). Biased retellings of events yield biased memories. *Cognitive Psychology, 40*(1), 1–38.

Whitney, C., Huber, W., Klann, J., Weis, S., Krach, S., & Kircher, T. (2009). Neural correlates of narrative shifts during auditory story comprehension. *NeuroImage, 47*(1), 360–366.

Wolpert, D. M. & Flanagan, J. R. (2001). Motor prediction. *Current Biology, 11*(18), R729–R732.

Wood, J. N. & Grafman, J. (2003). Human prefrontal cortex: Processing and representational perspectives. *Nature Reviews Neuroscience, 4*, 139–147.

Zacks, J. M. (2004). Using movement and intentions to understand simple events. *Cognitive Science, 28*(6), 979–1008.

Zacks, J. M., Braver, T. S., Sheridan, M. A., Donaldson, D. I., Snyder, A. Z., Ollinger, J. M. . . . & Raichle, M. E. (2001). Human brain activity time-locked to perceptual event boundaries. *Nature Neuroscience, 4*(6), 651–655.

Zacks, J. M., Kumar, S., Abrams, R. A., & Mehta, R. (2009). Using movement and intentions to understand human activity. *Cognition, 112*, 201–216.

Zacks, J. M., Kurby, C. A., Eisenberg, M. L., & Haroutunian, N. (2011). Prediction error associated with the perceptual segmentation of naturalistic events. *Journal of Cognitive Neuroscience, 23*, 4057–4066.

Zacks, J. M., Speer, N. K., & Reynolds, J. R. (2009). Segmentation in reading and film comprehension. *Journal of Experimental Psychology: General, 138*(2), 307–327.

Zacks, J. M., Speer, N. K., Swallow, K. M., Braver, T. S., & Reynolds, J. R. (2007). Event perception: A mind/brain perspective. *Psychological Bulletin, 133*(2), 273–293.

Zacks, J. M., Speer, N. K., Swallow, K. M., & Maley, C. J. (2010). The brain's cutting-room floor: Segmentation of narrative cinema. *Frontiers in Human Neuroscience, 4*(168), 1–15.

Zacks, J. M., Swallow, K. M., Vettel, J. M., & McAvoy, M. P. (2006). Visual movement and the neural correlates of event perception. *Brain Research, 1076*(1), 150–162.

Zwaan, R. A. (1999). Five dimensions of narrative comprehension: The event-indexing model. In S. R. Goldman, A. C. Graesser, & P. van den Broek (Eds.), *Narrative comprehension, causality, and coherence: Essays in honor of Tom Trabasso* (pp. 93–110). Mahwah, NJ: Lawrence Erlbaum Associates.

Zwaan, R. A., Langston, M. C., & Graesser, A. C. (1995). The construction of situation models in narrative comprehension: An event-indexing model. *Psychological Science, 6*(5), 292–297.

13

WHAT ARTISTS DO (& SAY) WHEN THEY DRAW

A Cognitive Ethnographic (and Arts-Based) Study of Eight Contemporary Artists' Improvisational Drawing Practices

Andrea Kantrowitz

What ARTISTS do (& say) when they DRAW

a cognitive ethnographic (and arts-based) study of eight contemporary artists' improvisational drawing practices

Andrea Kantrowitz
State University of New York @ New Paltz

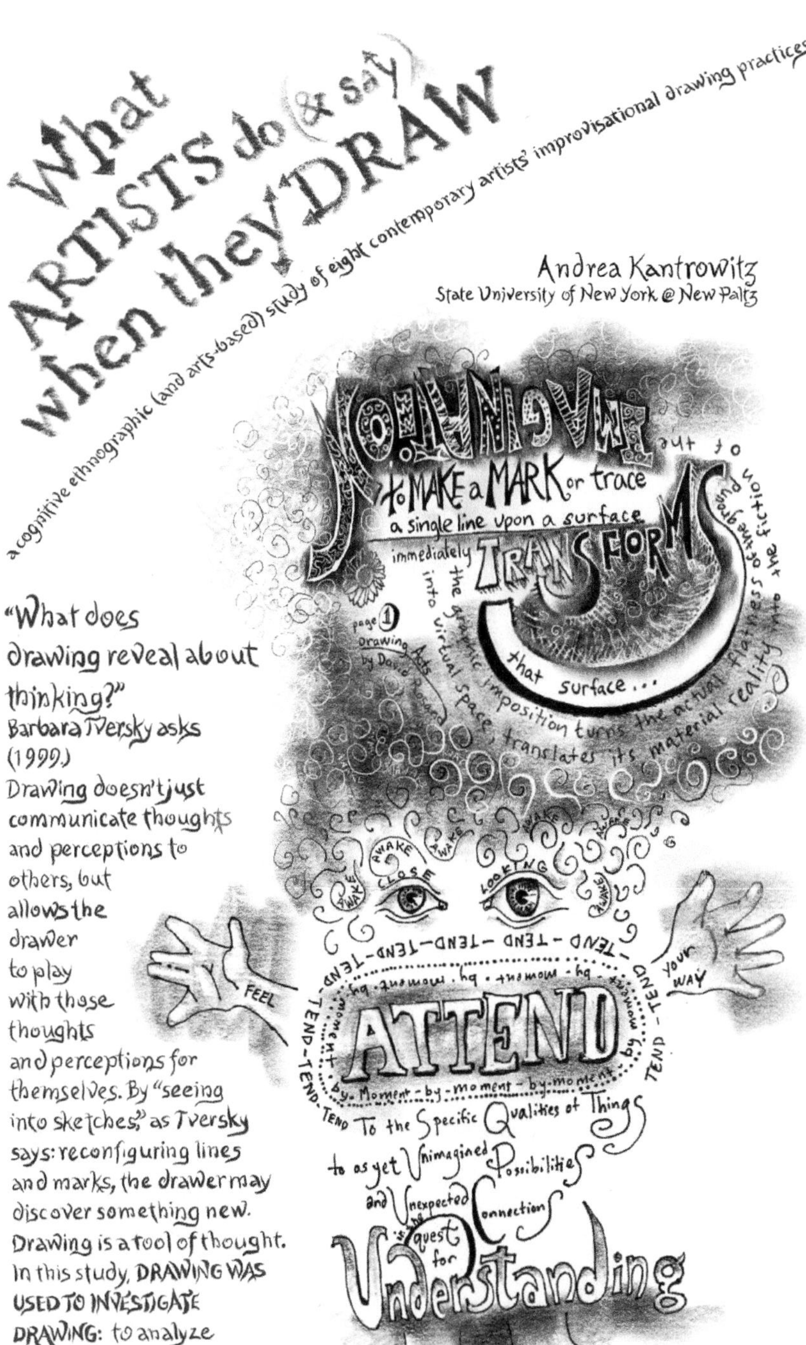
to MAKE a MARK or trace
a single line upon a surface
immediately TRANSFORMS
that surface...
out to
the graphic imposition turns the actual flatness of the ground
into virtual space, translates its material reality into the fiction
page 1
Drawing Acts
by David Rosand
AWAKE
CLOSE
LOOKING
TEND-TEND-TEND-TEND-TEND-TEND
moment-by-moment-by-moment
ATTEND
FEEL
YOUR WAY
To the Specific Qualities of Things
to as yet Unimagined Possibilities
and Unexpected Connections
the quest for
Understanding
SLOW
DOWN

"What does drawing reveal about thinking?" Barbara Tversky asks (1999.) Drawing doesn't just communicate thoughts and perceptions to others, but allows the drawer to play with those thoughts and perceptions for themselves. By "seeing into sketches," as Tversky says: reconfiguring lines and marks, the drawer may discover something new. Drawing is a tool of thought. In this study, **DRAWING WAS USED TO INVESTIGATE DRAWING:** to analyze the data and visualize underlying concepts.

Knowing **"how to draw"** is often understood to mean being able to reproduce a known target But artists often say they draw to see and play with their thoughts on paper: The writer and artist John Berger has explained, **"Every artist discovers that drawing~when it is an urgent activity~ is a two-way process. To draw is not only to measure and put down, it is also to receive"** (2005, p. 77.)

Improvisational drawing practices invite the unexpected. Without a clear end in mind, forms and shapes emerge and seem to take on a life of their own

"All instrumentalists... feel that their instrument is an extension of themselves... and improvisation is not just making it up as you go along, its the ability to be creative within and around a known set of boundaries for which you've prepared a great deal ... and that is right in line with the ethos of the Marine Corps."

– Staff Sgt. Ken Ebo
Marine Corps Jazz Ensemble

this is Wynton Marsalis

DRAWING IS A WAY TO HAVE A CONVERSATION WITH YOURSELF. Thinking, according to the theory of situated cognition, doesn't just happen in the brain, but is a complex series of iterative top-down, bottom-up interactions, flowing between the brain, the whole body and surroundings. Cognitive acts such as planning, analyzing and evaluating, are task-directed and top-down, initiated by explicit reasoning.

Bottom-up processes include learned and automated routines, multi-modal perceptions, and emotional responses. Emotions, coming from the bottom up, below the level of conscious awareness, serve to filter perceptions, guide attention and are, in turn influenced by top-down thoughts and judgments. (Damasio 1999, 2006.)

COGNITIVE ETHNOGRAPHY is the study of "cognition in the wild," outside the laboratory (Hutchins, 1995.) Artists were videotaped for a half hour as they drew in their own studios. Immediately following these sessions, artists narrated the thought processes that guided specific actions.

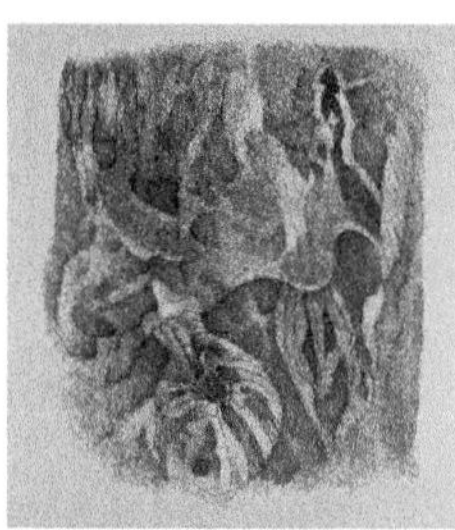

Michael Moore draws on memories

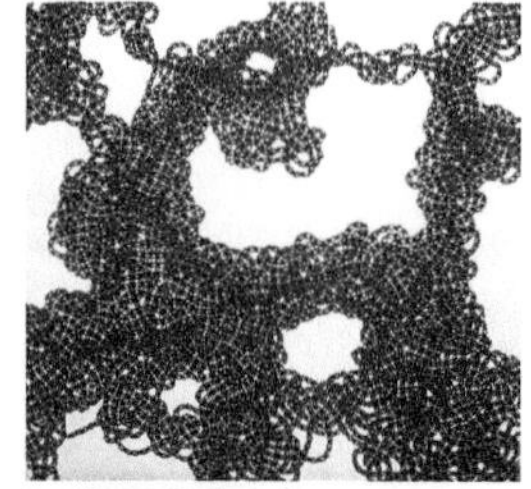

William Holton is interested in biological processes

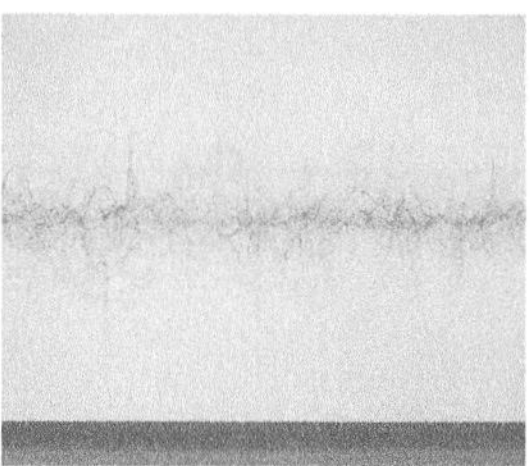

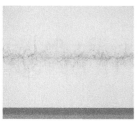

Margaret Neill responds to a sense of place in her site-specific wall drawings

Jane Fine is inspired by Krazy Kat comics

Tara Geer observes bits of stuff in the world

Josette Urso looks out her window

Sharon Rosensweig makes comics based on her observations of people in her life

Wennie Huang reflects nostalgia for a far away country.

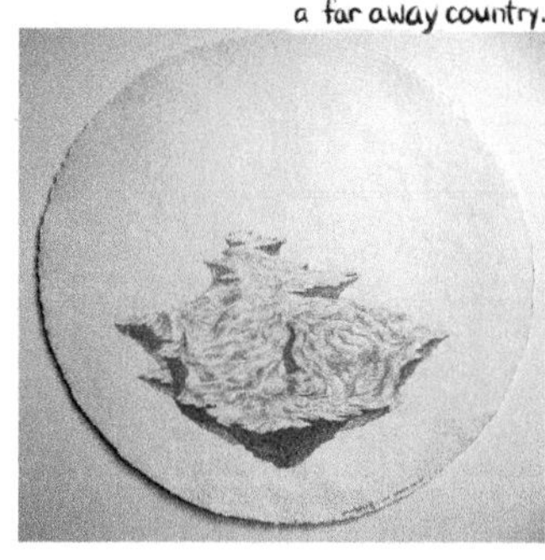

Research drawings based on the videos helped identify patterns of activity, types of actions and spatial location.

Five (5) TYPES of

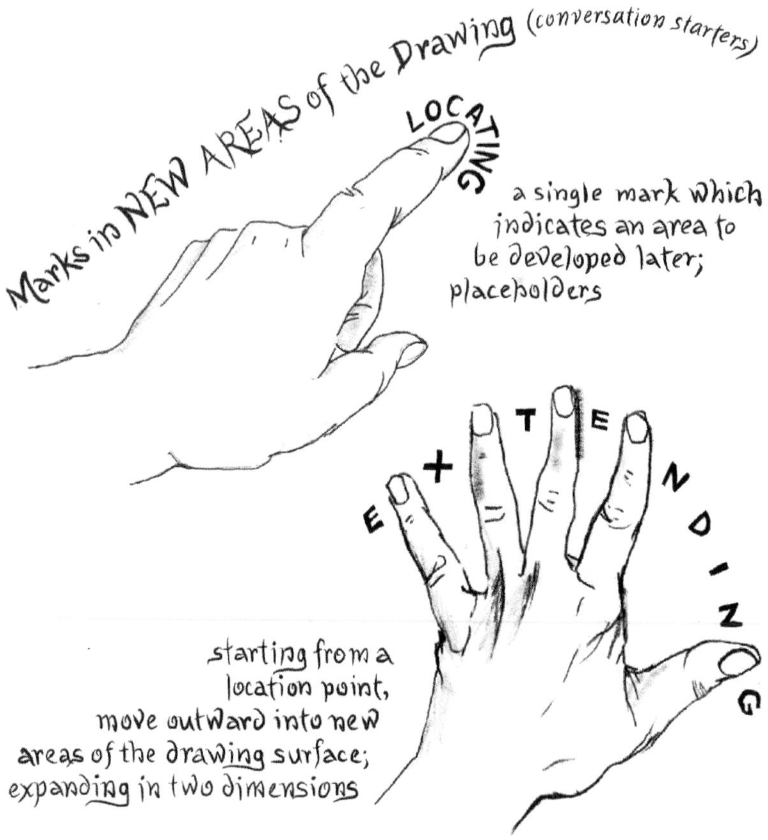

Marks in NEW AREAS of the Drawing (conversation starters)
LOCATING
a single mark which indicates an area to be developed later; placeholders
EXTENDING
starting from a location point, move outward into new areas of the drawing surface; expanding in two dimensions

Artists made five different kinds of marks:
to **LOCATE, EXTEND, CONNECT, REINFORCE** and **REVISE.**

These categories were observed in the video without needing any interpretation or explanation. The taxonomy was discussed and shared with other researchers and artists, and provides a flexible and comprehensive framework for analyzing many different kinds of drawing, beyond the specific examples analyzed in this study.

DRAWING ACTIONS

Revisits to ESTABLISHED AREAS (the drawing talks back)

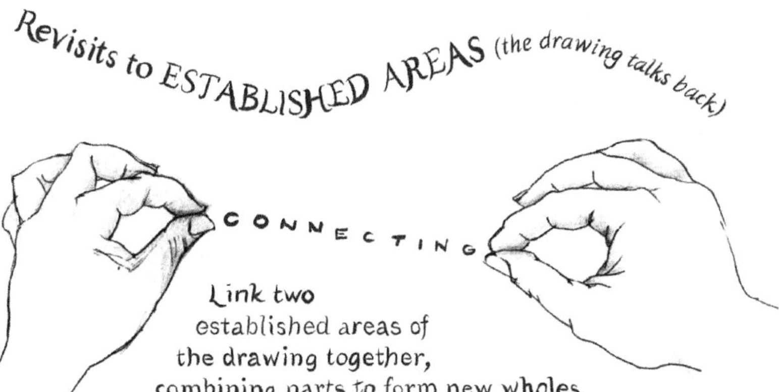
CONNECTING
Link two established areas of the drawing together, combining parts to form new wholes.

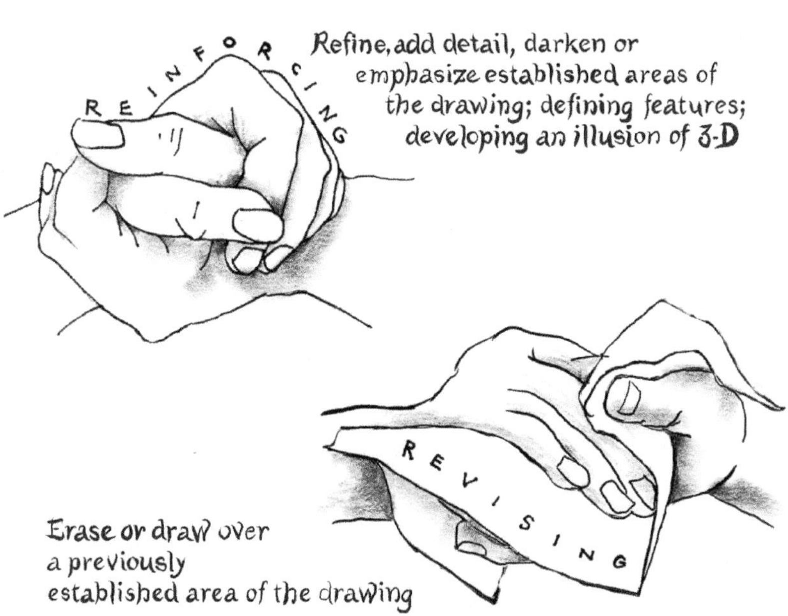
REINFORCING
Refine, add detail, darken or emphasize established areas of the drawing; defining features; developing an illusion of 3-D
REVISING
Erase or draw over a previously established area of the drawing

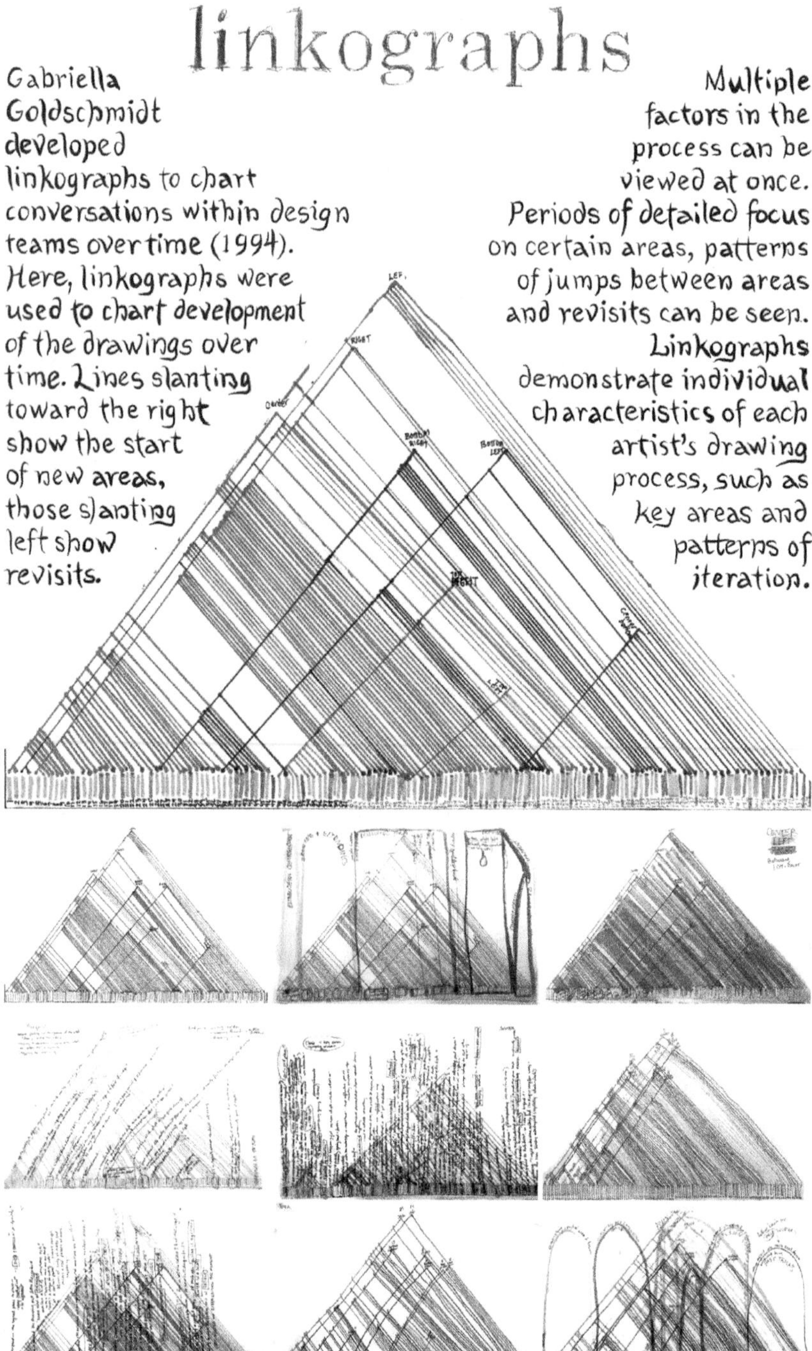
linkographs
Gabriella Goldschmidt developed linkographs to chart conversations within design teams over time (1994). Here, linkographs were used to chart development of the drawings over time. Lines slanting toward the right show the start of new areas, those slanting left show revisits.
Multiple factors in the process can be viewed at once. Periods of detailed focus on certain areas, patterns of jumps between areas and revisits can be seen. Linkographs demonstrate individual characteristics of each artist's drawing process, such as key areas and patterns of iteration.
LEFT
RIGHT
CENTER
BOTTOM RIGHT
BOTTOM LEFT
TOP RIGHT

As marks accumulate, borders and edges, figure and ground begin to emerge. Artists combine parts into new wholes, noticing and reinforcing opportunities to create a sense of three-dimensional form and space. Accidental variations generate further development.

Oscillations between action and reflection become feedback loops that drive the drawing forward. Each artist seemed to have developed their own rhythm of moving between focus on specific details of the drawing and working on overall coherence, pulling it all together.

node

consecutive repeated visits to the same area. (*different actions, i.e. contour line, followed by cross-hatching.*)

multiple incidents of consecutive repeated visits to the same area

jump between the same two areas

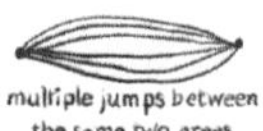

multiple jumps between the same two areas

These diagrams are simplified MAPS of action locations. They show the spatial distribution of marks over the drawing surface and patterns of breaks between individual action segments. Each artist demonstrated a unique pattern of oscillation between periods of concentrated activity in single areas, and jumps between areas.

Key areas of concentrated activity emerged in most of the drawings which seemed to guide the process.

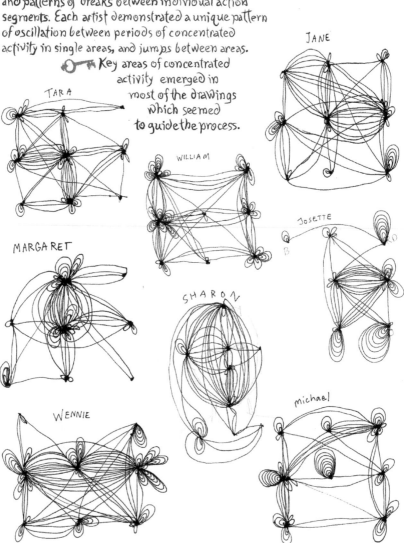

TARA

JANE

WILLIAM

JOSETTE

MARGARET

SHARON

WENNIE

michael

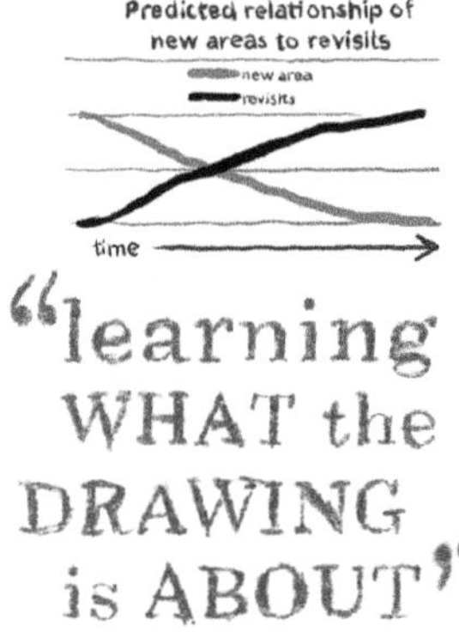

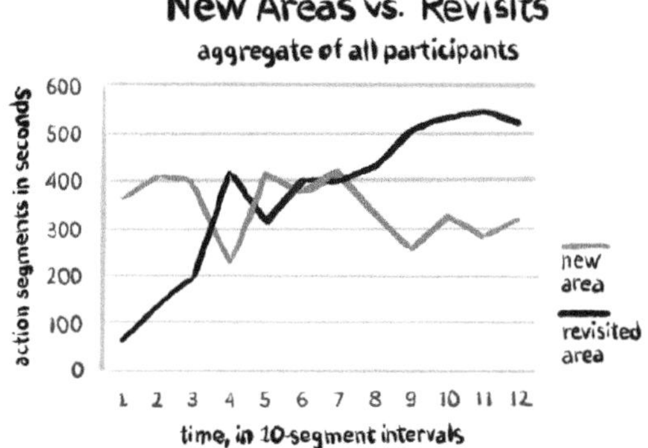

The charts above show the predicted and actual marks made in new areas, compared to revisited areas, over time. The early peak of revisits in the aggregate graph coincided with artists' reports that early on, they were searching for clues in key areas of the drawing that could guide its progress. The artist-participant Sharon Rosensweig explains that the pleasure of drawing comes "when the formless void of marks and erasures burp up something funny or alive." As the drawing develops, the artist imaginatively projects her or himself into a virtual world, pokes around, turns corners, encounters the unexpected and fleshes out details. The image below contains artist-participants' observations during that first peak of revisits, when they are "learning what the drawing is about."

REFERENCES

Berger, J. (2005). *Berger on drawing.* J. Savage (Ed.). Cork, Ireland: Occasional Press.

Damasio, A. R. (1999). *The feeling of what happens: Body and emotion in the making of consciousness.* Boston, MA: Houghton Mifflin Harcourt.

Damasio, A. R. (2006). *Descartes' error.* New York: Random House.

Goel, V. (1995). *Sketches of thought.* Cambridge, MA: MIT Press.

Goldschmidt, G. (1991). The dialectics of sketching. *Creativity Research Journal*, 4(2), 123–143. doi:10.1080/10400419109534381

Goldschmidt, G. (1994). On visual design thinking: the vis kids of architecture. *Design Studies*, *15*(2), 158–174.

Hutchins, E. (1995). *Cognition in the wild.* Cambridge, MA: MIT Press.

Kavakli, M., Suwa, M. Gero, J. S. and Purcell, T. (1999). Sketching interpretation in novice and expert designers, in J. S. Gero and B. Tversky (Eds.), *Visual and spatial reasoning in design.* Key Centre of Design Computing and Cognition, University of Sydney, pp. 209–219.

Kozbelt, A. (2008). Hierarchical linear modeling of creative artists' problem solving behaviors. *The Journal of Creative Behavior*, 42(3), pp. 181–200.

Rosand, D. (2002). *Drawing acts: Studies in graphic expression and representation.* New York: Cambridge University Press.

Schmuckler, M. A. (2001). What is ecological validity? A dimensional analysis. *Infancy*, *2*(4), pp. 419–436.

Schön, D. A. (1983). *The reflective practitioner: How professionals think in action.* New York: Basic Books.

Suwa, M., Tversky, B., Gero, J. and Purcell, T. (2001). Seeing into sketches: Regrouping parts encourages new interpretations. In J. S. Gero, B. Tversky, T. Purcell (Eds.), *Visual and spatial reasoning in design.* Key Centre of Design Computing and Cognition, University of Sydney, pp. 207–219.

Tawil, F. F. (2007). A problem solving approach to understanding thought processes in a creative task: A protocol analysis comparison of artists and non-artists. New York: City University of New York, ProQuest Dissertations Publishing.

Tversky, B. (1999). *What does drawing reveal about thinking? A workshop on visual spatial reasoning in design.* Cambridge, MA: MIT Press.

Tversky, B. and Suwa, M. (2009). Thinking with sketches. *Tools for Innovation*, *1*(9), 75–85.

Verstijnen, I. M., van Leeuwen, C., Goldschmidt, G., Hamel, R. and Hennessey, J. M. (1998). Sketching and creative discovery. *Design Studies*, *19*(4), 519–546.

Whale, G. (2006). An investigation of spatial strategy in observational drawing. Ph.D. thesis. Loughborough: Loughborough University.

Drawing is a Tool of Thought

Dr. Barbara Tversky
Cognitive Psychologist
Columbia University

INDEX